John Phin

Practical Hints on the Selection and Use of the Microscope

For Beginners

John Phin

Practical Hints on the Selection and Use of the Microscope
For Beginners

ISBN/EAN: 9783744689489

Printed in Europe, USA, Canada, Australia, Japan

Cover: Foto ©Andreas Hilbeck / pixelio.de

More available books at **www.hansebooks.com**

PRACTICAL HINTS

ON

THE SELECTION AND USE

OF THE

MICROSCOPE.

INTENDED FOR BEGINNERS.

By JOHN PHIN,

EDITOR OF "THE AMERICAN JOURNAL OF MICROSCOPY."

FOURTH EDITION.

THOROUGHLY REVISED AND GREATLY ENLARGED.

Illustrated with Six Plates and Numerous Figures in the Text.

PRICE ONE DOLLAR.

NEW YORK:
THE INDUSTRIAL PUBLICATION COMPANY.
1881.

COPYRIGHT SECURED.

TO

Mrs. Lucy G. Winton,

OF HAVANA, N. Y.,

IN MEMORY OF MANY PLEASANT HOURS SPENT OVER THE MICROSCOPE WITH DEAR ONES WHO "HAVE GONE BEFORE," THIS LITTLE BOOK

IS DEDICATED,

BY HER SINCERE FRIEND,

THE AUTHOR.

CONTENTS.

DEDICATION. - - - - - - - - - - iii
PREFACE. - - - - - - - - - - vii
INTRODUCTION. - - - - - - - - - xi

THE MICROSCOPE.

What it Is; What it Does; Different Kinds of Microscopes; Principles of its Construction, and Glossary of Terms; Essential Parts of the Microscope; Names of the Different Parts, - 15

SIMPLE MICROSCOPES.

Hand Magnifiers, with One, Two, and Three Lenses; Doublets; Power of Two or More Lenses When Used Together; Watch Makers' Eye-Glasses—Single Lenses and Doublets; Engravers' Glasses; Linen Provers; Stanhope Lens; Stanhope Collecting Microscope; Coddington Lens, Achromatic Doublets and Triplets; Twenty-five Cent Microscopes—Their Construction, and How to Make Them; Penny Microscopes, to Show Eels in Paste and Vinegar; Craig Microscope; Novelty, Globe, etc., - 28

DISSECTING MICROSCOPES.

Essentials of a Good Dissecting Microscope; Cheap Stands for Simple Microscopes, Excelsior Microscope; Raspail's Microscope, Compact Dissecting Microscope; Binocular Dissecting Microscope, - - - - - - - - - 40

COMPOUND MICROSCOPES.

Cheap Foreign Stands; French Vertical Microscopes; Conversion of Vertical Microscope into Collecting Microscope; the Ross Model; The Jackson Model; The Continental Model; The New American Model; Cheap American Stands; The Binocular Microscope; The Binocular Eye-Piece; The Inverted Microscope; Lithological Microscopes; The Aquarium Microscope; Microscopes for Special Purposes; "Class" Microscopes, - - 46

OBJECTIVES.

Defects of Common Lenses; Spherical Aberration; Chromatic Aberration, Use of Diaphragms; Corrected Objectives; Defining Power, Achromatism; Aberration of Form; Flatness of Field; Angular Aperture; Penetrating Power; Working Distance; Immersion and "Homogeneous" Lenses; Lens Systems; Duplex Fronts, French Triplets; Focal Length of the Numbers used to Designate Objectives by Nachet, Hartnack and Gundlach; - 61

TESTING OBJECTIVES.

General Rules; Accepted Standards—Diatoms, Ruled Lines, Artificial Star; Podura; Nobert's Lines; Moller's Probe Platte; Table of Diatoms on Moller's Probe Platte, with the Number of Lines to the Inch on the Several Diatoms; Methods of Testing for Flatness of Field, Penetration, etc., - - - - - 84

SELECTION OF A MICROSCOPE FOR PRACTICAL PURPOSES.

Must be Adapted to Requirements and Skill of User; Microscopes for Botany; For Physicians; For Students; Magnifying Power Required; The Stand; The Stage; Mechanical Stages; Revolving Stage; Stages for Special Purposes; Diatom Stage, Safety Stage, etc.; Sub-Stage; Mirror; Body; Draw-Tube; Adjustments for Focussing; The Diaphragm; Objectives; High *versus* Low Angles; Eye-Pieces, - - - - - - 95

ACCESSORY APPARATUS.

Stage Forceps; Forceps Carrier; Object Holder; Plain Slides; Concave Slides; Watch-Glasses; Watch-Glass Holder; Animalcule Cage; Large Zoophyte Trough; Small Zoophyte Trough; Walmsley's Zoophyte Trough; The Weber Slide; The Cell-Trough; The Compressorium; Gravity Compressorium; Growing Slides; Frog Plate; Table; Double Nose-piece, - - 127

ILLUMINATION—SOURCES OF LIGHT.

Sun-Light; Artificial Light—Candles, Gas, Lamps, Magnesium. Oxyhydrogen Light; Parallel, Convergent and Divergent Rays, 143

ILLUMINATION OF OPAQUE OBJECTS.

Diffused Light; Bulls-Eye Condenser; Side Reflector; The Lieberkuhn; The Parabolic Reflector; Objectives with Tapered Fronts; Smith's Vertical Illuminator; Tolles' Vertical Illuminator. - 147

ILLUMINATION OF TRANSPARENT OBJECTS.

Direct and Reflected Light; Axial or Central Light; Oblique Light; The Achromatic Condenser; The Webster Condenser, and How to Use it; Wenham's Reflex Illuminator, and How to Use it; The Wenham Prism; The Homispherical Illuminator; The "Half Button"; The Woodward Illuminator; Tolles' Illuminating Traverse Lens; The Spot Lens; The Parabolic Illuminator; Polarized Light, - - - - - - - 152

HOW TO USE THE MICROSCOPE.

General Rules; Simple Hand Magnifiers; Compound Microscopes; Practical Notes on Illumination; White Cloud Illumination; Monochromatic Light; Blue Cell; Opaque Objects; Hints to Beginners. - - - - - - - - - 164

HOW TO USE OBJECTIVES OF LARGE APERTURE.

Illumination; Collar-Correction for Cover-Glass, - - - 171

CARE OF THE MICROSCOPE.

Should be Kept Covered; Care of Objectives; Precautions to be Used when Corrosive Vapors and Liquids are Employed; To Protect the Objectives from Vapors which Corrode Glass; Cleaning the Objectives; Cleaning the Brass Work, - - - 175

COLLECTING OBJECTS.

Where to Find Objects; What to Look for; How to Capture Them; Nets; Bottle-Holders; Spoons; Collecting Walking Cane; Water Strainer; Wright's Collecting Bottle; Aquaria for Microscopic Objects; Dipping Tubes, - - - - - - - 177

THE PREPARATION AND EXAMINATION OF OBJECTS.

Cutting Thin Sections of Soft Substances; Valentine's Knife; Sections of Wood and Bone; Improved Section Cutter; Sections of Rock; Knives; Scissors; Needles; Dissecting Pans and Dishes; Dissecting Microscopes; Separation of Deposits from Liquids; Preparing Whole Insects; Feet, Eyes, Tongues, Wings, etc., of Insects; Use of Chemical Tests; Liquids for Moistening Objects; Refractive Powers of Different Liquids; Iod-Serum; Artificial Iod-Serum; Covers for Keeping out Dust; Errors in Microscopic Observations, - - - - - - - - 187

PRESERVATIVE PROCESSES.

General Principles; Preservative Media—Canada Balsam, Solution of Balsam, Colophony, Damar Medium, Glycerine, Glycerine Jelly, Hantzsch's Fluid, Glycerine and Gum, Deane's Gelatine, Alcohol, Thwaite's Fluid, Beale's Liquid, Goadby's Fluids, Pacini's Fluid, Castor Oil; General Rules for Applying Preservative Fluids, - - - - - - - - - 198

APPARATUS FOR MOUNTING OBJECTS.

Slides; Covers; Cells; Turn-Tables—Plain, Matthew's, Kinne's, Cox's; Cards for Making Cells; Hot-Plate; Lamps; Retort Stand; Centering Cards; Mounting Needles; Cover Forceps; Slide Holder; Water Bath; Simple Form of Spring Clip, - 206

CEMENTS AND VARNISHES.

General Rules for Using; Gold Size, Black Japan, Brunswick Black, Shellac, Bell's Cement, Sealing Wax Varnish, Colored Shellac, Damar Cement, Marine Glue, Liquid Glue, Dextrine, 221

MOUNTING OBJECTS.

Mounting Transparent Objects Dry; Mounting in Balsam; Mounting in Liquids; Mounting of Whole Insects; How to Get Rid of Air-Bubbles; Mounting Opaque Objects; Wooden Cells; Leather Discs; Pierce's Cell; Prof. Smith's Wax Cell; Deep Cement Cell, 224

FINISHING THE SLIDES.

Covering with Paper; Varnishing for Preservation; Labeling; The Maltwood Finder, - - - - - - 229

PREFACE TO THIRD EDITION.

This might with propriety be called the fourth edition—the main idea of the work having been embodied in a pamphlet under the same title, published in 1873. but long since forgotten. The successive editions have reached their present form by accretion, rather than by development; like Topsey, the book has "growed," rather than been ' brought up, and just as that young lady exhibited numerous traits which were inconsistent with a proper training, so this book shows patch-work and inequalities which do not add either to its value or its attractiveness.

Of all this the author is fully conscious, and if he could possibly have secured the necessary leisure he would gladly have rewritten the entire volume. But pressing, or rather imperative calls upon his time, have prevented this, and he has, therefore, been compelled to feel satisfied with such general revision and additions as were necessary to bring the work up to the present state of our knowledge.

The book is still intended for beginners and has changed nothing of its elementary character. It is true that we have inserted a few pages relating to the higher class of objectives, and the accessories used with them, but those who do not possess such apparatus can easily skip these passages.

That it is suited to the purpose for which it was intended, we have evidence, not only in the extended sale which it has secured, but in the fact that it has been adopted as an auxiliary text-book in several of our schools and colleges.

New York, January, 1881.

PREFACE TO SECOND EDITION.

The fact that an unusually large edition of this work has been sold in a comparatively short period, is, to the author, evidence that such a work was needed, and that the present volume has, to a certain extent, supplied the want. In the present edition, therefore, he has endeavored to introduce several important improvements, while at the same time the elementary character of the work remains unaltered. With a few very slight and unimportant exceptions, the entire matter of the former edition has been incorporated in the present, and in addition several important subjects, particularly the chapter on objectives, have been greatly enlarged.

Many important points still remain untouched, but it is believed that in its present form most beginners will find in it all the information that they may require upon general topics.

As the want of all illustrations of the stands of different makers, and of many accessories, has been urged as an objection to the first edition, and as we have not deemed it advisable to fully supply this omission in the present issue, a word of explanation may not be out of place. One great object in view in the preparation of this book was the furnishing of a *cheap* manual for those who cannot afford the more expensive books of Carpenter, Beale, Frey, etc. To have given anything like a fair representation of the products of the different makers of this country and of Europe, would have nearly doubled the size and price of the volume. But if the reader will examine the engravings of stands, etc., in the books just mentioned, he will find that, even in the best of them, these illustrations are mere reproductions of the figures found in the descriptive lists of the various dealers. As new editions of these lists are being constantly issued, and as they may in most cases be obtained without cost from those that publish them, we have thought it best to refer our readers to these catalogues for information in regard to the construction of the instruments of different makers. For the addresses of the prominent microscope makers of this country and Europe we refer our readers to "The Microscopist's Annual."

In this, as in the previous edition, we have omitted all descriptions of objects, believing that the proper aim of a book on the microscope should not be to teach the general principles of botany, zoology or histology, but simply the best methods of using the microscope in the pursuit of these studies. The proper books in which to find a description of objects, are those which treat of that department of science which takes cognizance of the special subject under consideration. The present volume is intended merely as a guide to the best general methods of using the microscope.

It has been a source of great satisfaction to the author to be assured by those whom he deems good authority, that this little book has done much to foster the use of the microscope in this country, and he hopes that the present improved edition will tend to still further increase the deep interest which is already felt in an instrument which has done more than any other to extend our knowledge of organic nature.

New York, August, 1877.

PREFACE.

The Microscope and its applications in the Arts, and in general science, having deservedly occupied a prominent place in the pages of THE TECHNOLOGIST, OR INDUSTRIAL MONTHLY, a very large number of enquiries in regard to the best methods of using and applying this useful instrument have been directed to us. It would have been easy to answer these enquiries by a reference to some one of the many treatises that have been published on this subject, but as most of these works are expensive, and as many of our correspondents desire an answer in a more concise and simple shape, we have endeavored to give, in cheap and compact form, the information that is most usually demanded.

It is an unfortunate fact that while the microscope is daily growing in favor with those who know anything of its achievements, the operations of certain parties, too well known to the public, have brought a certain degree of suspicion upon all attempts to popularize this most valuable instrument. Microscopes, varying in price from twenty-five cents to two dollars and a half have been offered for sale, and the claim made for them that they are capable of showing clearly the structure of the more minute tissues, and that they may be used to advantage by physicians and naturalists. To the young student whose means are limited, and to the country practitioner, whose ability to supply himself with needed books and instruments often falls far short of his desires, the offer of a serviceable microscope for a couple of dollars is a great temptation, and when the instrument in question is endorsed by a long list of clergymen, lawyers, and even editors, this temptation becomes irresistible. And if the purchaser should happen to be unfamiliar with really good microscopes, and unable to discriminate between a clear and accurately defined view of any object and one that is distorted and incorrect, he may be led to use it, and so fall into the most serious mistakes. That this, unfortunately, does happen too often must be well known to all who are familiar with the subject, and it is within our own knowledge that the most worthless caricature of a microscope has been purchased and used under such circumstances.

We indulge a faint hope that the information conveyed in the following pages will enable the inexperienced reader to avoid these mistakes, and to assign a proper value to the certificates of clergymen and editors who vouch for the excellence of articles concerning whose properties and uses they are profoundly ignorant. These two classes we single out for reprobation, because—in this respect, at least—they seem to be sinners above all other men.

As stated in the title page, it is intended for beginners, and not for beginners in the use of the microscope only, but for those who have had little or no experience in the use of instruments of any kind. Hence the directions that are given are of the very simplest kind, and all theoretical explanations have been avoided, for the reason that any person that is desirous of studying the optical principles upon which the microscope is constructed will find in the ordinary text books on natural philosophy all the information he may want. Our object has been solely to impart such information as will enable the reader to make a beginning in the practice of microscopy, hoping that the start thus given will lead him to proceed with his studies, and ultimately acquire that knowledge, skill and dexterity which will enable him to avail himself of the extraordinary powers and advantages which the use of this instrument confers, both in scientific pursuits and in everyday life. Above all things, therefore, we have endeavored to be accurate in our statements and judicious in our directions, and the reader is assured that no processes or methods are given which we ourselves have not frequently and successfully put in practice.

JOHN PHIN.

New York, January, 1875.

INTRODUCTION.

Thousands of microscopes throughout the country are at the present day lying idle, simply because their owners do not know how to use them. If properly employed they might be made to afford an incalculable amount of instruction and amusement; but, as it is, they are a drag upon the popularization of science, because they convey the idea that the microscope is a difficult instrument to use, and that it is not of much account after we have learned to use it. The owners of these microscopes have examined all the mounted objects at their command, the entire number of which probably does not exceed two or three dozen, and they have no information as to the best methods of preparing common objects for examination or preservation. Even the objects that they possess have never been explained to them, and are merely pretty toys. The fly's eye is interesting because it looks like a piece of netting, and the butterfly's wing is attractive because it is probably a little more brilliant than the most brilliant silk dress, but neither of these objects interests of itself and because of its beautiful structure.

Moreover it often happens that an instrument which, when first purchased, was of very fair quality, has, through ignorance and carelessness, become so soiled and dimmed that it no longer serves the purpose intended. On more than one occasion have we seen a fine microscope leave the dealer's hands in excellent order, and return in a week entirely unfit for use. Microscopes in this condition, instead of being a source of instruction and pleasure, are an eyesore and an occasion of annoyance. They continually serve as reminders of awkwardness and failure, of wasted time and ill-spent money. And yet with proper instruction and a due amount of care all this might have been avoided.

It is also a fact to be regretted that heretofore the microscope has not been extensively employed in the arts, and in everyday life, simply because practical men have not been taught how to use it, and consequently have been unable to avail themselves of the advantages which it offers; but if carefully and judiciously selected, and properly handled, it is capable of affording an amount and kind of assistance which cannot be safely neglected. It may be made to aid in the examination of raw materials, and of the finer kinds of work; it will enable us to measure spaces which would otherwise be inappreciable, and this, in an age when even in ordinary machine shops the thousandth part of an inch is frequently an important quantity, renders it indispensable to the careful and skillful mechanic; on the farm it will enable the agriculturist to examine closely and minutely the various noxious insects and forms of fungi and blight, and thus aid him in identifying them and applying the proper remedy; and in the examination of minute seeds, such as timothy, clover, etc., it will prove a very valuable assistant, enabling him to detect any inferiority in the quality, or any impurity or adulteration. Frequently the agricultural seeds offered in market contain minute seeds of offensive weeds, many of which are so small that they are not easily discovered by the naked eye.

Every farmer and mechanic knows the value of a good pair of eyes, and he also knows that an agent which doubles or trebles our power in any given direction at once confers upon us in that respect a superiority over our fellows. Very few men are twice as strong as their comrades; still fewer have three times the strength of ordinary men, and it may be safely affirmed that no man possesses the power of ten ordinary men. But a microscope of very ordinary capacity at once multiplies our powers of sight by ten, twenty, or even a hundred times, while those of the better class enable us to see things with a keenness and clearness which, when compared with that afforded by the naked eye, is as more than a thousand to one.

There are four distinct and important directions in which a microscope may be made to serve us: 1. It is capable of affording the most refined and elevating kind of pleasure by the exhibition of objects of extreme beauty and interest. There are few more splendid sights than the gorgeous colors displayed by some objects when viewed by polarized light, and even the tints of certain minerals, and the brilliant scales of certain insects, when viewed as opaque objects, by means of a good condenser, surpass anything that is familiar to us in our ordinary experience. On the other hand the exquisite beauty of form which is characteristic of most of the objects with which the microscopist concerns himself can be fully appreciated only by those who have seen them. As a source of innocent amusement and pleasure, therefore, the microscope has few or no equals; for it may be safely affirmed that a five-dollar instrument is capable of affording gratification of greater variety and intensity, and of longer continuance, than that yielded by anything else of the same cost. This arises chiefly from the fact that most other instruments, when once exhibited, with their slides or fixtures, lose their freshness and interest, and become old. While for the microscope, a few fibres of wool from the carpet, a few grains of sand from the sea-shore, or a handful of wild flowers from the field, yield objects of surpassing beauty. Everything in nature and in art may be subjected to inspection by it, and will then disclose new beauties and fresh sources of knowledge. Under it the point of the finest cambric needle looks like a crow-bar, grooved and seamed with scratches; the eye of the fly is seen to consist of thousands of eyes; and the dust on the butterfly's wing appears to be what it really is, scales laid on with all the regularity of shingles or slates on a house; while to prepare and examine these simple objects requires no great skill and no elaborate apparatus.

2. As a means of imparting instruction to the young, the microscope has now become indispensable. The changes which of late years have taken place in the views held by our ablest men in regard to the best education are too well known to need even mention. No education that does not include a knowledge of natural science is now regarded as complete, and there is a very wide range of the most essential and practical knowledge that can be reached only through the microscope. Thus, when we look at a leaf with the naked eye, we see but a green mass of matter, possessing a certain beautiful form, it is true, but disclosing none of those organs which render it more complicated and wonderful than anything ever produced by our most skilful mechanics. Looked at by the microscope, however, this same leaf is found to be made up of innumerable parts, each one of which is highly complex and beautiful; it is furnished with mouths for breathing, with cells for storing, digesting and assimilating nutriment, and with ribs for strengthening its structure; and all this, which is perfectly invisible to the unassisted vision, becomes distinct and obvious when we call to our aid a microscope of even moderate power. It is true that much of this may be taught by means of books, engravings and verbal descriptions, but every one knows that for distinctness and impressiveness the very best engravings fall far short of a view of the real object.

3. As an instrument of research, the microscope now occupies a position which is second to none. There is hardly any department of science in which a student can hope to reach eminence without a familiarity with the microscope. Botany and Zoology have been developed almost wholly by its aid, and so necessary is it in the study of these sciences, that Schleiden, one of the most successful of investigators says of it: "He who expects to become a botanist or a zoologist without using the microscope, is, to say the least of him, as great a fool as he who wishes to study the heavens without a telescope." In chemistry its services have been very important, and in geology and mineralogy it has opened up new fields of research which almost promise to revolutionize these sciences. Medicine has

long acknowledged the microscope as one of its most efficient assistants, and in the practice of the best physicians it is regarded as an indispensable means of diagnosis in some diseases.

4. As an assistant in the arts. Its importance in this department is but just beginning to be recognized, and in a former paragraph we have endeavored to point out a few of the subjects to which it may be applied with good hopes of success.

These important and obvious advantages are not difficult to secure, provided we avoid two mistakes which are very commonly made by beginners. One of these consists in supposing that it is only by means of very expensive and complicated instruments that anything of value can be accomplished in microscopy. Now while it is certain that, in some departments of study, none but the very best microscopes are of any value at all, it is equally certain that a very wide range of study and of practical work can be thoroughly cultivated by means of apparatus of very moderate cost, and of great simplicity of construction. The great discoveries of Ehrenberg, which opened up entire new fields of research and of thought, were made with a microscope which at the present day would not command $25. Indeed some of the French instruments that are sold for $15 will show a very large proportion of the objects that are figured in his earlier works. Most of the great anatomical and botanical discoveries were made with simple microscopes of no great power, and it is not many years since one of the most successful workers in the field of botany gave it as his opinion that a power of 300 diameters is capable of showing everything that is of importance in this science.

The other error is of precisely the opposite kind. It is not at all unusual to meet persons who seem to think that all that is necessary in order to become a microscopist is to buy a microscope and place objects under it! Such people always entertain an exaggerated idea of the power of the microscope as an instrument of research. For example, they think that in order to detect adulteration all that is necessary is to place a sample under the microscope, when all impurities will at once stand out conspicuously! To their imagination every blood corpuscle is clearly marked with the name of the animal from which it was obtained!

Truth lies between these extremes. No progress can be made without steady application and persistent labor, but any person of fair average ability and a moderate degree of perseverance can soon learn to follow the beaten track at least, if not to branch out into original research.

THE SELECTION AND USE

OF

THE MICROSCOPE.

What is a Microscope?—The microscope is an instrument which enables us to see either very minute objects or very minute parts of large objects. It is a very popular idea that the name *microscope* is applicable only to complex instruments of considerable power; but this is clearly wrong. A ten cent magnifying glass has as good a right to the name *microscope* as has a complicated binocular instrument with all the latest improvements. By common consent, however, the small hand instruments, without stands, are generally called *magnifiers*. An attempt has been made to introduce the foreign word *loupe* as an equivalent of magnifier. The word *loupe* is, however, superfluous, and is used only by ostentatious pedants, and by foreigners who are ignorant of English.

What the Microscope Does.—It is well known that the further off any object is, the less it appears. A house at a distance appears less than a man who is close by, and the distinctness with which an object is seen depends largely upon its apparent size. Thus, at a distance, a house not only appears very small, but the windows cannot be distinguished from the rest of the building. As we draw nearer it becomes apparently larger, and the different parts become more distinct. First the windows are seen clearly, then the individual panes of glass, then the bricks, and finally the grains of the material of which the bricks are made. When, however, we approach too closely we again find it impossible to see distinctly, as may easily be proved by a very simple experiment. Place some fine print, such, for example, as the present page, at a distance of six feet from the eye, and gradually move closer to it. At six feet the letters will be indistinguishable; at two feet they will be quite distinct; at one foot still more distinct; at three inches they will be quite blurred. There is, therefore, a limit to the degree of closeness with which we can approach any object for the purpose of examining it, and the object of a microscope is to enable us to get close to it, as it were, without blurring our view. If, without changing the distance of the eye from the paper (three inches) we introduce between the two a lens of one inch focus, and bring it into proper position, we will find that the indistinctness formerly complained of disappears, and the object is now not only seen clearly, but appears very much magnified. That objects appear large in proportion to their nearness to the eye may be thus shown: Take two slips of paper printed with type of the same size (two clippings from a newspaper answer well) and place one at a distance of ten inches from the eye and the other at a distance of five inches— the edge of the upper slip being placed so as to lie about the middle of the lower one. In this way we can readily compare the apparent sizes of the type on the two slips, and one will be found to appear just twice as large as the other, though, of course, we have the evidence of our senses to prove that they are precisely of the same size. Moreover, as the usual distance for distinct vision is about ten inches, in persons of middle age, it will be found that a lens which enables us to view any object clearly and distinctly from a distance of one inch, will enable us to see it just ten times larger and ten times more distinctly than we could do when looking at it from a distance of ten inches. A consideration of these facts led the late Dr. Goring to propose the name *engiscope* as a substitute for the word *microscope*—the word *engiscope* signifying to see things at a very short distance.

The facts which we have just detailed must, however, be regarded as illustrations, rather than explanations of the action of the microscope. It is evident that the power of a lens to increase the distinctness with which any object is seen, depends not only upon the action of the lens upon the rays of light, but upon the influence which such modified light exerts upon the organs of vision. Now, the eye, considered merely as an optical instrument, is in reality a small *camera obscura* in which the cornea, crystalline lens, and other transparent portions, combine to throw upon the retina an image of external objects. That the transparent portions of the eye do in fact act as a lens, and throw a real image upon the retina or posterior portion of the eye, is easily shown by taking the fresh eye of an ox and gradually shaving off the coating at the back until it becomes transparent. If the eye, so prepared, be then held towards a window or any very bright object, a distinct but inverted image of the window or other object will be seen on the coat of the eye.

The action of the eye in this case is the same as that of a lens, and the general mode of action of lenses under such circumstances may be easily illustrated by means of a common hand magnifier or even a spectacle glass. If the reader will hold before a window, at a distance of, say, six feet, a sheet of white paper, and will place a magnifier in front of the paper, then by properly adjusting the distance between the magnifier and the paper, a picture of the window will be thrown on the latter. If the magnifier and paper be now removed to a distance of twelve feet from the window, the picture of the latter will be only half as large as it was in the first place, and it will also be found that the distance of the lens from the paper will have to be readjusted and made less.

That the eye possesses this power of adjustment we are all conscious, for we feel that if, when the eye is adjusted for the distinct vision of distant objects, we suddenly look at those which are near, the condition of the eye requires to be changed before a distinct view can be had, and to make this change requires an effort of which we are perfectly conscious.

When a lens is held in front of a sheet of paper, so as to throw on the latter a distinct image of the objects in front of it, the distance between the paper and the lens is called the *focal distance* or *focal length* of the latter. This, as we have just seen, varies with the distance of the object which gives the image. In order, therefore, to secure a standard in this respect the object selected is always one whose distance is so great that it may be practically regarded as infinite.

When we examine an object, first at a distance, and then close at hand, we see it through the medium of two different sets of rays, those in the latter case entering the eye in such a direction that the image thrown on the retina is larger than the image produced when the object is more distant. The lens acts, however, by bending the rays so that the same set, which, if allowed to pursue their natural direction would not produce a distinct image, are caused to enter the eye in such a direction that the image is large and clear. The manner in which the lens acts to produce these effects is not difficult to understand. It is true that the *ultimate causes* which produce these phenomena are beyond our knowledge, but in this respect the ablest philosopher has very little advantage over the veriest tyro. It may be difficult also for the general reader to follow the mathematical demonstrations of the action of lenses. There are, however, a few simple facts which are easily understood, or at least demonstrated and accepted *as facts*, and which, when clearly and firmly grasped by the mind, render the construction of the microscope comparatively easy of comprehension.

There are two ways in which the subject may be studied. We may examine the facts experimentally, by using lenses and actual eyes in the way we have described, or we may follow the course of the rays as laid down in any good book on optics. A combination of both methods will of course give the clearest views on the subject, and we would therefore advise the reader to provide himself with a few lenses of various degrees of curvature, and consequently of various magnifying powers, and test all the statements made in the text. He will thus acquire such a practical knowledge of the action of lenses as can be obtained in no other way. For this purpose the cheapest lenses are good enough. One or two cheap magnifiers and a few glasses from old spectacles will serve every purpose. The simplest methods of arranging such lenses will be found in a note on a subsequent page, and although very accurately made tools are required for the construction of serviceable optical instruments, it will be found that a very large number of simple but valuable experiments may be worked out with the aid of a few wooden rollers and a little paper and paste.

While the magnifying power of lenses depends upon their focal length, this in turn depends upon the material of which the lens is made, and also upon the curvature given to its surfaces. Lenses of precisely the same form, and made respectively of diamond, flint glass, crown glass and Canada balsam would possess different magnifying powers; the diamond magnifying most, the flint glass next, crown glass next, and Canada balsam least of all. On the other hand, of two lenses composed of the same material, that which has the sharpest curvature to its surfaces will magnify most. Now, on reflection, it will be evident to even the least mathematical mind that lenses which have very sharp or *quick* curves must of necessity be small. Suppose the curve which bounds the figure of a lens has a radius of half an inch, it is evident that the largest lens which could be made with this curve would be one inch in diameter, and then it would be a perfect sphere. Most lenses, however, resemble thin slices off the spheres, or in some cases two such slices joined together, so that the diameter of the lens is in general greatly less than the radius of the curves which form its surface. Therefore, we see that all lenses of high power are of necessity small, and when lenses are required of very high power they become so minute as to be handled only with great difficulty. Indeed, before the modern improvements in the microscope, many of the lenses used by scientific men were nothing more than little globules of glass, brought to a round form by fusion.

We have made this lengthened explanation of a very simple matter because we have found amongst beginners in microscopy a very general idea that large lenses are the most powerful. "Send me one of your largest and most powerful magnifiers," is an order with which every optician is familiar, and yet such an order contains a contradiction in terms. A lens cannot possibly be large and magnify greatly at the same time.

The Different Kinds of Microscopes.—Microscopes are divided into two classes—simple and compound—the difference between them being purely optical, and not mechanical; for a simple microscope may be very complex and expensive, while, on the other hand, a microscope may be *compound* and yet contain very few parts. Thus the little vertical French microscopes, which cost only $2,50, are *compound*, although very simple in construction, while a *simple* microscope, if binocular, and provided with all desirable adjustments, might be a very complicated affair. The difference between simple and compound microscopes is this: in the simple microscope we look at the object directly, while in the compound microscope we look at a magnified image of the object. In the simple microscope, objects are always seen in their natural position, while in the compound microscope they are inverted, and right becomes left, and left becomes right. This makes it very difficult for beginners to work upon objects under the compound microscope; and hence simple microscopes are almost always used for dissecting and botanizing.

It is true that by adding more lenses, and making the instrument still more compound, we can again invert the image, and thus bring it back to its original and natural position, and almost all the very expensive microscopes are furnished with these extra lenses arranged in a piece of accessory apparatus technically known as an *erector*. The distinguishing feature of the compound microscope remains, however, the same. Certain forms of the microscope, in which *concave* lenses are substituted for the usual convex form, also give erect images, but this does not affect the general truth of the statement just made.

Simple microscopes frequently consist of more than one lens. Thus, in using the ordinary pocket magnifiers with two or three lenses, it is usual to employ all the lenses at once, looking at the object through two or three lenses at the same time when a high power is required. In this case, however, the two or three lenses are placed close together and act in the same way as a single lens, with surfaces more sharply curved than those of any of the lenses forming the combination. Under such circumstances the image is not inverted, but if we now separate the lenses sufficiently, we will find that on again bringing the object into focus, the image is inverted and greatly enlarged. Moreover, it will be found that the magnifying power may be greatly increased by increasing the distance between the two lenses, and it will also be found that as the distance of the two lenses from each other is increased, the distance at which the combination is placed from the object must be made less and *vice versa*.*

The early forms of the compound microscope consisted of little more than the two lenses we have just described, but the modern instrument, even in its simplest form, is a vastly more complicated arrangement. In the best forms, for the lens next the eye there is substituted an eye-piece consisting of two lenses with a diaphragm between them, while the objective, or lens next the object, is composed of from four to ten different pieces of glass, forming two or more lenses, which are so arranged that each shall correct the defects of the others, and this optical combination is mounted on a stand which is sometimes a marvel of mechanical ingenuity.

*The student who possesses a little mechanical genius and a desire to become *experimentally* acquainted with the properties of lenses and the construction of the microscope, would do well to procure a couple of cheap lenses, say one of half inch focus, and one of about two inches focus, and test by actual trial the statements made in the text. Such lenses may be conveniently arranged in a tube formed of writing paper and gummed on the edges. All the most important properties and defects of lenses may be thus illustrated and studied. By means of a little extra care, two such lenses, arranged as we have described, in tubes blackened on the inside, and mounted on a little wooden stand, the focus being adjusted by sliding the tube holding the lenses within another tube, also of paper, will give not only a very fair view of such objects as the wing of a fly, the scales on a butterfly's wing, and even the barbs on the sting of a bee, but it will show the globules of blood quite distinctly, and we have even given a very interesting exhibition of the circulation of the blood in the foot of a frog by means of a temporary arrangement of this kind, which we put together for the purpose of explaining to a little girl the construction of the microscope. We would not recommend any one to use such a microscope for purposes of work or study, because the fallacies to which it may give rise are too numerous and too serious. But any boy, or even girl, who will undertake the construction of such an instrument, cannot fail to obtain thereby an amount of information which the perusal of volumes would not give. As hints towards aiding our young friends, we may remark that our tubes were made of the best stiff paper, rolled up tight and pasted only along the outer edge. The lenses were secured in their places by being attached to the bottoms of pill-boxes, holes being punched through to admit the light. Pill-boxes with holes were also used for diaphragms to reduce the effects of aberration. A piece of mirror reflected the light, and the sides etc., of an old cigar box furnished material for the stand. Fifty cents covered all expenses.

Essential Parts of the Microscope.—When a good lens is held steadily at a certain distance from an object which is properly illuminated, this distance depending upon the form and material of the lens, we are enabled to see the object clearly and distinctly. When, however, this distance is either increased or diminished, the object becomes blurred and indistinct. The point at which vision is most distinct is called the *focus** of the lens, and when we are able to see it clearly the object is said to be *in focus;* when the distance is either increased or diminished, it is said to be *out of focus*. An object is said to be *within* the focus when the lens is too near it, and *beyond* the focus when the lens is too far away.

The performance of any lens depends greatly upon the accuracy with which it is adjusted to the correct focal distance, and the steadiness with which it is held there. For all ordinary purposes, lenses which do not magnify more than ten diameters may be very conveniently held in the hand without any special means of support; but when the power is much greater than this, or where, as in the compound instrument, the microscope is bulky and heavy, it becomes necessary to use some mechanical contrivance which will hold the microscope steadily in its position in relation to the object, otherwise the view becomes indistinct. Thus a good lens, magnifying from thirty to forty diameters, will very readily show the individual corpuscles or globules in the blood of the frog, provided it is arranged on a steady support and accurately adjusted for focus. But if the lens be merely held in the hand, without any firm support, it will be impossible for the observer to see the corpuscles.

Another important point is the illumination of the object. Unless the object be properly illuminated it cannot be dis-

---

* It is scarcely necessary to inform the reader that the focus described in the text is not precisely the focus of the lens itself, but the focus of a compound lens of which the eye forms one element. Hence the focal distance varies with different eyes, and so does the apparent size of objects. To short-sighted people objects appear of larger size than they do to persons of ordinary eye-sight. In working with the compound microscope we frequently find that different people require a different focal adjustment.

tinctly seen, and consequently all microscopes, except the simplest forms of hand magnifiers, are provided with means for throwing the light upon the object, and for regulating the amount which shall either fall upon it or pass through it.

Hence the importance of providing efficient means for adjusting the focus and holding and illuminating the object, and the purpose which the stand is intended to fulfil, is to furnish these means in a compact and convenient form. Every microscope, therefore, of a grade above a hand magnifier, whether it be simple or compound, must possess :

1. Suitable means for supporting the object, and placing and maintaining it in proper position.

2. Means for illuminating the object, either by throwing the light upon it when it is opaque, or transmitting the light through it when it is transparent.

3. Means for transmitting to the eye an enlarged image of the object.

The different parts which are employed for securing these several ends, have been constructed of an almost endless variety of forms, according to the fancies of the different makers and the requirements of different microscopists. As it is important that the student should familiarize himself with the names of these different parts, we give a definition of them, and in order that there may be no opportunity for mistake or misapprehension, we have also engraved an outline of one of the ordinary forms of the microscope, and on this we have marked the names of the different parts.

NAMES OF THE DIFFERENT PARTS.

The following are the names of the essential parts of a compound microscope of ordinary construction. The names of the different parts of the simple microscope are the same as those of the compound microscope, but the latter has several parts which do not exist in the former.

The *Stand* is the name properly applied to the entire frame used for supporting and illuminating the object, and for carrying and adjusting the optical part, the latter consisting of the

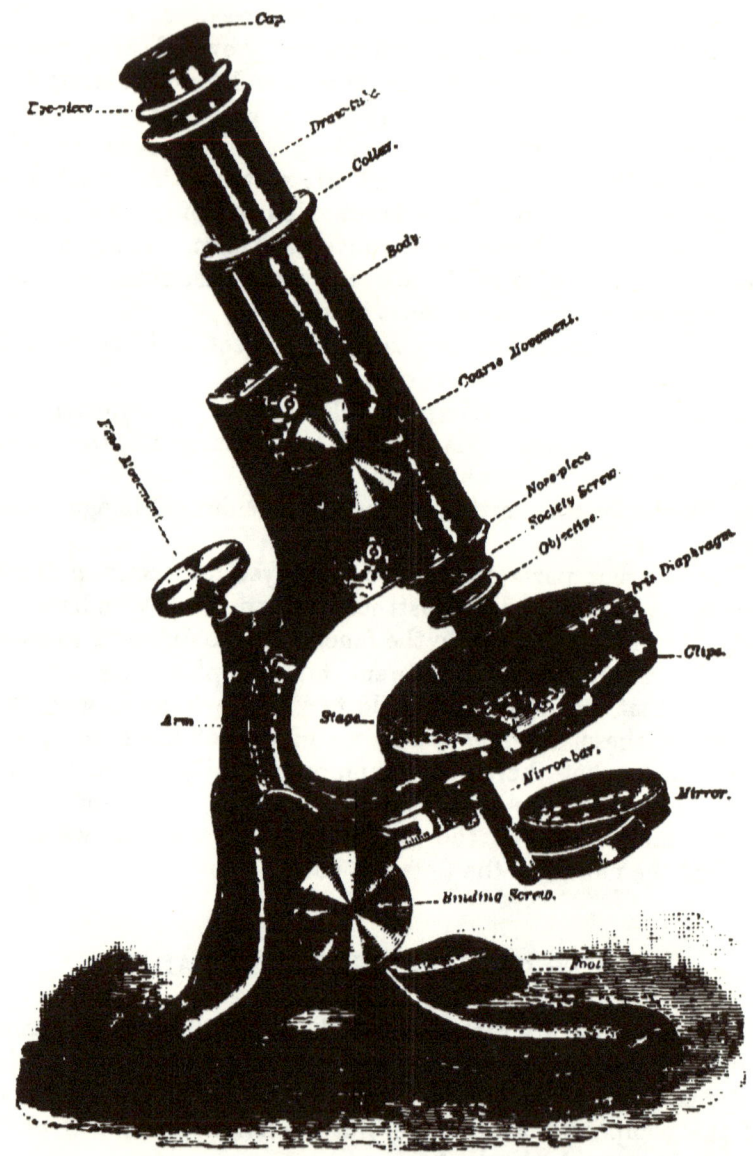

Fig. 1.—DIAGRAM SHOWING THE DIFFERENT PARTS OF THE MICROSCOPE, AND THEIR NAMES.

eye-piece and the objective. Stands are frequently sold separately, or furnished with eye-pieces only—the purchaser making such a selection of objectives and other accessories, as may best suit his special needs.

The *Base* or *Foot* is that part which supports the rest of the stand.

The *Body* is the tube to which the eye-piece and objectives are attached.

A *Draw-tube* is a secondary body which receives the eye-piece, and slides within the main body like the draw of a telescope. It enables us to increase the distance between the eye-piece and the objective, and thus to change the magnifying power, as explained in a previous paragraph.

A *Collar* is a short tube through which either the body, the draw-tube, or the eye-piece slides.

The *Arm* is that part which carries the body.

The *Stage* is the plate upon which the object is placed for examination.

Clips are springs attached to the stage for the purpose of holding in place the glass slide or plate carrying the object.

A *Sub-stage* is furnished with some instruments. It is used for holding and centering various means of illumination. No sub-stage is shown in the diagram, Fig. 1. The sub-stage, with its centering arrangements, is shown very clearly in the Ross model, Plate I.

Sub-stage Ring.—Instead of being provided with a sub-stage, many cheap microscopes are furnished with what is known as a *sub-stage ring or tube*. This serves to receive the polarizer, paraboloid, etc.

The *Object-Glass* or *Objective* is the lens or lenses which are placed next the object. The term Object-glass is sometimes applied to the glass plate or slide upon which the object is placed, but this use of the word is entirely wrong, and tends to produce confusion.

The *Society Screw* is a screw of a certain standard size for connecting the objective to the body. In microscopes furnished with a screw of the Society's standard, the objectives of any American or English maker may be used. The makers on the continent of Europe have now very generally adopted the Society Screw. In this country the Society Screw has been universally adopted, but as it has been found too small for low-power objectives of wide angle, another screw, named the

Broad Gauge, is sometimes used in addition to the Society Screw.

In all microscopes, means are provided for moving the objective to and from the object, so as to bring the latter *into focus*, as it is called. According as the device used for this purpose acts coarsely but rapidly, or slowly but delicately, it is called a *coarse or a fine adjustment*. The best microscopes are provided with both kinds, so that the object is first brought approximately, but rapidly, into focus by one, and then adjusted more slowly, but with great accuracy, by the other.

The *Coarse Adjustment* has several forms. In Fig. 1 it consists of a rack and pinion. In some cases it is a chain movement; very often it is effected by merely sliding the body up and down through a tubular collar by hand, as in Fig. 12.

The *Fine Adjustment* usually consists of a fine screw, sometimes called, improperly, a *micrometer screw*, which moves either the entire body or the lower part of it, called the nose-piece. In some cheap stands, the fine adjustment is effected by moving the stage towards the objective.

The *Nose-piece* is a short tube, which fits into the lower end of the body, and carries the Society screw at its lower end. Sometimes it is made to slide out and in, and thus forms part of the fine adjustment. In the instrument figured in the diagram, it is immovable. The term *nose-piece* is also applied to certain accessories which enable us to attach different pieces of apparatus to the microscope, as, for example, two or more objectives at one time, the analyzer of the polariscope, etc.

A *Diaphragm* is usually a thin plate of metal pierced with a hole, the size of which regulates the diameter of the pencil of rays that pass through. There is a diaphragm in the eye-piece which contracts the field of view, and cuts off those rays which tend to confuse the images, and all good microscopes have a diaphragm attached to the stage, whereby the amount of light passing through the object to the objective may be regulated. Instead of a thin plate of metal, an arrangement known as the "Iris diaphragm" is used in the microscope shown in the diagram.

The *Eye-piece* or *Ocular* is the short brass tube, with its lenses, which is next the eye. The eye-piece contains an *Eye-Glass*, which is that next the eye; a *Field-Glass*, placed next the objective, and a *Diaphragm*, consisting of a brass plate with a hole through it, and so arranged as to cut off the outer rays of light. The tube in which these lenses are secured is in almost all cases removable, and the best microscopes are furnished with several eye-pieces of different powers, which may be changed at pleasure. We may here remark that where a microscope is furnished with several eye-pieces, the *shortest* eye-piece gives the greatest magnifying power.

The *Cap* is a cover which fits over the top of the eye-piece. It is pierced with a hole, to allow the rays which pass through the instrument to reach the eye. This cap is sometimes covered with a second cap, which has no hole, but which is intended to exclude dust from the eye-lens, and which is removed when the instrument is in use.

The *Mirror* reflects the light, and causes it either to fall upon the object or to pass through it, so as to render it visible.

The *Mirror-bar* is a bar attached to the stand and carrying the mirror. It is usually made to turn on a pivot, and in the microscope shown in Fig. 1, it consists of two parts sliding upon each other, so that it may be shortened or lengthened, as circumstances require.

Accessories are those parts of the microscope which are used only for special purposes, such as the paraboloid, the camera lucida, stage forceps, etc.

The *Object* is that which is subjected to examination. It is usually mounted upon

A *Slide*, or plate of glass, which is laid upon the stage.

All these parts will be fully described in a subsequent part of this volume, and their utility and importance explained. It is greatly to be desired that the young microscopist should familiarize himself with the terms employed, so that he may always use them accurately. Anything that he may say or write will then be clearly understood by all who have given careful attention to the subject. So important does the author deem this matter, that he has in an advanced state of preparation an extended glossary or dictionary of microscopical terms.

SIMPLE MICROSCOPES.

The simple microscope is an indispensable assistant to those who use the compound instrument, as well as to those who rely upon it alone for the examination of flowers, seeds, minerals, textile fabrics, etc. We shall therefore devote some space to a consideration of its various forms, though even then we shall be unable to do more than describe certain typical models which, however, afford variety enough for all practical purposes.

Hand Magnifiers.—These are so generally useful and applicable that they are used by all who wish a cheap and yet efficient aid to natural vision. They are found in market in a great variety of forms, styles of mounting, and price, and are too well known to need minute description. Large lenses, magnifying two or three times, are mounted singly, and used chiefly for the examination of pictures, and as reading glasses; the smaller sizes of the same style serve for the examination of fine engravings. Very small lenses of considerable power, and simply mounted in a frame, are also sold by most opticians. They are known as "watch-charms," and magnify about fifteen diameters. We have also seen a very powerful magnifier mounted in a little ring attached to a pair of eye-glasses.

For the purpose of the student and naturalist, a very excellent form is that shown in Fig. 2. It consists of a lens of suitable magnifying power set in a frame, which folds into a case, just as the blade of a pocket knife folds into its handle, thus allowing the instrument to be carried in the pocket without liability to injury. Similar magnifiers are made with two, three, and even four separate lenses, as shown in Fig. 3. The lenses are usually of different powers—a 2 inch, 1 inch, and ½ inch, forming a very useful combination. Each lens may be used separately, or two may be used together, or all three may be used at once, a considerable range of magnifying power being thus secured.

Fig. 2.—HAND MAGNIFIER—SIMPLE LENS.

The magnifiers shown in Figures 2 and 3 are furnished with what are called *diaphragms*—that is to say, each one has a thin plate of some opaque material, having a hole of suitable size through its centre. This plate is placed over the lens when

Fig. 3.—HAND MAGNIFIER—THREE LENSES.

but one lens is used, and between the lenses when two or more are employed. It serves to cut off the marginal rays which do not give a clear image, and in this way it greatly improves the definition of the object.

Two or more lenses, properly adapted to each other, and used together, give results greatly superior to anything that can be obtained from a single lens, at least so far as clearness and accuracy of definition is concerned. But when used as a working or dissecting microscope, they are open to the objection that the distance at which they must be placed from the object is very small, and hence it is frequently inconvenient to use them for working upon objects. Thus, if we have a plano-convex lens of a quarter of an inch focus, and one of three quarters of an inch focus, and place them at a distance of a sixteenth of an inch from each other, we will have a very good magnifier which will enlarge objects about fifty times, but we must place it at but a very short distance from the object. If we separate the lenses a little, the definition will be improved, but the working distance, as it is called, will be diminished. Those who have studied optics are quite familiar with these facts, but the ordinary reader does not always think of them, and yet they are very important when we come to choose a microscope for working or dissecting purposes.

Where two or more simple lenses are used together (without being combined so as to form a compound microscope) the power of the combination is always equal to the *sum* of the powers of the separate lenses. Thus if we have a lens of half an inch focus and one of one inch focus, one magnifying ten and the other twenty diameters, the resulting power is thirty and not two hundred times. In the compound microscope, on the other hand, the combination of an objective magnifying twenty diameters with an eye-piece magnifying ten diameters, gives a magnifying power of two hundred diameters.

Watch-Makers' Eye-Glasses.—These are well known, and may be obtained of almost any power within the useful range of a singe lens. They are called "eye-glasses" because when in use they are held by the muscles around the orbit of the eye, and consequently require no extraneous support. Fig. 4 shows the bell-mouthed form of the frame, which enables us to secure this result. The eye-glass ordinarily used by watch-makers magnifies about eight times, but glasses magnifying twenty diameters are not uncommon. Glasses of the latter power are usually *doublets*, that is, they consist of two lenses, arranged together, one being of much longer focus than the other. If well made they give excellent definition and a large field, and, when mounted on a stand, are very serviceable as *dissecting microscopes*, especially in working upon coarse objects, and picking out shells, the larger foraminifera, etc. Their form enables us to support them by means of a small wire ring, arranged as in a retort stand, and the large bell-mouth of the frame prevents any light from entering the eye, except that which has passed through the lens. They are very cheap, and any intelligent boy can make a tolerable stand for one. The same stand will answer for several glasses of different powers.

Fig. 4.—WATCH-MAKERS' GLASS.   Fig. 5.

The eye-glass shown in Figure 4 is a doublet, the front lens of which is set in a separate piece, shown in Figure 5. When the latter is removed, the remaining part forms a very serviceable low-power glass; when both are used together, the combination forms an excellent high-power magnifier. This form is one made by the Bausch & Lomb Optical Co.

Engravers' Glasses.—These are mounted in frames, similar to that of the watch-makers' eye-glass, but as they are larger, and are therefore not so readily held in the eye, after the fashion of the latter, they are always used with a stand of some kind. Those of the best quality are, in general, doublets, consisting of two plano-convex lenses, and as they give a large field of view, with very good definition, they are altogether the best microscopes for examining bank bills, fine engravings, and similar objects. The general form is shown in Fig. 6.

Fig. 6.—ENGRAVERS' GLASS.

Linen Provers.—These are a very old form of the simple microscope, and being in very general use, they are manufactured in large quantities, while as it is necessary that they should be of good quality they afford an opportunity of getting a good magnifier at a moderate price. The general form is shown in Fig. 7, in which the instrument appears as in use. The upper plate carries the lens, and the length of the upright is such that when the base is placed upon any flat surface, that surface will be in focus. The base is pierced with a hole one quarter of an inch square, and when placed on a piece of cloth the lens enables us to count the number of threads which occupy that space. This indicates the fineness of the fabric.

Fig. 7.—LINEN PROVER.

The Stanhope Lens consists of a cylinder or rod of glass, one end of which is rounded so as to form a lens, while the other end is either flat or slightly curved. The distance between the lens and the flat surface is exactly equal to the focal distance of the lens. Transparent objects, such as the scales of insects, animalculæ in water, etc., are simply placed on the flat surface of the glass cylinder, and when looked at through it, they appear greatly magnified. It is easily used, but can not well be employed as a working microscope. It is this kind of lens that is used in the construction of those watch charms in which a large picture is seen on looking through a very small hole. The picture is a photograph attached to the flat end of a small glass rod, the other end of the rod being formed into a lens of exactly the right focal length required to show the picture clearly and considerably magnified. Lenses and photographs of this kind are usually mounted as miniature opera-glasses.

The Stanhope lens seems to be a favorite in France, where it is manufactured very extensively, and sold under the name of the *Stanhoscope*. One advantage claimed for it is that no adjustment for focus is required, the flat surface of the lens being

Fig. 8.—STANHOPE COLLECTING LENS.

exactly in the focus of the curved surface. This feature, while presenting some slight advantages, has also the great disadvantage that objects covered with thin glass cannot be examined by such lenses, and neither can objects having a sensible thickness. The feature which we have just mentioned is imitated in some cases by placing a piece of thin glass in front of a small lens, and at such a distance that the outer surface of the thin glass will be exactly in focus, as is hereafter described when speaking of the Craig microscope.

There is one purpose, however, to which this form of lens is applied with good effect, and that is to the construction of a "collecting lens" as it is called—that is, a lens for examining drops of water when searching for diatoms, algæ, animalculæ, etc. Fig. 8 shows a lens of this kind made by Jas. W. Queen & Co., of Philadelphia. The lens is set in a brass frame, provided with a handle, and after a drop of water has been placed on the flat surface of the lens, the cap, c, is screwed on, and the object examined by simply holding the instrument up to the light.

A very excellent collector's microscope will also be found described amongst the compound instruments.

The Coddington Lens.—This lens was devised by Sir David Brewster, but having been made by a London optician for Mr. Coddington, it was called by his name, which has stuck to it ever since. It consists of a cylinder of glass, the two ends of which have been ground so as to form portions of the surface of the same sphere. A deep groove is cut around the cylinder, midway between the ends, and a diaphragm is thus formed between the two lenses. In Figure 9 is shown a very neat and convenient method of mounting the Coddington.

This form of lens gives very sharp definition, so that whenever a power greater than twenty diameters is required for *examining* objects, a Coddington, if well made, will be found to be the best lens in use, always, of course, excepting the carefully corected doublets and triplets hereafter described. The price of the latter, however, is in general four to eight times that of a good Coddington. But it has this defect, that the working focus is very short, and therefore for a dissecting microscope a doublet is to be preferred. In using a Coddington lens, great care must be taken to secure good illumination of the object, and the shortness of the focus makes this difficult to those who have had no experience.

Fig. 9.—CODDINGTON LENS.

Those who desire to acquaint themselves with the structure and peculiarities of the most important simple microscopes, will find this subject very fully and very clearly treated in the article contributed by Andrew Ross to the "Penny Cyclopædia," published by the Society for the Diffusion of Useful Knowledge. This article has been republished in book form.

Achromatic Doublets and Triplets.—Magnifiers, composed of two or more lenses, are to be had of two very distinct kinds. The lenses may either be simply united in one frame, without any special adaptation to each other, or the instrument may consist of two or more achromatic lenses combined together in a fixed and accurately determined relation. Examples of the former are found in the ordinary two and three lens magnifiers we have just described; the latter are not so common, since they are somewhat expensive when well made. They are known as achromatic doublets and triplets, and one maker in this country, Mr. Tolles, of Boston, has long been noted for the excellence of the simple achromatic microscopes of this class made by him.

The advantages possessed by lenses of this kind are the larger field of view which they give, thus enabling us to obtain a clear view of objects of considerable size; and the wonderfully increased sharpness of definition which they afford, owing to their wide angular aperture. They are usually mounted in the same style as the Coddington (Fig. 9), but are readily distinguished from the latter by the absence of any diaphragm. The lenses of which these magnifiers are composed are so constructed and combined that the field is perfectly flat and well defined in all its parts, so that a diaphragm is not necessary. Mere common lenses, put together so as to resemble these achromatic doublets, and without a diaphragm, would give such a misty view of objects that they would be at once condemned.

With the exception of the low and medium-power achromatic objectives used with the compound microscope, these doublets and triplets, when well made, are altogether the most satisfactory simple microscopes in use, and several firms now make a specialty of their manufacture. Amongst others we may name the Bausch & Lomb Optical Company, Messrs. R. & J. Beck, Browning, whose magnifiers of this kind are known as *Platyscopic* lenses, and Steinheil, of Munich.

To some it may appear that we have devoted more space to the simple microscope than its importance demands. Our excuse is that simple microscopes, of the different kinds we have just described, are not in such general use as they ought to be. This, however, seems to be the case even in France, the country of Raspail, who was the great advocate of the simple microscope, for Chevalier, in his work, says: "It is a matter of regret, from a scientific point of view, that the simple microscope is not more extensively used in France than it is, because in minute dissections it is capable of rendering immense service."

Twenty-five cent Microscopes.—Before leaving this subject it may be well to say a few words about those very cheap microscopes which have been so extensively advertised. We frequently see in the papers an advertisement in which some person offers to send for twenty-five cents a microscope which will show animalcules in water, globules of blood etc., etc., and the question naturally arises, Are these microscopes good for anything, or is the advertisement a swindle—the advertiser taking the money and sending nothing in return?

As a general rule, those who send to such advertisers, receive in return, a plate of brass or lead, with a glass bead fastened in a hole in the centre. The glass bead is formed by fusion and is frequently ground flat and polished on the side by which it was attached to the thread or rod of glass from which it was made, forming in such cases a hemispherical lens. Such lenses are very easily made by any one. Take a strip of flint glass, such as a piece of flint glass tubing, or a piece of glass rod, draw it out to a thread in the flame of a spirit lamp, fuse the end and allow it to gather into a drop. Give plenty of time and a good strong heat, so that the surface of the little globe may become well-fused and truly round. The best results are always obtained by holding the thread perpendicularly, as when held horizontally the globule is apt to become distorted. Make one or two dozen of these, and in separating them from the glass rod leave about an eighth of an inch of the latter attached to each globule, to serve as a handle, in the next step of the process, which consists in inserting them to about half their depth in a plate of cement, consisting of shellac thickened with very dry and finely powdered pumice-stone. To form such a wax plate, melt some shellac in a ladle or large iron spoon, mix it carefully with as much powdered pumice-stone as can be conveniently stirred in, remove it from the fire, stir well until it begins to stiffen, and then pour it out on a flat metal plate—the surface of a smoothing iron answering very well. The plate of cement should be from one-half to three-quarters of an inch thick, and the little globules are easily fastened into it by seizing them by the small handles left on them, holding them by a pair of forceps in a lamp flame until they are hot enough to melt the cement, and then pressing them in to about half their depth or a little more. When quite cold they will be very securely held. The little handles, or tails, are now nipped off with a pair of cutting pliers, and the globules ground all at once on a fine grindstone, or still better on a metal plate charged with emery. When they have been reduced nearly to the surface of the plate of cement, they should be ground with emery of the finest kind, and as soon as all coarse scratches have been removed they should be polished on a buff leather with crocus martis or putty powder. When finely polished they may be removed from the cement by means of a small chisel, and any cement that adheres may be dissolved off by means of alcohol. They are then mounted in thin plates of lead, brass, or, what is better still, vulcanite. Out of two dozen such globules, carefully made and well polished, three or four may be obtained that will give satisfactory definition, and it was with such lenses that the early microscopists made many of their discoveries. These men, however, took great pains in making and polishing them, and rejected hundreds as unfit for use. The objections to the microscopes of this kind, that are ordinarily sold, are that they are badly made, and that good and bad are sold together without any selection being exercised. But, even if well made, they are very difficult to use, and very unsatisfactory in their results, even in the hands of persons of great skill. The polish of a fused surface never equals that of a surface finely cut and polished, as every housekeeper that is familiar with common, and with cut glass, very well knows. The fused surface of these little globes is, therefore, always more or less, covered with striæ or very minute ridges which interfere with their defining powers, and we have described thus minutely the process of their manufacture, rather for the purpose of giving our readers such information as will enable them to understand how they can be sold so cheaply, than in the hope that they will endeavor to make them for themselves.

Penny Microscopes.—A few years ago a man in London made a living by selling through the streets a microscope which would show the eels in paste and vinegar, and of which the price was only one penny, (equal to two cents.) These microscopes were thus made: In the bottom of a pill-box he punched a small hole and then blackened the inside of the box. In this hole was placed a drop of Canada balsam or damar varnish, which was allowed to dry. When hard, the balsam formed a very tolerable lens.

A drop of water, balsam, or varnish, laid on the under side of a slip of clear glass will often enable us to extemporize a microscope capable of doing good service in the hands of a skillful observer. The outline of the drop should be perfectly round, and the glass plate should be held as level as possible. We have derived great assistance from such a lens, when better could not be had.

The Craig Microscope.—This microscope at one time attained an unprecedented degree of popularity, not on account of its merits, but because of the extensive puffing and advertising which it received. It consists of a vertical frame, somewhat like that of the cheap French microscopes, having a mirror, but no sliding tube, as there is no occasion for any. The slide which holds the object is slipped through a horizontal slit cut in the stand, and the lens with its frame is laid on it.

The lens is a fused bead of glass set in a little frame, to the under side of which is attached a thin plate of glass, whose lower surface is exactly in the focus of the bead, so that when a drop of water or vinegar is placed on the glass plate, or such objects as insects' scales, wings, etc., are laid on it, they are exactly in focus. Hence, this microscope is said to require no adjustment for focus. This is true when the objects to be examined are actually in contact with the glass plate, but when we wish to examine objects that are covered with thin glass (as all valuable preparations should be) or objects having a perceptible thickness, it is *impossible* to adjust it for focus, and hence it is impossible to examine such objects satisfactorily. Besides this, nine-tenths of the microscopes of this pattern in market, are very badly made, and distort objects to such an extent that one who has been accustomed to employ a good microscope cannot recognize them. It has unquestionably done a great great deal to impede the progress of microscopy in this country, and we have been led to give this extended description of it, chiefly because so many editors and clergymen have praised it in the highest terms. It has even been patented, although the principle upon which it is constructed is very old; but then we must remember that under our present administration the patent office seems to be conducted rather for the *dis*couragement than the *en*couragement of progress and invention. We daily see patents issued for old and worthless devices, while it is well-known that the author of a really meritorious invention will have the hardest work to obtain protection.

Of the Novelty, Globe, and other similar microscopes, it is unnecessary to speak. In all the microscopes of this kind that we have seen, the optical part is utterly worthless. The lenses are mere fused globules of glass, and they distort beyond recognition the image of any object.

Strange to say, however, even this fact has been used as an argument to sell them. They have been sold chiefly by newsdealers and stationers, and as the purchasers did not know how any given object *ought* to appear, the fact that it looked so very different from what they expected was considered an evidence of the power of the microscope ! !

In regard to all microscopes in which fused globules are used, it must be remembered that the lower the power of the lens the more apt it is to be imperfect. No lens of this kind, magnifying from 100 to 150 times, (according to the estimates of those who deal in them, which, however, is in fact only from ten to twelve times, as measured by proper methods), can be good for anything. On the other hand, it must be borne in mind that when we attempt to examine objects under high powers, obtained by the use of very small single lenses, we subject our eyes to an almost destructive strain.

DISSECTING MICROSCOPES.

The term *Dissecting Microscope* is applied to all microscopes used for working upon objects under moderate magnifying powers. They are used not only for dissecting, properly so called, but for the study of botany, mineralogy, etc., as well as for numerous investigations in the arts. A good microscope of this kind is absolutely indispensable to those who hope to do more than merely look at objects prepared by others.

For ordinary purposes of examination, the different magnifiers previously described serve very well when merely held in the hand, but their performance is greatly improved when they are mounted on appropriate stands, which not only enable us to adjust the focus with great accuracy, but which hold the lens steadily in relation to the object, and thus prevent any necessity for that constant adjustment of the eye itself, which always occurs when a lens trembles, and which is so fatiguing and injurious to the sight. A complete dissecting microscope should, therefore, be furnished with stand, mirror, etc., and if the student can afford it, there should be some good mechanical means of adjusting the focus. The importance of dissecting microscopes being generally recognized, even if the instruments themselves have not come into general use, nearly every manufacturer of microscopes has devised a stand of his own, some of which are very complete, and as a consequence very expensive. We shall, therefore, rest content with describing a few of the simpler forms.

The microscopist can easily construct a dissecting microscope for himself, by means of a cork and some wire, for whenever a piece of apparatus is to be supported steadily, while at the same time it is necessary that it should be easily moved and adjusted, nothing serves so well for a temporary expedient as a fine cork sliding on a smooth wire. Consequently a very serviceable stand for a simple microscope is easily extemporized as follows: Procure a good sound wine cork, and bore two holes through it, the holes being at right angles to each other, and to the axis of the cork. The holes should be of the right size to slide easily, but firmly, on a wire rather more than the sixteenth of an inch in diameter. One piece of such wire is stuck perpendicularly in a wooden foot, and serves as a stand upon which the cork slides up and down; another piece of wire, having a ring at one end for holding the magnifier, is thrust through the second hole in the cork, and is supported by it in a horizontal position. The horizontal wire should be so long that there will be no danger of injury to the eye or face from the upright wire. A piece of white paper makes the best mirror, as it gives sufficient illumination with low powers, and besides this, it diffuses the light very equally over the object. This, of course, is for use with transparent objects; when opaque objects are under examination a condensing lens must be employed.

The Excelsior Microscope.—The accompanying engraving gives a very clear view of this microscope, which is constructed as follows:

To one end of the lid of a small wooden case or box, is attached one of the ends of the box; and when the lid is reversed and turned upside down, it may be slid into the groove which usually receives it, and then forms a stand for the lenses and glass stage, as is shown in engraving. The lenses and stage are supported by a steel rod, D, the lower end of which is hinged to the lid, so that it may be turned down and lie in a groove provided for it. When raised into the position shown in the figure, it is held very securely in place by means of the button, E; and this button also serves to retain it in the groove when it is turned down. The glass stage, G, which is fitted into a frame of hard rubber, slides easily on the stem, D, so as to be readily adjustable for focus, while at the same time it may be firmly fixed, by means of a set-screw, at any desired height, and will then serve as a stage for dissecting purposes. The frame which holds the lenses fits on to the top of the stem. A mirror, H, is fitted into the case, and is readily adjustable by means of the button shown on the outside, so that light may be reflected up through the stage when the objects to be examined are transparent; and when they are to be viewed by reflected light there is a dark ground of hard rubber (not shown in the engraving) which is also carried by the stem, D, and may be turned under the stage, so as to cut off all transmitted light. Dissecting needles (K and L), with neat handles, fit into appropriate grooves. When the lenses and stage are removed from the stem they are readily packed in the case; the

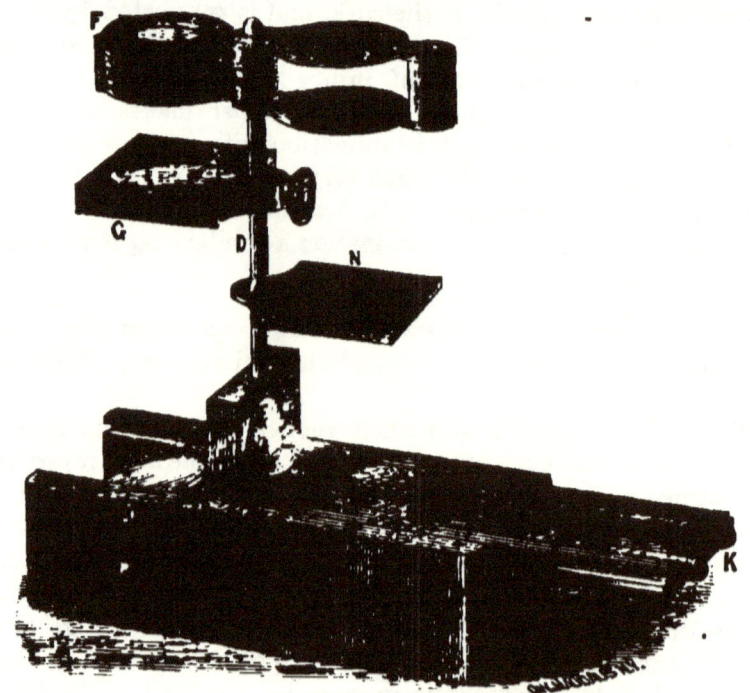

Fig. 10.—THE EXCELSIOR MICROSCOPE.

stem is then turned down and held in its groove by the button, E; the lid is drawn out of the groove, turned over, and replaced so that the vertical piece (C) closes the open end of the box, and the whole thing is packed into a compass which readily admits of its being carried in the vest pocket.

The lenses are well made, and being provided with a proper diaphragm, great clearness of definition is secured. Two styles of frame are sold, one containing two, and the other three lenses, the latter being altogether the cheapest, in proportion to the power furnished. The magnifying powers are about as follows: With the lens of longest focus, five diameters; with the lens of medium focus, eight diameters; with the lens of shortest focus, ten diameters. When the lenses of shortest and medium foci are combined the magnifying power is about eighteen diameters; all three lenses together give a power of twenty-five to thirty diameters.

In using a combination of two or more lenses, the lens of shortest focus should always be placed nearest to the object.

As a dissecting microscope for botanical, entomological, and physiological work, this instrument is very efficient and convenient. The glass plate is fitted into the stage so as to form a cell capable of holding water, so that dissections may be carried on under that liquid, or aquatic animals may be kept alive and examined at leisure. The stage may also be turned, so that the flat side will be up when so desired, in which position it is most convenient for some purposes, such as dissections and the teasing out of tissues by means of needles. The only serious defect in the Excelsior microscope is that it is not sufficiently steady for ordinary work, the case which forms the base or foot being, for portability's sake, made quite small. This difficulty is, however, easily remedied by screwing the case to a piece of pine board six inches long, four inches wide, and three-quarters of an inch thick. A single small screw, which does not deface the instrument, is sufficient, and when the microscope is to be carried in the pocket it is easily detached from its temporary stand. Its low price, $2.75, is a strong recommendation.

Raspail's Microscope.—This was the instrument so largely used by Raspail in his investigations into the structure of plants, and having been fully described by him, it has been called by his name, though Chevalier tells us that it was really invented by Cuff, of London, and ought to be called the Cuff microscope. It consists of a pillar which screws into the top of the box in which the whole instrument packs when the microscope is not in use. This pillar carries the mirror, and also a fixed stage. It is hollow, and in it slides a rod which may be moved up and down by means of a rack and pinion, so as to adjust for focus. This rod carries a horizontal arm, into one end of which the lenses fit, and the arm itself may be moved back and forth across the top of the vertical rod, so as to bring the lens over any part of the object. The great objection to this microscope, as usually constructed, is its want of steadiness, and this is a vital defect.

The Compact Dissecting Microscope —Those who desire a really serviceable and substantial microscope for dissecting purposes, will find that several manufacturers have recently endeavored to supply the demand for an instrument

Fig. 11.—THE COMPACT DISSECTING AND MOUNTING MICROSCOPE.

of this kind at a moderate price. We select one by the same firm that manufactures the Excelsior Microscope—the Bausch & Lomb Optical Co. It is called the "Compact Dissecting and

Mounting Microscope," from the fact that it may be folded together so as to occupy very little space, and may then be packed in the case which contains the compound microscope, or carried in its own little box. It is capable of receiving lenses of long focus, as the rod which carries the horizontal arm slides up and down in a tube upon which a rack is cut. This sliding movement serves for a coarse adjustment, the rack and pinion just mentioned serving for the fine adjustment. The mirror is hung with all necessary movements, and the arm which carries the lenses is provided with the Society screw, so that ordinary achromatic objectives may be used—thus saving the expense of extra lenses.

The engraving fails to show an important feature which is provided by the makers. This is a joint in the arm, which, in connection with the rotation that may be given to the rod to which the arm is attached, enables the operator to place the lens over any part of the preparation. We call this an important feature, for we hold it to be essential to the convenient use of the dissecting microscope that the preparation should remain stationary and firm during the processes and operations to which it is subjected. This is just the reverse of what is found to be most convenient and efficient in the compound microscope. There the objective should be immoveable (horizontally), and the object should be adjusted to a proper position in relation to it.

Rests for the arms, when using the dissecting microscope, are easily improvised out of books or blocks of wood. We prefer, to anything else, good-sized blocks of wood, having the form of a wedge with the point cut off. They are clumsy, it is true, but very comfortable. Small rests may be fitted like wings to each side of the stage, and these are furnished at a slight extra cost by the makers of the microscope just described.

Cheaper forms of this microscope are also made. In these the instrument is not made to fold up, and there are a few other points (not essential to the *efficiency* of the microscope) in which expense is avoided. But as improvements are being constantly introduced, those who require a good dissecting microscope should procure the catalogues of all the various dealers before they decide.

Binocular Dissecting Microscope.—The binocular principle, when applied to the dissecting microscope, is of the greatest value, as it enables us to estimate accurately the positions, vertically, of the several parts, and we can thus direct needles, knives, scissors, etc., to the exact point that we wish to operate on with an accuracy that is impossible with the monocular dissecting microscope. Nachet and Beck manufacture very excellent binocular dissecting microscopes, and the only thing to be regretted is that the price is necessarily somewhat high.

PRINCIPAL FORMS OF THE COMPOUND MICROSCOPE.

The variety of models, styles, or patterns which have been devised for the stands and for the general arrangement of compound microscopes, is almost infinite, and as they are continually changing, it would be a hopeless task to attempt to give a description of all, or even of any large number of them. Fortunately, from motives of self-interest, the manufacturers of these instruments promptly publish full descriptions and engravings of new styles as soon as they bring them out, and therefore the best plan for those who desire to make a judicious selection, is to procure the catalogues of as many manufacturers as possible, and carefully compare the several advantages of the different forms. The addresses of all the prominent manufacturers are published from year to year in the "Microscopist's Annual," a cheap little volume devoted to statistical information of this kind.

Cheap Foreign Stands.—A few years ago, the only stands attainable by those who could not afford an expensive article, were the cheap French and German microscopes. These were imported in large numbers by dealers in optical goods, and were distributed to different parts of the country through the agency of watchmakers, jewellers, booksellers, and those who dealt in spectacles and opera glasses, and consequently were *called* "opticians." Fortunately the production of really good and cheap American microscopes has almost driven this class of instruments out of market, but as they are still to be found on sale, a few words in regard to them may be necessary. One of the most common models is that shown in Fig. 12. This form, although modern when compared with the microscopes of Adams, Baker, etc., is one of the oldest in use. It was, we believe, devised by Wollaston, as a stand for his doublet, and was afterwards modified by Fraunhofer, whose microscopes on this model were almost identical with that shown in the engraving. It is now too well known to need elaborate description, and the smaller sizes are still sold extensively for the use of young people. Being manufactured in large quantities, they are sold very cheaply, when the quality of the lenses is taken into consideration. Therefore, until some manufacturer concentrates his efforts upon the production of the more convenient forms, and turns them out in very large numbers, the vertical microscope will probably maintain its place in the market, and many beginners will be led into buying an instrument which, even in its most complete and perfect form, will almost certainly be a source of dissatisfaction.

Fig. 12.
VERTICAL MICROSCOPE.

Aside from any deficiencies which may exist in the optical parts of the instrument, the objections to this model are the small size and inconvenient form of the stage ; the fact that the microscope can be used only in the vertical position, which, although occasionally very useful, is the worst position in which the instrument can be placed for protracted observations, and the arrangement of the mirror, which renders the proper management of the illumination impossible. Therefore, whenever there is a possibility of choice, some form other than the vertical should be chosen.

Occasionally microscopes of this kind are furnished with achromatic objectives of pretty fair quality. In such cases the objectives and eye-pieces, if they could be applied to a better stand, would be worth more than the whole microscope in its original form.

There is, however, one very useful purpose to which cheap microscopes of this kind may be applied. They make a very convenient and efficient pocket microscope for collecting. The stand should be cut off *above* the mirror, the flat stage being left with enough of the tube adhering to it to give it stiffness. A drop of water being placed in a cell, and covered with thin glass, is laid on the stage and held there with the fingers. To illuminate the object the microscope is simply held up to the sky. Those who object to holding the slide with the fingers, can have a round plate of metal soldered to the under side of the stage, so as to make it even. Movable clips, made by bending a narrow strip of hard sheet brass, so that both legs are even, can then be slipped on so as press on the slide, and on the under side of the stage. Such a microscope is very light, and may be readily carried in a tubular pasteboard case, which any one can make.

Setting aside these obsolete forms, as well as those models which have been devised for special purposes, we find that of the stands which are best suited to the purposes of the physician, the naturalist, the student, and the family, there are four distinct styles, which may be distinguished as follows: The Ross, the Jackson, the Continental, and the New American models. In order to give the reader an idea of these different models, and to explain the advantages and disadvantages of each, we give engravings and such descriptions as will enable him to form some idea of the stand best suited to his special wants. In selecting illustrations of the different types, we have taken the cheaper forms in preference to the more perfect, but more expensive models; and as our object is to describe the general features of the stands themselves, and not to detail the merits and point out the faults of those parts which may be easily changed or altered, we have omitted all description of diaphragms, eye-pieces, objectives, etc.

The Ross Model.—The distinguishing characteristic of this model is the mode in which the body is supported. By referring to Plate I, it will be seen that the body is attached at its lower end to a transverse arm, which in turn is supported by a stout bar, which is moved up and down by means of a rack and pinion. This movement constitutes the coarse adjustment, the fine movement being effected by means of a lever which is concealed in the transverse bar, and acts upon the nose-piece.

So far as mere questions of convenience and adaptability to different kinds of work is concerned, this model is all that can be desired, and as made by Ross & Co., the workmanship is so perfect, and the finish so exquisite, that it has long maintained a high position in public favor. It has, therefore, had numerous imitators, and has probably been copied more extensively than any other model in existence. At the recent Centennial Exhibition there were microscopes on this model from the most widely scattered localities. Canada was represented by two microscopes made after this design. Unfortunately, however, this model is one of the very worst that a poor workman can attempt to imitate, for unless the workmanship is far above the average, the results are execrable. The reason for this is very obvious. The body, being supported only at the lower end, every vibration causes the upper end to swing through a comparatively large arc, and hence any motion arising from looseness in the joints is multiplied a hundred fold. And even when the joints are firm and without shake, any vibration communicated to the table on which the instrument stands, is greatly increased in its effects when it reaches the upper end of the body. In addition to this, the unsupported part of the body acquires, by each movement, a momentum which reacts powerfully on the lower part, and consequently on the objective.

These defects have induced Messrs. Ross & Co. to bring out a new pattern designed after the Jackson model. This design has been carefully worked out by Mr. Wenham, and is certainly very beautiful in appearance, and very efficient and convenient in use. Our readers will therefore bear in mind, that all microscopes made by Ross & Co., are not made on the "Ross model."

The Jackson Model.—The special characteristic of this model lies in the fact that the "ways" of both the coarse and fine movements are brought as close as possible to the optic axis of the instrument. In the Ross model the coarse movement is at a considerable distance from this axis, and any lateral motion which may take place on the sliding part is greatly magnified at the axis of the body—the transverse bar, which supports the latter, acting like the long arm of a lever to greatly multiply that which at first was very insignificant. Hence the advantages which this model presents are great steadiness and the fact that, in common with the Ross model, it affords abundant room underneath the stage for those accessory methods of illumination which are indispensable in the highest class of work. It is almost impossible to attach to the smaller patterns of the Continental model a convenient sub-stage, carrying polarizer, achromatic condenser, paraboloid, etc., while the model under consideration is specially designed to receive these important accessories.

This model is a very general favorite both with English and American makers. Amongst the latter it has been adopted as the best for all first-class stands. The engraving, Plate II, shows a very excellent form of this model by the Bausch & Lomb Optical Company, and known as their Large Student Stand. It will be observed that the body of the microscope is supported along its whole length by means of a tube attached to the arm, which is hung between two pillars, so as to give great steadiness. To add to this steadiness, all sharp angles are avoided, and the arm is gracefully curved instead of joining the body at a right angle, as in the Ross model, and all of those made strictly after the so-called Continental pattern.

The Continental Form.—Most of the stands made by the better class of French, German, and Austrian microscope makers are characterized by a low, compact form, and great solidity and simplicity of construction. They are intended to be used chiefly in a vertical position, and hence the bodies are short, and the space beneath the stage is contracted to the last degree. And as a low price is an important feature in these microscopes, the coarse movement is generally secured by simply sliding the body through a tube or collar. In the higher-priced stands the coarse movement is effected by means of a rack and pinion, arranged as in the "Jackson" model, but in both styles the fine movement is generally arranged in the place where the coarse movement is located in the "Ross" stand. These features will be found to characterize the microscopes of Chevalier, Hartnack, Nachet, Zeiss, and others.

The term "Continental" model has been applied by ourselves and others to any low, compact form of microscope, but a careful study of the subject has satisfied us that this is not correct. The characters above given are peculiar to what ought to be known as microscopes of the Continental model.

The Continental model has some advantages on the score of convenience, and as large numbers of our medical students have been educated to its use, it has been such a favorite that many of our prominent makers have imitated it to a certain degree. For the ordinary work of the physician and the histologist, a low microscope, which may be easily arranged for work, and which may be used conveniently in a vertical position, is certainly desirable, but other forms, possessing the same advantages and without the objectionable features of the Continental model, are now in market, and have taken their place.

The objections to the Continental model as a microscope for the higher classes of work, are the want of space below the stage for illuminating accessories, and the liability of the fine movement to get out of order. For it is obvious that a very little wear on the "ways" or "slides" will allow the body to have considerable lateral motion, the distance of the "ways" from the optic axis of the instrument being very great. Some of our American makers, who have adopted this fine motion, have gone so far as to use hard steel pins sliding on hardened ways as guides, but with all their care lateral motion ensues after a time.

The New American Model.—The more general employment of objectives of wide angles of aperture, and of improved methods of using them, have led American manufacturers to introduce certain improvements in stands of moderate price, and the stands which embody these improvements and modifications are so distinct that they form a class by themselves, which may be designated the "New American Model." None of the individual features found in this model are new, the most important of them having been embodied many years ago in the English patent of Grubb, while others were used long ago by Spencer in this country. But Grubb's invention, so far as we know, never came into use, and it was not until the year 1875, that the importance of the improvements in question became generally recognized. Towards the close of that year, and the beginning of 1876, four of the prominent microscope makers of this country, viz., Bulloch, Gundlach, Tolles, and Zentmayer seem to have turned their attention to the subject, and shortly after brought out models on the new plan, the distinctive features of which are the swinging of the mirror around a centre which lies in the plane of the object; the combination of a swinging with a longitudinal movement in the sub-stage, and the use of a very thin stage. Prior to this time, in all the best microscopes of English and American make (at least as described in the catalogues of the dealers), the sub-stage was made to move only in the line of the optic axis of the instrument; the American makers took a new departure, and the new model is the result. In its popular forms this model is characterized by great simplicity in its working parts, while at the same time, being provided with the very best means for adjusting and registering the illumination, it is a stand which is sufficient for the highest class of work, except, of course, in a few special departments.

So far as our knowledge goes there are at present before the public four stands of comparatively low price, which may be relegated to this class They are: The "Acme" of J. W. Sidle & Co.; the "Biological" of Bulloch; the "Histological" of Zentmayer, and the "Investigator" of the Bausch & Lomb Optical Company. The large stands of the Bausch & Lomb Optical Co., of Beck, Bulloch, Ross, Tolles, Zentmayer, and others, are of course quite as efficient as the small stands we have named, but the price is greater, and the convenience of the small stands, when used as working microscopes, is in their favor. At the end of this volume the reader will find plates of the "Acme," the "Biological," the "Histological" and the "Investigator" stands, and we would recommend the reader to study carefully their several special features.

The "Acme" will be described in its binocular form, and we therefore pass, in alphabetical order, to the "Biological" stand of Mr. Bulloch, which is shown in Plate III.

It will be seen at once that this stand is substantial and firm in all its parts. The coarse movement is by rack and pinion, and the body is supported, as in the Jackson model, along nearly its entire length. The fine movement acts upon the entire body, the coarse movement included, so that the distance between the eye-piece and the objective is not affected by it. The stage is thin, but substantial, and is so cut away at the well-hole that light of great obliquity can be used. The stage-plate rotates in a ring, and may be clamped when necessary by means of the small screw seen in front. By loosening this screw the plate may be entirely removed, and then, when the body stands upright, a simple plate of glass may be used for a stage, and thus all danger of injury from acids is avoided. The ring in which the stage-plate rotates is held in place by two capstan-headed screws, and when these are slacked it is easy to adjust the stage so that it shall be concentric with the optic axis. The sub-stage is arranged for adjustment in the same way. It is adapted to carry the standard size accessories, and is furnished with an adapter which has the Society screw, so that ordinary objectives may be used as condensers. Mr. Bulloch also furnishes a diaphragm of peculiar form (shown in the engraving), which we have found very efficient, both with direct and oblique light. The special feature of models of this class is, however, shown in the method of hanging the mirror and sub-stage. These are attached to separate bars, which rotate on an axis, the plane of which is a little above the level of the stage. A stop is also provided, whereby they may both be placed precisely in the line of the optic axis. Both mirror and sub-stage may be moved towards the stage and from it, and the movements of both are entirely independent. The consequence is that the various forms of illuminating apparatus have a range of adjustment that cannot be obtained with the older models.

The instrument, as shown in the cut, is about two-fifths of the real size. When the draw-tube is out, the body has the standard length of ten inches, and it is furnished with the "broad-gauge" screw, to which is fitted an adapter carrying the standard Society screw.

The first stand placed in market at a moderate price, and embodying the special features of the new American model, was the Histological stand of Mr. Zentmayer, which is shown in Plate IV. The base and uprights of this stand are one piece, of a peculiar shape, of great rigidity, to which the bell-metal bar is attached by a joint, allowing the use of the instrument at any angle of inclination ; the perpendicular and horizontal positions are indicated by stops. The coarse adjustment is by a rack and pinion, or in cheaper forms by a sliding tube.

The fine adjustment is by a concealed lever, acted upon by a delicate screw, and moving the entire body, which is fitted to the grooved bar, giving a steady and delicate movement. The arrangement of the swinging sub-stage and mirrors is easily understood from the engraving.

The removable sub-stage carries the diaphragms, which can be shifted up close to the object.

The stage is a modification of the glass stage, and consists of a glass bar kept down by two spring clips, against which the object rests. By this method the object may be moved in the latitude, the longitudinal movement being accomplished by hand. The spring clips may be used independently for holding anything in a fixed position, by simply placing them in the extra holes provided for that purpose.

The "Investigator" stand is shown in Plate V, and also presents the special features which we have mentioned. The mirror-bar is swung so that its axis of motion lies in the plane of the object, and it carries the sub-stage, which may thus be inclined to any angle with the plane of the stage, or it may be brought entirely above the latter. The mirror is attached to the mirror-bar by means of a secondary bar, which thus permits the use of the mirror independently of the sub-stage, and both mirror and sub-stage may be moved to and from the object. The sub-stage may be removed entirely when desirable.

In order to secure the convenience of the low Continental

model, this microscope is provided with *two* draw-tubes, sliding one within the other, so that the body may be shortened as much as possible when desired. The first draw-tube has the Society screw at the lower end, so that low-power objectives of very great working distance may be used; and as, by means of the second draw, the draw-tube may be made of the usual standard length (ten inches), it may be used as the body for any objective, and quickly focussed by sliding it in the outer tube, the same as in instruments without rack and pinion adjustment. The " broad-gauge " screw has been added, so that low-power objectives of wide angle may be used to the greatest advantage.

Cheaper Stands.—The stands which we have just described, are, of necessity, somewhat expensive, because, unless the workmanship is of the very best, the performance is quite unsatisfactory; and as a stand alone is of no use, an outfit which includes such a stand is frequently beyond the means of students and others. To meet the wants of such persons, the various manufacturers we have named, together with Klein, Pike, Schrauer, and others, have brought out stands, which, when complete, with case and objectives, are sold for about the price of the stands we have described. For the study of elementary botany, histology, etc., many of these cheap microscopes answer a very good purpose. They enable us to follow the descriptions given in the books, and the view of any object which we obtain from even the poorest of them, is infinitely better than any representation which can be given by an engraving. The better class of these microscopes answer well for the ordinary purposes of the physician, and, as they are simple and easily used, they are frequently preferred to more expensive and more complicated instruments.

The Binocular Microscope.—More than two hundred years ago, attempts were made to construct binocular microscopes, and yet a good and efficient binocular is a thing of yesterday. The first really efficient binocular microscope was constructed by Prof. Riddell, of New Orleans, about the year 1853, and to this fact Mr. Wenham has borne free and generous testimony in a letter addressed to the *English Mechanic.* To Mr. Wenham, himself, however, is due the honor of having devised a form of the binocular which is at once efficient and of moderate price. Mr. Wenham's form has been adopted by all the American and English makers that manufacture binoculars, and he has, therefore, laid all microscopists under deep obligations, not only by devising such simple and efficient means of accomplishing a most desirable result, but by giving the use of his invention freely to the world.

Of the value of the binocular, there is a wide difference of opinion, some regarding it as a mere toy, altogether beneath notice as an instrument of scientific research, while others consider it a most important addition to our means of investigation. Since, however, it will almost always be found that those who place a high value on the binocular are those who have used it most, while those who decry it know absolutely nothing of its merits, and in some cases are even ignorant of the manner of using it, the reader will have but little difficulty in deciding on which side the truth lies. In England, where cheap and good binoculars are common, this form of instrument has become a great favorite with all the noted microscopists, and we refer not merely to men who own microscopes as a means of amusement, but to those, who, like Carpenter and others, have enlarged the boundaries of knowledge by their researches. At present the binocular is gaining rapidly in favor in this country, and very excellent instruments are now turned out by several of our American microscope makers.

There are, of course, certain limits to the range of usefulness of the binocular microscope. As at present constructed, it is most efficient in the use of the low powers, and hence, there are certain classes of work to which it is peculiarly applicable, while in other branches, particularly certain departments of histology, it is of comparatively slight advantage. And it will in general be found that the principal opposition to the binocular has come from continental histologists, who, because they found it of little use to themselves, concluded that it could not possibly be of use to any one else.

The advantages presented by binocular instruments are twofold; the relief to the observer arising from the ability to use both eyes is very great, and the view which is obtained of any object is so much clearer and more realistic, that we at once perceive, by our mere sense of vision, those features which we would otherwise have to work out by tedious mental processes. It has been said by some that the binocular is apt to exaggerate the stereoscopic effects, and give false views. This is certainly not the case under ordinary circumstances, and we doubt much if it ever occurs.

We have selected as an illustration of the binocular microscope, one of moderate cost, which combines the binocular feature with those peculiar to the new American model—the "Acme," made by J. W. Sidle & Co., of Lancaster, Pa. This instrument, in its monocular form, was, we believe, arranged by Prof. J. Edwards Smith, and the details of its construction were worked out with special reference to the use of objectives of high angles. So far as this purpose is concerned, the "Acme" has many points in common with the "Biological" stand of Mr. Bulloch, the "Histological" of Zentmayer, and the "Investigator" of the Bausch & Lomb Optical Co., the differences being chiefly in details of construction, which leave room for choice on the part of intending purchasers. We therefore turn to the binocular feature as being that with which we are now more immediately concerned.

The binocular in general use, being that in which the Wenham prism is used, consists of a main body through which the half of the rays transmitted by the objective pass directly to the eye-piece. In the figure (Plate VI) this body is the one nearest to the reader, and connected with it is another body, through which the other half of the rays pass—they being diverted in this direction by the prism, which, when in place, cuts the cone of rays from the objective in two. The frame which carries this prism is seen just above the point at which the objective is attached, and it is so arranged, that when desirable it may be drawn out, and thus the prism becomes inoperative, and the instrument is practically converted into a monocular one. This is one of the important advantages which are peculiar to the Wenham prism. In some forms of the Acme binocular the entire fittings of the prism may be removed, so as not to interfere with **wide-angle lenses of low power.**

As eyes differ greatly in their distance apart, the eye-pieces in the binocular are made variable in this respect by being pushed out or in, either by a lever or a rack and pinion. As the bodies are not parallel, but form an angle with each other, it is evident that the further the eye-pieces are drawn out the wider apart do they become.

Binocular Eye-Piece.—A very valuable and efficient means of converting an ordinary monocular microscope into a binocular, has been devised by Mr. Tolles. The one which we possess gives excellent results with objectives of higher power than those available with the Wenham prism as ordinarily constructed, and it is greatly to be regretted that its high price ($80) places it beyond the reach of those for whom this work is chiefly intended. It has been copied extensively in Europe, but we believe that it is now definitely settled that the honor of the invention belongs to Mr. Tolles.

The Inverted Microscope.—Some years ago, Professor J. Lawrence Smith devised a microscope specially adapted to chemical investigations. In this instrument the stage is placed *over* the objective, which is inverted, and the rays from the object, after being reflected *down* through the objective, enter a prism, which so changes their direction that they pass up the body to the eye-piece, and thence to the eye of the observer. For very many investigations the inverted microscope is a very useful instrument.

Lithological Microscopes.—The application of the microscope to petrology, or the study of rocks, has now become such an important department of scientific research that microscopes specially adapted to this purpose are manufactured by several makers. These microscopes possess several very important conveniences, which are almost indispensable for such work, but which the limits of the present volume forbid us to describe at length.

The Aquarium Microscope.—The importance of the compound microscope in the examination of small portions (*in situ*) of large objects, without any preparation whatever, has led to the construction of microscopes consisting simply of a body with its adjustments for focussing arranged on the simplest kind of a support—usually a rod and foot somewhat like a retort stand. Such microscopes have been used largely for examining objects in aquaria, and hence the name. They are also applicable to the examination of writing, the sheet of paper being simply spread out on a table and the microscope placed on it; to the examination of portions of the surface of the human body in various cases of skin disease, and, in short, to the examination of any object which cannot be conveniently placed on the stage of an ordinary microscope.

Microscopes for Special Purposes.—In addition to the microscopes which we have described, some of which have been devised with a special view to certain particular lines of research, it often happens that a microscope is needed for a single purpose, and for no other. Thus, for example, in Germany, a few years ago, microscopes were made and sold for the sole purpose of examining flesh for trichinæ. These microscopes were very simple, and when their quality was considered, they were very cheap—the cheapness being due, in a great degree, to the fact that no provision had been made for a multiplicity of conveniences, which, in the case of these special instruments, would never be of any use. As the microscope becomes more generally used, and the people at large become more thoroughly acquainted with the extraordinary aid which it is capable of rendering to those who are engaged in the arts, it is probable that the numbers of these cheap microscopes will increase, in which case we may expect to see the price greatly reduced in proportion to the quality.

"Class" Microscopes.—When a number of objects are to be shown to a class or to a scientific meeting, it is desirable to avoid the inconvenience arising from each individual having to go to the instrument, and this is unavoidable where ordinary microscopes are used on fixed tables. Prof. Quekett got over this difficulty by having his class-room or theatre fitted up with rails upon which the microscopes with their lamps were passed from one to another, and where the company is small, the common revolving table meets every requirement. But where the class or meeting is large, the best device is that of Prof. O. W. Holmes, whose class microscope, as made by Messrs. J. W. Queen & Co., is shown in Figure 13. This instrument is of the simplest construction, so as to reduce the cost as much as possible, and it is made largely of wood, so as to be light and easily held in the hand. The objects are viewed by direct light, without the intervention of a mirror. The lamp used is a flat-wicked one, the edge of the wick being turned towards the

Fig. 13.—HOLMES' CLASS MICROSCOPE.

object when high powers are used, and the flat side of the wick when the powers are low.

For opaque objects, the lamp is raised to the top of its stand, and its rays allowed to fall upon a small concave mirror attached to the iron frame by a universal joint, whence they are reflected upon the object. The coarse adjustment is effected by sliding the body through a short split tube, and the fine movement by means of a delicate screw, which acts on the stage. The entire height of the instrument is about twelve inches, size of base twelve by four inches.

OBJECTIVES.

The modern compound microscope owes almost all its value to the high degree of perfection which has been attained in the construction of the objectives used with it. Some of the old microscope stands were quite as elaborate, and quite as costly, as anything that can be found in the workshops of our modern opticians, but from the fact that the objectives were defective, their value as instruments of research was of a very low degree. In these old microscopes even the highest power objectives were simply bits of ground glass, such as with our modern appliances might easily be produced for ten cents apiece, while a modern objective of the same power, by any of our first-class makers, would cost at least one hundred dollars. In mechanical execution the modern objective approaches more nearly to theoretical perfection than any other instrument made by man, but the reader must not infer from this, as some have done, that it has reached the limit of perfection, and that nothing more is to be expected. This was said ten, twenty, and thirty years ago, and in each case the words had hardly been committed to paper before some optician proved their falsity by accomplishing that which had just been declared to be impossible! Within the past few years the most wonderful improvements have been effected, and from present indications it would seem that we are on the eve of still more startling developments.

Since, then, the objective is really the most important part of every microscope, seeing that the quality and trustworthiness of the work done must depend to a very great extent upon its efficiency, it is of some importance to the microscopist that he should have at least a fair understanding of the causes to which the superiority of modern objectives is due.

When we use a simple glass lens as an objective for a compound microscope, we find, on attempting to examine objects under powers of more than one hundred diameters, the following defects and difficulties: The field of view is so dimly illuminated that objects are seen with difficulty; the outlines of the different parts, instead of being sharp and clear, are thick and hazy; several of the lines are fringed with brilliant colors, but colors which do not belong to the objects, and finally, if the outlines of the object should happen to be straight lines, and be known to be such, it will be found that they will appear to be curved and distorted. It is evident, therefore, that a simple lens cannot be used as an objective in any important work; its indications are unreliable, and the imagination is allowed full scope, so that the eye is enabled to see whatever the mind desires to see.

The defects which we have just detailed, and which are found in every simple glass lens, whose surfaces are bounded with curves that are parts of circles, are largely due to what is called *spherical* and *chromatic aberration*. As these terms are probably not familiar to many of our readers, we will give as full and simple an explanation of the subject as can be done without the formal aid of mathematics.

Spherical Aberration.—The enlarged image formed at the focus of any lens, and rendered visible on a screen or sheet, is produced in this way: The rays proceeding from the object, and passing through the lens, are, by the action of the glass, bent from the path they would otherwise pursue. The object may of course be supposed to consist of an infinite number of points, and from these points rays proceed in every direction, and consequently through every part of the lens. If the lens were perfect, all the rays from any one point would be brought together at a second point corresponding with the first. Unfortunately, however, the ordinary lens does not do this; the central portions of the lens and the outer portions act differently; the one brings the rays to a focus at a point a little nearer to the lens than the other, and, consequently, although we move the screen to a slightly greater or less distance, we still get an image of about the same degree of distinctness. It is obvious, therefore, that when placed at any distance within certain limits, the screen will receive not one image, but a series of *layers* of images as it were, and this consequently gives an indistinctness to the resulting image.

Our readers will find no difficulty in thinking out this matter for themselves, and when they have arrived at clear ideas upon the subject, they will see that spherical aberration is caused by the difference between the extent of the refraction produced at different parts of the lens, and this applies not only to all the rays proceeding from each individual point, but to the several pencils which proceed from different points.

It is evident that if some parts of the lens bring the rays to a focus at a shorter distance than others, these parts must magnify more, and such is in reality found to be the case. But if one part of an object is magnified more than another, the image will be distorted, and hence we have what is sometimes known as *aberration of form*. This distortion is easily seen by examining a piece of muslin with a magnifier of high power and large diameter. The threads in the centre of the field of view* will appear to be straight, while those at the outside will appear to be curved.†

Chromatic Aberration.—This is a defect of ordinary or uncorrected lenses, whereby they not only act as magnifiers, but as prisms, decomposing the light, and causing objects seen through them to appear with a fringe of color. Common hand magnifying glasses, used in the ordinary way, do not exhibit this defect to a very marked degree, but when the images formed by lenses of this kind are again magnified, as is done in the compound microscope or telescope, the color becomes very disagreeably perceptible.

* By field of view is meant that portion of the object which is visible through the magnifier.

†In ordinary lenses and microscopes, in which this defect is not corrected by the structure of the glasses themselves, the effects of spherical aberration are lessened by contracting the field of view, so that only those parts of the object which are seen through the centre of the lens or objective are looked at. This contraction is usually effected by means of diaphragms, or round plates of metal pierced with a central hole, which are so placed as to cut off the rays which pass through the edge of the lens, and leave only those that are central. This plan, however, is only the substitution of one defect for another, for by lessening the field of view of the lens, we are prevented from seeing more than a very small portion of the object, and in addition to this the light is so much reduced that the object is seen only with very great difficulty, and not at all clearly.

Corrected Objectives.—The defects which we have just described have been the chief difficulties in the way of perfecting both the microscope and the telescope. In the case of the latter, however, it was long ago found that very excellent results could be obtained by forming the lenses of two or more pieces of glass of different kinds, and numerous attempts were made to apply the same principles to the construction of the microscope, but without marked success. The small lenses used for the microscope seemed to defy the skill of the practical opticians of those days, and resort was had to such devices as lenses made of precious stones, and the use of light which could not be decomposed—*mono-chromatic* light as it was called, or light of one color. Such light is readily procured by the combustion of alcohol mixed with common salt, and when illuminated solely by such a light, a brilliantly colored painting looks exactly like a plain black and white engraving. But although the use of such a light lessens the evils caused by chromatic aberration, they introduce another which is quite serious—objects which are really colored, appear in black and white only. Moreover, such a light cannot easily be obtained of a brilliancy sufficient to afford good illumination, and in addition to this all the defects due to spherical aberration still remain in full force.

The first attempts made to perfect the object-glasses of microscopes, consisted in the use of doublets and triplets, it having been found that the spherical aberration is greatly lessened, when the total refraction is divided up amongst several surfaces of moderate curvature, instead of one surface in which the curvature is excessive, and this plan is still pursued in the construction of what are known as French triplets, which will be described hereafter. About the year 1829, however, Mr. J. J. Lister, of London, England, published an elaborate paper upon the subject, and it was from the principles laid down in this paper, that all the important improvements in the modern objective took their rise. These principles were embodied in the practical construction of objectives by Andrew Ross, who suggested the important improvement known as the adjustment for thickness of cover. To Lister and Ross, therefore, it may be justly said that we owe that optical wonder, the modern objective, for although great improvements have been made within the past few years, it is upon the results of their labors that these improvements have been based. And yet, notwithstanding this well-known fact, the names of these distinguished microscopists are not so much as mentioned in this connection in the recent work of Dr. Frey, which has been lately translated into English, and extensively circulated in this country!

In estimating the quality of an objective, there are certain features to which especial attention must be given. Aside from magnifying power, which, of course, cannot be regarded as affecting the *quality* of an objective, these points are: 1. Defining power; 2. Achromatism; 3. Freedom from aberration of form; 4. Flatness of field; 5. Angular aperture; 6. Penetration; 7. Working distance.*

Defining Power.—This is undoubtedly the most important quality to be sought for in objectives. A glass that is deficient in this point is absolutely worthless. Want of defining power is shown by a general haziness and thickening of the outlines, together with a want of clearness in the details. It arises from the presence of either spherical or chromatic

*The authors of the Micrographic Dictionary enumerate the following points as those in which object-glasses differ from each other: 1. Magnifying power. 2. Defining power. 3. Penetrating power. 4. Their corrective adaptations. The functions attributed to "defining power" are the same as those given by other writers; "penetrating power" seems to be equivalent to what is generally called "resolving power;" "corrective adaptation" is merely the presence of a means of adjusting for thickness of glass cover. Frey distinguishes two attributes of object-glasses, viz., defining power, and penetrating or resolving power—penetrating power and resolving power being considered by him to be the same thing. Carpenter enumerates four distinct attributes of object-glasses, viz., "(1) *Defining power*, or the power of giving a clear and distinct image of all well marked features of an object, especially of its boundaries; (2) its *penetrating power* or *focal depth*, by which the observer is enabled to look into the structure of objects; (3) its *resolving power*, by which it enables closely approximated markings to be distinguished; and (4) the *flatness of the field* which it gives." We cannot regard any of these classifications, as strictly logical. Beale makes no formal statement, but gives some very excellent practical directions in regard to the selection of objectives.

aberration, or both. It might be caused by a want of finish on the surfaces of the lenses, but this is seldom the case in practice, except where the objective has been exposed to some corroding fumes or liquids. Old objectives that have been very excellent in their day, sometimes fail in defining power, from the fact that the surface becomes covered with a greasy deposit, very slight, it is true, but just enough to destroy the efficiency of the glass. Objectives in this condition should be returned to the makers to be cleaned. In one case we found that in a lens which failed to show anything clearly, the difficulty arose from the fact that the cement used for uniting the glasses of the combination had become affected. The objective was by a well-known maker, but was over twenty years old

Achromatism.—When an objective shows much color, it fails to define well except by monochromatic light, such as that obtained by passing sunlight through a cell filled with the blue solution of copper in ammonia. A very slight degree of color is not regarded as objectionable, and indeed it has been found almost impossible to secure the requisite angular aperture and absence of spherical aberration without leaving a little color. Some of the best objectives, therefore, show such objects as the *P. angulatum* with decided colors, and yet well resolved.

Aberration of Form.—An objective may appear to define an object perfectly, and yet give a very distorted figure of it, just as a cylindrical mirror gives a perfectly definite, though very distorted, image of objects seen reflected in it. Aberration of form may arise either from over or under correction of the spherical aberration, or from want of homogeniety in the glass used for making the lenses, or from a want of perfection in the workmanship—the surfaces of the lenses not being perfectly spherical. Sometimes this defect is shown very clearly on one side of an objective, while the other side is not affected, and this fact may give rise to very curious results when the objective is tried on different stands, and with oblique light. Owing to a variation in the point at which the screw threads begin in the different stands, the objective, when fairly screwed up, may have a different position in each, as regards the direction from which the illumination comes. The consequence is, that an objective which may give excellent results on one stand, may fail on another. An easy way of testing this fact, is by means of a rotating adapter. Of course the best test for aberration of form is the artificial star, though in the hands of the beginner, a micrometer, ruled into squares, is probably the most available test. Any trace of the defect under consideration will be shown by the lines being curved.

When the lines appear curved, from the fact that the spherical aberration has not been properly corrected, the nature of the error may be determined as follows: When the micrometer lines are widest apart at the centre (like the lines on a map of a hemisphere) the spherical aberration has been over-corrected. It is under-corrected when the reverse is the case.

Aberration of form is one of the worst faults with which a lens can be affected, and experience has shown us that it is the one which is least apt to be detected by a beginner. An objective may give a "beautiful" image, and yet be worthless because affected with this defect.

Flatness of Field.—If, when we examine a perfectly flat object, every part included in the field of view is clearly in focus, the objective is said to have a *flat field*. Want of flatness of field is shown by some parts of a flat object being clear and well-defined, while other parts are out of focus. In general it happens that where this defect exists, the centre and circumference of the objective do not act together.

Angular Aperture.—This subject has given rise to some of the most vexatious questions connected with microscopy, for a discussion of which we must refer our readers to the pages of the microscopical journals published during the past few years. The views which have been promulgated by the two schools into which microscopists have been divided on the questions affecting angular aperture, have been of an extremely opposite nature, and few scientific disputes have been waged with more bitterness and personalities than that which has been called the "Battle of the High and Low Angles." Now that the smoke has in a measure cleared away, and that we are able to take a calm view of the actual results which have been attained, there is little room for doubting that the wide angles have gained the victory in all the most important points. In a subsequent section we shall give our view in regard to the circumstances

Fig. 14. Fig. 15.

DR. GORING'S FIGURES ILLUSTRATING ANGULAR APERTURE.

which ought to influence the beginner in the selection of objectives of high or low angles; at present we shall confine ourselves to a discussion of what angular aperture is, and its influence upon the working qualities of the objective.

The reader who will carefully look over the pages of the microscopic journals published during the last few years, will probably find that amongst the combatants even the *definition* of angular aperture seems to be undecided, all of which is, of course, very puzzling to a beginner. We do not propose to decide this vexed question, but the following statement will, we hope, enable our readers to form a clear idea of what the older writers meant by this term.

It was Dr. Goring, we believe, that first pointed out the special advantages of high angles, and suggested the use of test objects, and the figures on the preceding page were used by him to define and explain what he meant by angular aperture.

In these figures, L L and L' L' are two lenses of the same magnifying power, but different angular apertures. It will be seen that the cone of rays proceeding from O, is substantially the same as that from O', but that the lens L L takes in a larger part of the cone from O, than the lens L' L' does of the cone from O'. The angles L O L and L' O' L' are the respective measures of the angular apertures of the two lenses.

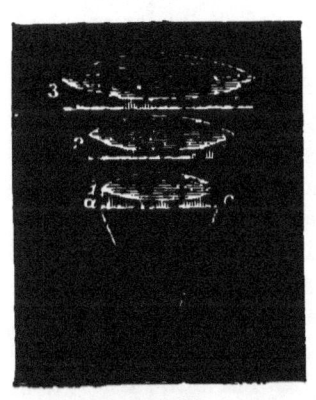

Fig. 16.

The definition of angular aperture, given by Goring, has been followed by all subsequent writers, the accompanying figure being that used by Dr. Carpenter for the purpose of explaining and defining the same thing. In this figure the compound lenses, 1, 2 and 3, are parts of an achromatic objective without its brass mounting. The line, *a c*, is the front of the objective, and *b* is the object. In this case the angle, *a b c*, is the angle of aperture, and it is evident that if *a c* had been made of a larger diameter, or if the curvatures of the lenses, 1, 2 and 3, had been such that the distance of *a c* from *b* had been lessened, the angle, *a b c*, would have been increased. The points that we have mentioned as governing the angular aperture are in general controlled by the character of the glass used, and by the formula (as regards curves, distance, etc.) employed by the optician, and he cannot deviate from them without an entire change of design.

Dr. Goring devised several practical methods of measuring the angular aperture of different objectives, and he gives a very full and clear description of an arrangement adapted to his own instrument, in which the foot was made to rotate on a carefully centered and graduated base, and modifications of this plan have since been adopted by several of our prominent microscope makers. It has been pointed out, however, that, as usually employed, the angle which is measured by this method is not the angle $a\ b\ c$, and although the angle which is actually determined may be of great value in determining the qualities of an objective, it can hardly be denied that to apply the term angular aperture to any other angle than the one that has been described, must tend to introduce a confusion of terms, and is altogether wrong. But in order to be strictly accurate, this statement presupposes a condition which is unfortunately too frequently overlooked, and that is that all the proportions and curves of the different parts of the objective are perfect. To make this clear, let us assume that Fig. 16 truly represents an objective of which the diameters, curves, and distances apart of the several lenses, are absolutely correct for the kind of glass used. It is obvious that by slightly increasing the diameter of lens 1, or by changing the relations of the three lenses, the apparent angular aperture might be considerably increased. We would soon find, however, that this increase was of no advantage, because after passing a certain degree the back combinations would fail to utilize the additional rays admitted, and the result would be that the performance of the lens would be injured rather than improved. Therefore, although in a *properly constructed* lens the angle $a\ b\ c$ shows the true angular aperture, this will not be the case if the optician has made the front, $a\ c$, larger than it ought to be in relation to the other parts of the objective.*

It is an unfortunate, but an indisputable fact, that this very mistake is frequently committed by makers of objectives, who either have not studied, or do not appreciate the qualities of lenses of wide angles. They therefore make objectives which

---

* The reader who desires to pursue this subject will find it fully discussed in Dr. Blackham's paper on Angular Aperture, which has been published in a separate form.

admit widely divergent pencils, but which fail to give distinct and sharply-defined images. Such lenses, when measured by the older methods, indicate extraordinarily large angles, and yet fail to have a resolving power at all commensurate with the aperture claimed. Indeed, when such objectives are diaphragmed down to moderate angles, their performance is frequently greatly improved. The action in this case is similar to that of the diaphragms in the hand magnifiers, shown in Figures 2 and 3. In these simple lenses, it is found that by cutting off the outer rays, which do not come to the same focus as the central ones, the definition is greatly improved.

It is a fact no longer open to dispute, that the efficiency of an objective, supposing it to be properly corrected, may be more nearly expressed by its angular aperture than by its focal length. For example, if we have two objectives, one of one-fifteenth of an inch focal length, and 150° angular aperture, and another of one-fifth of an inch focal length, and 180° angular aperture, the latter, although magnifying only one-third as much as the other, will actually show more of the more delicate structural features of any object; and if its magnifying power be increased by suitable eye-pieces until it is equal to the magnifying power of the one-fifteenth, it will give a better image than the latter. Our own experience has long since convinced us of the truth of this, and we believe that it is the opinion held to-day by all who are familiar with glasses of both kinds. Prof. Abbe, who is, perhaps, the highest living authority on the mathematics of the microscope, goes so far as to say that the angular aperture of an objective is an exact expression of its power, and he gives a table in which he lays down the number of lines to the inch which may be resolved by any given aperture.

It is not difficult to give a practical demonstration of the importance of a comparatively wide angle of aperture, for as we have just said, object-glasses possessing this feature are capable of giving important results, which cannot be obtained by means of lenses of lower angle. Thus, when we examine, by means of a superior French triplet of one-sixth of an inch focus, the silicious remains of certain very minute plants of the species *Pleurosigma Balticum*, we are able to see certain lines or markings which exist upon their surfaces. That we may be able to see these lines, it is necessary that the stand be a good one, and that the light be very carefully managed, but, even with the most perfect arrangements ordinarily used, we cannot, with such an objective, discover similar markings upon the *Pleurosigma Angulatum*, although they exist there in great perfection. But if for the French sixth we substitute a first-class objective of less than half its magnifying power, but of wider angular aperture, we shall be able to see the lines quite distinctly. We have now before us an objective of four-tenths of an inch focus, which does not correct for thickness of cover, but which, with any ordinary thickness of covering glass, is capable of resolving the lines on the *Angulatum* perfectly, and we have seen objectives of even lower magnifying power which would accomplish the same thing.

That the effect depends here chiefly upon angular aperture, was shown very clearly by Dr. Goring, from whose work we take the following figures, engraved from seven drawings showing the appearances presented by the scale of a butterfly's wing, viewed with the same magnifying powers, but different angular apertures. A well corrected lens of wide aperture showed the scale as in G; reducing the aperture, while all else remained the same, the appearance was as shown in F, and by successive reductions the stages shown in E, D, C, B, and A, were reached. The slightest examination shows that features which were quite distinct under a high angle, became invisible when the angle was reduced.

Fig. 17.

This quality of objectives of large angles, whereby they are capable of showing distinctly delicate lines or dots placed very closely together, is known as *resolving power*. In the early days of microscopy, it was called *penetrating power*, the term *penetrating* having been applied to that quality of the telescope by which it is enabled to show separately the individual stars of which the nebulæ are composed. In the telescope this was supposed to depend upon *space-penetrating power* as distinguished from mere magnifying power, and this space-penetrating power was found to depend very largely upon angular aperture. In the case of the microscope, however, it is now generally agreed that what was called penetrating power in the telescope, shall be called resolving power, while to the term penetrating power an entirely different meaning has been given.

Mere resolving power, however, or the power of showing separately lines placed very closely together, is not the only valuable feature of well-corrected object-glasses of high angles. They show delicate lines and fibres, and enable us to make out differences of structure which are entirely invisible to lenses of low angles. Thus, for example, it has been found during recent researches, that the delicate flagella of certain monads can be seen perfectly with high angle lenses, while with very excellent glasses of low angular aperture they are quite invisible. The same fact, probably, holds true in regard to the ultimate fibres of nerves and similar objects.

The researches of Lister and Ross formed, as we have just stated, the first great step in the direction of better correction and increased angular aperture. Whereas, 40° to 65° had previously been regarded as very high angles, even in objectives of the shortest focal distance, Ross, in his objectives, soon attained an aperture of 132° to 135° and, working with the glass at that time available, this was pronounced the highest attainable angle. Attempts had previously been made to obtain a higher angle by the use of the glass which Faraday devised for optical purposes, and which is in fact a borate of lead. But this compound is so easily tarnished and disintegrated, that it was found impracticable to use it. It happened, however, that a young American backwoodsman, Charles A. Spencer, of Canastota, N. Y., a graduate of Hamilton College, had his attention called to this subject, and after careful study he concluded that if he could only procure a durable glass of greater refracting power than that ordinarily attainable, the angular aperture might be greatly increased. He at once went to work, and after many experiments he succeeded in producing a glass which enabled him to attain immediately an angular aperture of 146°. As early as 1857 he had produced a 1-12th with an angular aperture of 178°. His objectives had corresponding excellence in other directions, and from that time forward this country has been noted for the excellence of its objectives, and especially for their great resolving power. We may note, in passing, that glass of great refractive power, combined with sufficient hardness and durability, is now produced as a regular article of commerce.

Penetrating Power.—As previously stated, penetrating power, in the early days of microscopy, meant precisely what is now understood by resolving power. Now, however, penetrating power is usually understood to mean the extent to which an object-glass shows the depth or thickness of an object. It is obvious that such a result can only be produced by the lens showing several layers of images, all of which are equally in focus, and consequently equally visible at the same time. In other words, instead of bringing only one given point sharply to a focus, the lens, which has great penetrating power, will bring several other points lying above and below this point equally to a focus. Hence, as Dr. Pelletan well observes in his work, "Le Microscope": "From a purely theoretical point of view, an objective with penetration is in reality a defective objective."

As this subject is one of great importance, we have introduced the two engravings, Figures 18 and 19, for the purpose of making it clear to our readers. In Figure 18 we have shown a small lens of half-inch focus, and with a very narrow angle. Figure 19 shows a lens of the same focal length, but with an angle of 90°. The points at which the lines $a\,c$ and $b\,c$ in Fig. 18, and $a'\,c'$ and $b'\,c'$ in Fig. 19 cross each other, are the respective foci of the two lenses at the centre of the field of view. Across the points where the lines $a\,c$ and $b\,c$, and $a'\,c'$ and $b'\,c'$

cross, we have drawn these lines, which may be supposed to represent respectively three layers of cells in a section mounted for microscopical examination. If the reader will examine the relation of these lines to the crossing lines in Fig. 18, he will find that the lines $a\,c$ and $b\,c$ coincide completely between the upper and under lines, and even outside of them, forming, in fact, a single line. In Figure 19, on the other hand, it is only the middle line that passes through the point at which the lines coincide; at the point where the upper and lower lines pass,

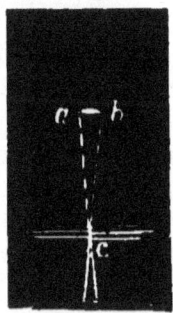

Fig. 18.

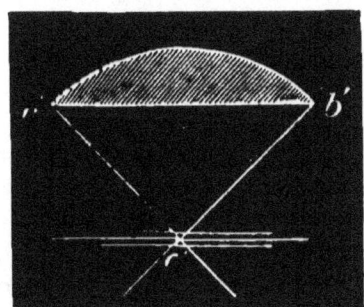

Fig. 19.

the lines, $a'\,c'$ and $b'\,c'$, have already separated to such an extent as to form distinct lines. If we regard the lines, $a\,b$, $b\,c$ and $a'\,b'$, $b'\,c'$, as rays of light, it is evident that while those in Fig. 18 will form images of the upper and lower lines, those in Fig. 19 cannot do so.*

Until within a few years it has been accepted, as a thoroughly demonstrated fact, that penetrating and resolving power always, *of necessity*, exist in inverse ratio to each other, for it is always found that, other things being equal, resolving power increases with the angle of aperture, while penetrating power decreases. Of late, however, it has been claimed that certain lenses of great resolving power possess considerable penetrating power.

* Those who wish to examine this subject more closely, would do well to examine an article on "Penetration in Objectives," by Dr. Geo. E. Blackham, published in the *American Journal of Microscopy*, for July, 1880, and the discussions which follow in succeeding numbers.

In attempting to reach a sound conclusion on this point, it must be borne in mind that resolving power does not depend *wholly* upon angular aperture. Two objectives of the same angle may have very different powers of resolution, on account of the degree of perfection to which the corrections have been carried, and it is quite possible that a lens of great resolving power may have a lower angle than another objective which it excels in this respect. In this case the lens of greatest resolving power might also have the greatest penetration. We confess, however, that we cannot see how great penetration can be combined with very high angular aperture, and in this view we believe that we are in accord with the majority of our best microscopists. Want of penetration has been urged against objectives of high angular aperture as a serious defect in many investigations in histology and natural history. The advocates of high angles claim that the best way to avoid this difficulty is to use objectives of less magnifying power, and to combine them with high eye-pieces. It is claimed that in this way the same amplification and penetration may be obtained as with low-angled objectives, and with greatly increased distinctness and improved definition.

Where stereoscopic effect is required by means of the ordinary binocular, low-angled objectives give better results than those of higher angle—one reason for this being that the corrections of such objectives are not so easily disturbed as those of the others. But it is a curious fact that low-power objectives of high angle, when used monocularly for examining opaque objects, frequently give an impression of stereoscopic effect which is startling. We feel certain that no one that has his attention once called to this point can ever forget it.

The late Henry J. Clark, in an article contributed by him to *Silliman's Journal*, many years ago, suggested another meaning for the term "penetration" in objectives. He referred to the power which objectives of high angle and perfect correction have of pasing through and *ignoring*, as it were, the various layers of cells or other elements which lie above the special layer in focus, which latter, when seen by a high-angle lens, is clear and distinct, while all the others are invisible. Mr. Stodder, who has recalled my attention to this article, which I had read many years ago but had forgotten, suggests that this be called the *penetration of high angles* in contradistinction to the penetration of low angles as understood by Dr. Carpenter, Frey, and others. Where the latter kind of penetration obtains, all the layers are visible at once, as we have previously explained.

Working Distance.—Considered as a quality of an objective, *working distance* is the distance between the front lens and the object, and it is this distance, and this only, which can guide us in forming an estimate of the quality of any given objective, as regards this particular feature. In practice, this distance is diminished by the amount of metal used in setting, which projects in front of the lenses, and also by the thickness of the cover glass. It is evident, however, that these are mere accidental circumstances which can be readily changed, and which have nothing whatever to do with the quality of the objective as regards its optical characteristics. Some writers have defined working distance to be the space between the front of the lens and the upper surface of the cover glass; but it is very evident that if we accept this definition we can no longer regard "working distance" as a quality of the objective, since an objective which might be notable for its great working distance with ordinary cover glasses, would have no working distance at all if very thick covers were used.

To avoid this difficulty, the term *frontal distance* has been introduced, and is used by some writers to signify the quality heretofore recognized as working distance. But since the term "working distance" has obtained a firm foothold in microscopical literature, as *expressing an important quality or feature of objectives*, we cannot see how any other meaning can be attached to it than that given above.

Working distance is a very important feature in all lenses, and good working distance is specially valuable to beginners. There are many objectives in market that have to be brought so close to the object that ordinary covering glass cannot be used, and even with the thinnest glass, the distance between the objective and the object is such that great skill and care are required to avoid accidents. Such objectives do excellent work in the hands of experienced microscopists, but beginners will find it difficult to use them. Objectives of very high angular aperture have in general very short working distances, but there are great differences in this respect amongst the products of different makers. Working distance does not depend upon angular aperture alone.

Immersion and "Homogeneous" Lenses.—Objectives which require a drop of liquid between the front lens and the covering-glass of the object are now in common use, and have been deservedly received with general favor. The liquid employed serves two important purposes. In the first place, it partially extinguishes two of the glass surfaces (the front surface of the objective and the upper surface of the covering-glass), and thus it prevents, to a considerable extent, the loss of light which always occurs at these surfaces; and in

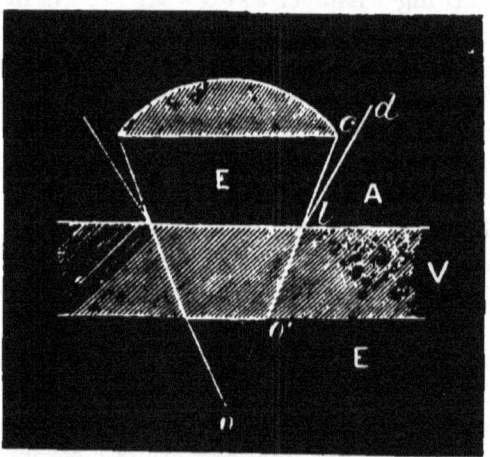

Fig. 20.

the second place, it enables the objective to gather up rays which otherwise would pass outside of it. In the ordinary immersion objective, water is the liquid which is used, and its action will be readily understood from an inspection of the accompanying diagram, where c is the front of the objective; V is the cover-glass; E the space between the front lens and the cover; *o* the object, and *o o'* a ray of light proceeding from that object. It is obvious that when the space, E, is filled with air, the ray, *o o'*, after passing through the cover-glass and suffering refraction within it, will, on emerging, pass on in a direction parallel to its original path, and so will pursue the line, *l d*, and pass outside of the objective. But if the space, E, be filled with water, it will take the course *l c*, and so will enter the front lens.

It is evident that if a fluid of greater refracting power than water were used, the result would be still more marked. This consideration led to the use of glycerine instead of water, with notably good results, and finally lenses have been constructed in which a liquid of the same refractive and dispersive power, as the glass of the thin cover, is used, and such lenses are known as "objectives of homogeneous immersion," or, for short, "homogeneous objectives"—the word *homogeneous* meaning *of the same kind*, and applying to the liquid and the cover-glass.

An immerson fluid, perfectly homogeneous with the cover-glass, would evidently obviate all necessity for what is known as "cover correction," provided certain other conditions in the mounting of the object and the construction of the microscope always remained the same, and most of the objectives made by Zeiss on the homogeneous system have no such correction. But since a difference in the quality or thickness of the medium in which the object is mounted, or a difference in the length of the tube or body of the microscope used with the objective, gives rise to serious disturbances, American makers have preferred to make their best homogeneous objectives "adjustable," as it is called; that is, provided with the usual means for cover correction.

It is a general impression that immersion objectives are more difficult to use than dry ones; such is not the case, however. Immersion objectives, with the same degree of effort and skill, give finer results than dry objectives of the same power, though of course for the ordinary rapid work of searching for known objects, dry lenses are to be preferred as being less troublesome, for it is undeniable that it is *some* trouble to apply the liquid and clean the lens, and also the cover, and where a large number of observations are to be made, even trifling delays must be considered. Some makers have endeavored to avoid this difficulty by supplying double fronts (a wet and a dry) to their objectives, while others have constructed objectives which work either wet or dry, according as the arrangement used for the ordinary cover-adjustment is set to the one or the other.

Lens Systems—Duplex Fronts—Formerly the term "system" was applied only to the entire combination forming the objective, and we had "immersion systems," "correction systems," etc. At present the word is used also to denote the individual combinations of two or more pieces of glass, which, when arranged together, form the whole objective, as will be understood from Fig. 16, where 1, 2 and 3 form the separate systems, each composed of two pieces of glass. Such a combination (the figure of which is, of course, only diagramatic) is said to form a three-system lens. Very low powers, formed of two achromatic lenses, are said to be two-system; four combinations, four-system, etc.

Some years ago, Mr. Tolles brought out objectives of remarkable power, which were known as "duplex fronts," or "four-system objectives. These objectives were so called because a second lens (nearly hemispherical) was added to the front combination, and this additional lens, added to the three already in use, made a four-system arrangement.

French Triplets.—A few years ago these objectives were used quite extensively. They are so called because they originated in the country after which they are named, while to further distinguish between them and objectives constructed according to the principles laid down by Lister, the latter were known as the *English* form. Good makers of the English form are now found in the United States, France, Germany, Austria, and Italy; and the French pattern is made in many of the cities of Europe outside of France, although as yet neither the English nor the American opticians have been able to manufacture them at prices which can compete with those of continental Europe. The best of the so-called French objectives consist simply of lenses in which the chromatic aberration is corrected by the usual plan of making each lens of two different kinds of glass, while the spherical aberration is corrected partly by the form of the lens, but chiefly by reducing the aperture, and by properly combining a series of single lenses, which, however, are never especially adjusted to each other, as in the English forms. Each objective, in its most perfect condition, consists of three lenses screwed together, and in the lower powers these lenses may be separated and used either singly or in combinations of two or three. As the magnifying power obtained with two lenses is less than that obtained by three, the defects of the double combination are not as obvious as they would be if the magnifying power were equal to that of the triple combination. As, however, the spherical aberration in the case of a single lens, whether it be a plain lens or an achromatic combination, is always greater than that of a doublet, and the aberration in the doublet greater than that in the triplet, it is never a good plan to attempt to obtain a low or moderate power by separating the lenses of a high power objective, and using them singly or in twos. Any person having a few French objectives at hand who will try this and attempt to secure the same magnifying power by the use of two lenses, and also by the use of three, the latter being a regularly adjusted combination, will find that the results obtained by the use of the latter are far superior to those afforded by the former.*

Considering their quality, these French objectives are remarkably cheap. Thus a French No. 2, which is nearly equivalent to the one-fourth objective of the English and American opticians, can be bought for $5, while the cheapest student's objective of this power would cost at least double that sum. In addition to this, the French objective may be divided so as to afford two other objectives of about three-quarters and one inch each, and although the performance of these is far inferior to English or American objectives of the same power, they are

*In making such a trial, it is, of course, necessary to use lenses of equal quality in both cases, since the quality of the professedly achromatic French objectives in market varies very much. We have seen objectives of this class of the same magnifying power, one of which would not resolve the markings on the scales of the clothes-moth's wing, while the other would resolve the *Pleurosigma Balticum*.

capable of showing a great deal that is interesting and instructive. Two or three years ago these lenses were the only ones furnished with microscopes costing less than $50, and in the very cheap instruments the different powers were always obtained by the division of one doublet or triplet, which was thus made to yield two or three different objectives. Those, however, who cannot afford American objectives, and who wish to do work that is of some real value, are advised never to separate their objectives, or at least never to separate any but the very lowest—that is the No. 1, and against even this we would protest were it not for the fact that cheap lenses of lower power than the half-inch are seldom found in market; and therefore, no other course except the division of a No. 1 is left to us when we wish to use a lens of lower power. But this system of dividing is often carried too far, and we find microscopes in market which are furnished with No. 2 or No. 3 objectives which are divided when lower powers are needed. This is decidedly wrong. If a power lower than No. 1 be needed, it may be admissible to divide this number, because this is in general the only course left to us, but a No. 2 should never be divided for the purpose of obtaining an objective equivalent to a No. 1.

The value of the numbers assigned to the different French objectives varies according to the fancy of the maker, but those of the better class usually found in market are about as follows:

Number.	1	2	3	4	5	6
Corresponding focus in parts of an inch	1-2	1-4	1-6	1-8	1-10	1-12

Frey, in his recent work on the microscope, regards the English system, whereby the focus is expressed in inches, as "peculiar." It certainly is "peculiarly" definite and positive, instead of being indefinite and arbitrary, as is the system adopted by the French and German opticians. According to the English and American systems, an objective of an inch focus ought to be the same, no matter by what maker it has been constructed, but when designated after the plan which Frey seems to prefer, it is impossible to tell what the focus of the lens may be, and consequently what its power is. Thus— a No. 2 of Nachet has a focus of half an inch, while a No. 2 of Hartnack has a focus of one inch, and a No. 2 of the ordinary French objectives is about a quarter of an inch in focal length. As it is often useful to the microscopist to know the powers of the different objectives made by prominent continental makers, we give the focal lengths of the objectives of Nachet, Hartnack, and Gundlach, premising, however, that by so doing we by no means intend to class these objectives with ordinary French triplets.

Nachet's ordinary objectives are as follows:

Number	0	1	2	3	4	5
Focus in inches	2	1	1-2	1-4	1-5	1-8

The immersion and correction objectives of the same maker are as follows:

Number	6	7	8	9	10	11	12
Focus in inches	1-10	1-14	1-15	1-20	1-30	1-40	1-50

Hartnack's objectives of recent construction are as follows:

Number	1	2	3	4	5	6	7	8	9
Focus in inches	2	1	3-4	1-2	1-4	1-5	1-6	1-9	1-11

Hartnack's new objectives with immersion and correction are as follows:

No.	Focus in inches.	No.	Focus in inches.
9	1-12	14	1-28
10	1-16	15	1-33
11	1-18	16	1-40
12	1-21	17	1-45
13	1-25	18	1-50

The following is Gundlach's scale:

No.	Focus in inches.	No.	Focus in inches.
I	1	VIa	1-12
II	1-2	VIb	1-12
III	1-3	VIIa	1-16
IV	1-4	VIIb	1-16
V	1-8	VIII	1-24
		IX	1-32

VIa and VIIa are not adjustable for thickness of cover, while VIb and VIIb are. VIIa, VIIb, VIII and IX are immersion lenses.

Since taking up his residence in this country, Mr. Gundlach has adopted the system of the English and American makers, and designates his objectives by their focal length. The table given above, however, will prove of service to those who either possess or intend to purchase specimens of his earlier work, some of which was very excellent.

Testing Objectives.—At first sight it would seem to be the easiest thing in the world to test an objective, and find out whether or not it is capable of doing certain work, but a little experience soon teaches those who are not too self-conceited, that it is the easiest thing in the world to be deceived. We have seen those who considered themselves the most capable of judges, condemn lenses that had received the approbation of the ablest microscopists in the world—lenses too that had shown their efficiency by doing really good work; showing that even those who consider themselves very expert, may sometimes arrive at wrong conclusions. If this is the case, then, with men of training and experience, how can a beginner, who has had no experience, hope to be able to form a correct judgment in regard to the quality of an objective?

But while it is difficult, or perhaps impossible, to pronounce a positive opinion in regard to the quality of an objective, especially those made for some of the higher departments of microscopic work, it is in general easy for those who have had experience, to form a judgment in regard to ordinary objectives, or at least those designed for ordinary purposes. The ability to form such a judgment depends rather upon experience and a comparison with the work of other glasses than upon a reference to any special standard; and therefore, as a general rule, we would advise beginners who are about to purchase objectives, to obtain the advice and assistance of some skilful friend. To those who cannot obtain such assistance, we offer the following hints.

The great difficulty in the way of arriving at a decision in regard to the quality of an objective, is the want of a standard with which to judge its performance. When we examine the image which an objective gives of any object, it is very difficult to decide whether or not that image truly represents the object. Take, for example, the podura scale: wide differences of opinion exist as to its structure, and how it *ought* to look; suppose, then, that two objectives show entirely different appearances of this object, who shall decide which one is correct? And if, even in the case of expert microscopists, this holds true absolutely, which it does, how shall a beginner determine that the images which he sees through an objective are true or false? In some departments, the most earnest and long-continued discussions have been maintained in regard to the accuracy or inaccuracy of certain images as seen by professional microscopists, and, strange to say, these disputes affect the very tests most commonly used, viz., the Podura scale and the test diatoms.

Makers of objectives, and skilful microscopists, being aware of the fallacies which beset examinations of this kind, resort to certain artificial standards of which the construction is positively known, and which should therefore give appearances conforming to this known structure. Numerous tests of this kind have been suggested, but the only ones generally accepted are the artificial star* and ruled glass plates. Of the latter, ordinary micrometers answer a very good purpose, but the most delicate tests are the famous ruled plates of M. Nobert.

In the examination of objectives, there are a few simple general rules which must be observed by the microscopist if he would secure accurate results.

The first important point, and one to which sufficient attention is not generally given, is the health of the observer at the time of making the trial. The eye is a very delicate organ, and the slightest derangement of the stomach or nerves affects it to an extent that few persons realize. We have an object-glass of comparatively low power, with which, when in good personal health, we find no difficulty in resolving the *P. angulatum*, though a very slight disturbance of the digestive organs, renders the lines perfectly invisible.

It must also be remembered that in the case of such delicate observations, personal peculiarities, irrespective of health or sickness, exert a marked influence, so that it does not follow that what one observer sees, all can see. We have frequently

---

*The artificial star is a very minute globule of mercury, obtained by crushing a small drop by means of a smart tap with a flat slip of iron or ivory. This globule is made to act as a small convex mirror, reflecting the light of a lamp, candle or window. It is not mentioned by modern writers on the microscope (Carpenter, Hogg, Beale, Frey, etc.), but is used by some of our best opticians. Dr. Royston Piggott, has recently revived its use. Goring devoted considerable space to an account of the best methods of using it.

seen those who could not distinguish lines that were visible to others, and we have also met those to whom an objective, in which the chromatic errors were very obvious, seemed to be perfect. This probably arose from a kind of color blindness. We have also met eyes which distorted objects, and those which saw fringes of color round objects viewed through an objective of generally recognized excellence.

Attempts have been made to get rid of the errors arising from personal peculiarities (or what may perhaps be called the "personal equation") by employing photography, it being assumed that if a lens will give an image which can be photographed, it must give an image that may be seen, and that whatever is photographed must of necessity be a real image. But from the known fact that the foci of the chemical and visual rays do not coincide, and that the corrections required in the one case are not those calculated to give the best results in the other, we have little faith in photography as the best test of the excellence of an objective, except, of course, in those cases where photographic work is the chief purpose in view. Lenses intended to transmit an image to the eye must be tested by the eye, and if certain eyes show peculiarities not possessed by the average eye, then lenses must be corrected specially for them.

It is scarcely necessary to say that when an objective is put upon its trial, the stand and means of illumination ought to be such as will do it justice. The best stand in the world cannot make a good objective out of a poor one, but a poor stand will give poor results even with the best objective. The eye-pieces also should be of good quality, and if an objective, which the microscopist has reason to believe is a good one, fails, it should not be condemned until it has been tried with eye-pieces either by the same maker, or of a known standard of excellence. And we must also remember that it is not sufficient to examine an objective in combination with a shallow eye-piece, or one giving a low magnifying power. An objective may perform very well if used with low eye-pieces, and utterly fail when a higher power is applied. Most makers of objectives test their glasses under eye-pieces of very high power—a quarter and even an eighth of an inch focus, or what would be equivalent to H or K on the usual scale.

The room in which the test is made must also be a subject of careful selection. Very many of our best microscopes are used in our large cities; at least they are very generally examined there with a view to purchase. Now, those who are familiar with the subject, know that during the day time the buildings along the principal thoroughfares in our large cities are in such a state of constant vibration, that good results are rendered impossible, and therefore that an objective and stand which, under such circumstances, fail to resolve difficult tests, or to define clearly, should not on that account be condemned.

The illumination employed must also receive careful attention. An objective which readily resolves the *P. angulatum* by central illumination, when lamp light or good daylight is used, may fail when poor daylight is employed. Special directions on this point are given under the head of light and illumination, and therefore we would merely say here that an object which has been tested only by the dull blue light of a northern sky, cannot be said to be inferior because it has failed either in resolving or defining power.

On the other hand, we must not place too high an estimate on an objective which, by the aid of monochromatic light, (the blue-cell, for example,) has resolved certain difficult tests. It is not uncommon to find that lenses of a quarter-inch focus will, with blue light, resolve the *Amphipleura pellucida*, but fail completely with ordinary light. Even eighths and tenths by the same makers, and of a grade quite as good as the fourths just mentioned, fail to resolve the *Amphipleura* by ordinary illumination, even when well managed. The aid which is derived from blue light in the resolution of difficult diatoms is unquestionable, but it is not quite so clear that this kind of light gives the same assistance in the matter of definition. Our own experience leads us to believe that the real assistance derived in the latter case is very slight. Therefore, we do not regard it as a very high recommendation for ordinary work that a lens can resolve the *Amphipleura* by blue light. We have, however, seen a fourth which would resolve the *Amphipleura* by the light of an ordinary hand lamp, aided by Wenham's reflex illuminator. The objective was made by Tolles, and manipulated by him.

To determine the quality of an objective it is best to take up in succession the several features which we have just detailed, and examine its efficiency in each of these directions. First of all, the defining power should be carefully tried, this being the most important quality that a glass can possess. No special test can be named for this, and in fact the formation of a correct judgment in regard to it will depend more upon the experience of the observer than upon any particular rules that can be laid down. As Carpenter well says: "An experienced microscopist will judge of the defining power of a lens by the quality of the image which it gives of almost any object with which he may be familiar." To which we may add that the *inexperienced* microscopist will in general fail to detect a want of defining power, no matter what object he may examine.

The chief points seem to be that the outlines should be sharp and clear, the blacks black, and the other natural colors clear and distinct. Frey compares the image given by a good lens to a good copper plate, or a print with sharp letters, and no illustration could be more to the point. He also states that an objective which is deficient in this respect, is best tested with a pretty strong eye-piece. In our own experience we have found no surer test of excellence than this; an objective which is deficient in defining power, is sure to "break down" under a high eye-piece. Deep eye-piecing does not effect the resolving power of a lens to the same extent that the defining power is lessened, and therefore, the fact that a glass shows lines under a high eye-piece, is not an absolute demonstration of its excellence as regards definition. At the same time, it will be found that considerable angular aperture is absolutely necessary to enable *any* glass to bear deep eye-piecing, because without this, the loss of light is so great that nothing can be seen clearly. Hence the truth of the somewhat paradoxical statement, that an objective may be really good under a low eye-piece, and yet fail under a high one.

With the English opticians a favorite test for definition is the *Podura scale*. Unfortunately, however, the structure of this scale and even the identification of the scale itself, seem to be a matter of doubt. Page after page has been written for the purpose of showing how the Podura scale ought to look, and still the question seems to be undecided. Carpenter, in his last edition (page 702) says: "The sharp and distinct bringing-out of the 'exclamation marks' of the Podura scale, constitutes, when it coexists with the greatest practicable freedom from color, and with adequate 'focal depth' or 'penetrating power,' the most valuable proof of the fitness of an Objective of high power for the purpose of scientific work."

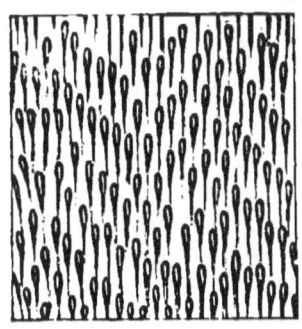

Fig. 21.

To give our readers an idea of how the podura scale ought to look, we give a figure copied from the engraving published by the late Richard Beck, in his work on the microscope. The figure shows "the appearance of the Podura scale when the adjustment of the object glass is correct and the markings are in focus." The objective used was a one-eighth, giving a magnifying power of 1,300 diameters.

It is, we believe, generally conceded that in the present state of the art, *perfect* correction for color cannot be obtained, but so long as the residuary chromatic abberration does not interfere with the defining power of the objective, it cannot be regarded as an objection. And yet we have seen a would-be critic reject a very excellent lens because it showed a little color, while he was loud in his praise of another lens which, although more perfect in this respect was almost worthless otherwise. Like specks of dirt on an eye-piece, which do no harm and are never even seen by experienced microscopists, slight color and want of flatness of field are the *bêtes noirs* of beginners. They are the defects which are most easily detected, and the detection gives the critic an air of knowledge which is to him a source of great pride.

The best English and American opticians now slightly undercorrect their best objectives, so that the field shows a slightly greenish hue, while any prominent markings on the object, such as the dots on the *Angulatum* stand out clear and well defined and of a very delicate ruby tint. According to Frey the majority of continental makers adopt the opposite plan. Their lenses are over-corrected, and objects show a bluish border.

A want of correction for color is shown when thin objects with many cross lines are examined, especially with slightly oblique light. As a test for achromatism in low powers, Carpenter prefers a section of coniferous wood, showing the glandular dots. He also recommends the tracheæ of insects, but almost any lined object will answer the purpose.

The existence of aberration of form is best proved by the use of a fine micrometer or a Nobert's plate. When this defect is very marked, it is easily seen in the curved and distorted lines of which the image consists, but such a state of things exists only in extreme cases. Where this distortion is not very glaring, it may be necessary to compare the magnified image of the lines in the stage micrometer with straight lines ruled on a thin plate of glass laid on the diaphragm of the eye-piece—in other words with an eye-piece micrometer in which the ruled lines are quite long.

For testing for flatness of field and aberration of form, Frey recommends "a slide thickly smeared with India ink, in which small circles or other figures are scratched with the point of a fine needle. * * * If the instrument is adjusted with transmitted light for such a circle, it should appear sharply cut on the black ground, and not surrounded by a halo of light. If the circle is then brought out of focus, it gradually enlarges, while its sharp borders disappear, without spreading a strong halo of light either inwards or outwards over the black field."

The angular aperture of an objective can be determined accurately only by measurement, and this is something that beginners will hardly attempt. To measure accurately the angular aperture of an objective, is a task requiring considerable skill and knowledge, and most of the appliances furnished by microscope-makers for this purpose, fail to give accurate results. It must be remembered that in measuring the angle of an objective, we must comply with the same rules that govern the accurate measurement of any other angle. Dr. Carpenter, in his work, gives a method which he calls "the simplest and most convenient." We venture to say, that none but an expert can obtain by it results that are anywhere near accurate, especially with high powers. We therefore consider that any directions upon this subject, addressed to beginners, would be worse than useless.

Since, however, the resolving power of an objective depends in a large measure upon its angular aperture, we may feel pretty certain that an objective which fails to resolve tests suited to its magnifying power, is deficient in angular aperture, unless, indeed, its inefficiency should arise from want of defining power, which may be tested by other means. Of ordinary working lenses, the half inch ought easily to resolve the *Pleurosigma Balticum*; the quarter inch should resolve the *P. angulatum* by oblique light, and those of a fifth or sixth inch focus should resolve the latter test by axial or central light. An eighth, tenth, or twelfth, ought to resolve all the diatoms on the *Probe Platte* below the 17th. It is true that objectives of a quarter inch focus have been made to resolve everything on the *Probe Platte*, but such glasses cost too much to render it likely that they will fall into the hands of ordinary students. Twelfths and sixteenths should go through the *Probe Platte* easily. If they cannot do this it would be better to take a lower power of better quality, and use it with a higher eye-piece.

We must also be on our guard against an old source of error— the use of lined tests which vary from the accepted standard.*
Great differences exist in the different specimens of the various test objects that are used, some, owing to individual characteristics and the methods employed in mounting, being much more easily resolved or shown than others. Conse-

---

*"The proof objects [finely lined insect scales] originally discovered by me, are sufficient for that purpose in *honest hands*, and when used with the precautions I have pointed out. But it is well known that they have been shamefully abused, owing to the various facilities of resolution which exist between different specimens of lined objects, the external characters of which closely resemble each other; so that it may be said that *there are proof objects to suit the capacities of all microscopes;* nay, they are actually perverted to the purpose of deceiving the unscientific part of the public in a much more effectual manner, than could possibly have been done without them."—*Goring*. What is true of the scales used by Goring is also true, though perhaps not to the same extent, of diatoms.

quently, because an objective resolves one specimen of the *P. Angulatum*, it does not follow that it will resolve all others. One of the most important steps in the direction of uniformity in this respect, at least so far as testing the resolving power of objectives is concerned, is furnished by the test-plate (Probe Platte) of J. D. Möller. Upon a slide of the usual size, he arranges twenty diatoms, carefully selected as to cleanness, and also as to resolvability. Those that he has chosen for the purpose are named in the accompanying table. They are arranged on the slide in a line which is about a quarter of an inch in length, the beginning and end of the row being marked by a specimen of *Eupodiscus Argus, Ehrbg*. The table on the opposite page gives the closeness of the lines and the direction of the markings in these diatoms according to the best authorities. In this connection it must not be forgotten, however, that mere closeness is not the only feature which makes a series of lines easy or difficult of resolution. Every micrometer maker knows that of two sets of lines, both ruled at 10,000 to the inch, one may be much more difficult to resolve than the other. The strength of the individual lines has as much to do with it as the mere distance at which they are placed apart. Möller's Probe Platte is furnished of two kinds, dry and in balsam, the latter being, of course, by far the most difficult test. It is an unfortunate fact, however, that even with all the care and skill exercised, even the test-plates of Herr Möller do not always conform to a standard; and, therefore, were it not for the facts just stated, it would seem that the most trustworthy tests are the ruled plates of M. Nobert.

It is not difficult to test an objective of moderate power for flatness of field, provided we have on hand a suitable object. For this purpose a thin section of wood, or of an echinus spine, is generally chosen. For low powers a very excellent test is one of those micro-photographs which are so common. One showing a sentence or sentences should be chosen in preference to a picture, since, unless the field of view be flat, the whole of the letters will not be clearly readable at once, while in a picture the effect known as aerial perspective may give rise to an impression of want of flatness of field. In applying tests for flatness of field, it is of course obvious that we must make sure

MÖLLER'S TEST PLATE. (PROBE-PLATTE.)

	Direction of Striæ.	Striæ in 1-1000 of an inch			
		Smith.	Sollitt.	Morley.	Others.
1. Triceratium Favus, Ehrbg............	......	....	....	3.06 to 3.08	4-5
2. Pinnularia nobilis, Ehrbg............	Transverse.	....	....	10.8 to 12.5	10-20
3. Navicula Lyra, Ehrbg. var...........	Transverse.	....	....	16.3 to 18.5	16-17
4. Navicula Lyra, Ehrbg...............	Transverse.	....	....	25.0 to 27.1	24-25
5. Pinnularia interrupta, Sm. var......	Transverse.	....	....	26.5 to 26.8	....
6. Stauroneis Phoenicenteron, Ehrbg...	Transverse.	....	....	31.1 to 33	....
7. Grammatophora marina, Sm.........	Transverse.	....	....	36.3	62
8. Pleurosigma Balticum, Sm..........	Transverse.	38	40-20	31.5 to 34.3	....
9. Pleurosigma acuminatum (Kg.) Grun.	Transverse.	....	....	42.7	....
10. Nitzschia Amphioxys, Sm...........	Transverse.	....	....	42.9 to 45.3	....
11. Pleurosigma angulatum, Sm.........	Diagonal.	52	51-46	43.8	....
12. Grammatophora oceanica, Ehrbg.... (= G. subtilissima.)	Transverse.	....	....	61.2 to 61.7	80
13. Surirella Gemma, Ehrbg.............	Transverse.	....	....	51.4 to 54.8	....
14. Nitzschia sigmoides, Sm.............	Transverse.	85	....	63.0 to 63.3	75
15. Pleurosigma Fasciola, Sm. var......	Transverse.	64	90-50	55.5 to 56.5	....
16. Surirella Gemma, Ehrbg.............	Longitudinal.	....	....	63.0 to 70.4	80
17. Cymatopleura elliptica, Bréb........	Transverse.	....	....	63.3	....
18. Navicula crassinervis, Bréb......... (= Frustulia Saxonica, Rabh.)	......	....	....	79.4 to 82.2	85
19. Nitzschia curvula, Sm...............	Transverse.	....	....	84.5 to 84.7	....
20. Amphipleura pellucida.............. (= Navicula Acus.)	Transverse.	....	....	130-120 92.7 to 92.9	95

that the test used is itself flat. Common glass slides are not flat, and as they are used for the cheaper kinds of microphotographs, this fact may give rise to errors if we are not careful in our selections. The best slides are cut from glass plate which has been ground and polished so that the sides are perfect planes, and it is this kind only that should be used. Care should also be taken to see that the object lies flat on the slide, and is not distorted by the cover. We have seen an objective condemned because it did not show all the diatoms in the field of view in focus at once, when the fact was that the diatoms were attached to the cover which was slightly wavy as covers often are. When it is suspected that the fault is not in the objective, but in the slide or cover, the object should be carefully passed across the field of view, and the changes in focus noticed. This will in general tell where the defect lies, for if the part that is apparently foggy should move as the object moves, it shows that the object itself is not flat. It has been recommended by high authority to test objectives for flatness of field by strewing some fine powder on a slide and seeing whether all the grains are in focus at once. For obvious reasons this is a very unreliable method.

Penetration in low powers is perhaps most readily determined by the examination of opaque objects of considerable thickness. The round pollen grains of the hollyhock, and the rounded forms of the polycystina are excellent tests for objectives of an inch or inch and a half. Lower powers ought to show coarser objects in all their dimensions, while for those of medium power the coarser cellular tissue of plants answers very well. It is more difficult to indicate a good test for penetration in the higher powers, in which, by the way, we have often seen want of penetration mistaken for want of flatness of field. This arose simply from the fact that scarcely any object is absolutely flat, and hence, as explained under another head, the curvature of the object is sometimes taken as an indication of a defect in the objective. Want of good working distance makes itself obvious during the examination of any object suited to the objective.

ON THE SELECTION OF A MICROSCOPE FOR PRACTICAL PURPOSES.

The object of all the information given in the preceding pages, is to enable the reader not only to understand the construction of the microscope, but to select one judiciously ; and, therefore, in every section we have offered hints bearing in this direction. We now propose to give the reader such special instructions in regard to the choice of an instrument as are necessary in addition to those previously offered.

Those who will examine the catalogues of the various makers of microscopes, will find the instruments divided into first, second, third, fourth, etc., classes, the microscopes in each succeeding class in this descending scale being smaller and less complete than those in the one preceding it. The first-class microscopes of almost all our prominent makers are large, beautifully-made instruments. They are provided with mechanical movements in every part, whereby the utmost delicacy and precision in making an adjustment, and in recording it, may be obtained, and as a natural consequence, such instruments are quite expensive. Indeed, it will often be found that the hanging and adjustment of the mirrors alone, of these fine stands, cost as much as an entire microscope of the lower grades.

Second-class stands are usually smaller than those of the first class, but they are frequently very complete as regards their adjustments and arrangements. Microscopes of the third and fourth class are usually much simpler in their construction, as well as less in size. In addition to these different classes, most manufacturers offer models adapted to special purposes, so that in setting out to procure a microscope, the beginner is very apt to be bewildered unless he has the guidance of some judicious friend. Of course those who are mere dealers always urge the purchase of the most complete and expensive microscope which the funds of the purchaser will enable him to procure, whereas a comparatively cheap microscope would frequently answer his purpose far better. The reader will of course bear in mind that by "dealer" we do not refer to experienced opticians, such as are most of our microscope makers. From these men the student will be pretty sure to get sound advice and efficient assistance. But, as is well known, every dealer in spectacles sets himself up as an optician, and professes to be competent to give advice in regard to the purchase of a microscope; and the microscope which these men always advise the purchaser to procure is *the one that will afford them the largest commissions*. It is unnecessary to say that this is not always the instrument that will afford the greatest amount of satisfaction to the beginner in microscopy.

In selecting a microscope, regard must be had, not only to the excellence of the instrument, but to its adaptability to the purpose for which it is intended, and to the person who is to use it. A complicated and expensive compound microscope, if placed in the hands of a person having little experience or skill, would evidently be worse than wasted, while to attempt to conduct elaborate and delicate investigations by means of a cheap non-achromatic instrument, would simply be to throw away time, and wantonly incur the risk of serious errors. And yet no mistake is more frequently made. A microscope is wanted; the purchaser is liberal with his means, and he is saddled with an expensive instrument entirely unsuited to his requirements. Or, on the other hand, a physician or student of limited means requires an instrument, and, being unable to afford the price of a really good one, he is induced to purchase a cheap affair, whose indications, when applied to the subjects for which he requires it, are entirely unreliable; whereas, he ought to be told that if he cannot afford a microscope which is at least provided with *good* objectives, and the necessary facilities for using them, he ought to leave microscopy in its applications to medicine and physiology alone. We feel it the more necessary to be emphatic on this point, from the fact that cases involving such errors have so often come under our own observation. Thus we have seen cheap French instruments, with poor triplets, in the hands of physicians, and used in cases where the safety of the patient depended upon a correct diagnosis!

The first point to be decided, is the *kind* of microscope that should be procured—that is to say, whether a simple or a compound microscope is wanted. If the student is desirous of *working* on objects under the microscope—making dissections of flowers, etc.—a simple microscope, of any of the kinds described in a previous chapter, will suit his purpose best. It should be arranged on a stand, and this he can either do himself, or he can procure one of the many *dissecting microscopes* which he will find described in the catalogues of the manufacturers. For such purposes a *simple* microscope is indispensable, though when we come to *examine* the results of our work, (dissections, etc.) a good compound microscope is equally necessary.

Attempts have been made to combine these two forms of the microscope in one instrument, and with considerable success, so far as increasing our power to examine our work as it progresses is concerned. This is accomplished by so arranging the simple microscope that a compound body with its eye-piece may be slipped on or off, as required. And by using a single concave lens as an eye-piece, we can secure considerable magnifying power and great working distance, while at the same time the object is seen erect and not inverted, as when the ordinary compound body is used. This form is called the "Brucké Loupe"—and is too little known in this country. But no such makeshift can take the place of a good compound microscope, although it may form a useful and convenient addition to the student's outfit.

The selection of a compound microscope will frequently be determined, not only by the wants, but by the means of the purchaser. To those who are obliged to put up with a cheap microscope, the only advice that we can give is to get the best they can for the money, and as newer and better microscopes are constantly coming into market, the best thing the student can do is to procure the latest catalogues of the different dealers, and examine and compare what they have to offer. There is no microscope in market to-day that will not probably be excelled by something better in less than twelve months from this time.

To those whose means enable them to procure whatever they

may require, a word of caution is also necessary. If your studies require the employment of the very best instrumental appliances, by all means procure either a first-class stand by some well-known maker, or a microscope made to suit your special requirements. But at the same time do not fail to provide yourself with one of what may be called the *third-class* instruments ; that is, a microscope of moderate size, and destitute of those complicated arrangements which are the glory of all first-class stands. With such a microscope you will be able to do twice, yes thrice as much work as with the large heavy stands. The physician or working naturalist that procures a very expensive stand for every-day use, makes a great mistake. It is very well to have such a stand for special occasions, but for "ordinary work" the small stand is to be preferred.

And this leads us to enquire what is or ought to be meant by "ordinary work ?" The expression is not an uncommon one, but it is one to which objection has been made on account of alleged indefiniteness.

If we exclude from consideration the employment of the microscope for purposes of amusement or of elementary instruction, almost all microscopic work may be divided into two classes, which may very properly be called, respectively, *ordinary work* and purposes of *research*. Ordinary work in this sense consists chiefly in searching for known forms, and does not demand anything like the instrumental perfection which is required for work which at all approaches the nature of original research. And by original research, we do not mean that research which is carried on for the purpose of making important scientific discoveries, but simply that which has for its end the examination of the structure and characteristics of objects which are unknown to the individual observer.

In support of this view, it would be easy to cite numerous instances. Thus every one knows, that for the examination of different kinds of starch, and the investigation of their peculiarities, very good microscopes and high powers ought to be used. But Hassal, in his work on adulteration, tells us that a quarter-inch objective, of ordinary quality, and used on a common stand, is sufficient to discriminate between the different starches when they are mixed together.

The study of the diatoms, in so far as their structure is concerned, confessedly requires microscopes and objectives of the very highest class. And yet we have been told by a gentleman, whose name deservedly stands very high in connection with the study of these interesting objects, that for the determination of species, and for most other points which he has studied, he has used a good non-adjusting quarter, on a simple stand, and that it is but seldom that he has recourse to better objectives, of which, however, he has a full series by the most eminent makers.

By the term "ordinary work," then, we may very properly designate all such examinations as lead us over ground that is well known, while no work that involves the examination of unfamiliar structures or the investigation of unknown processes, can be so called. But of all the work that is done with the microscope, four-fifths (including the work of the physician) is "ordinary work."

To those, therefore, who have abundant means at their command, we would by all means recommend the purchase of two microscopes—always, of course, getting the cheap one first. If, during the course of their "apprenticeship," this cheap instrument should get injured, the loss will not be very great, and by the time the student has learned to use the cheap instrument, he will have acquired intelligent views as to his special needs in the matter of a more complete one, and will not be dependent upon the advice of any one.

To those who cannot afford two microscopes, we would strongly recommend as a stand, one of the New American Models, previously described. If we except a few special departments, such as goniometry, etc., these stands are equal to all demands, and will do justice to any objectives or accessories, while at the same time they are sufficiently compact and handy to allow of the convenient and rapid accomplishment of all kinds of simple work.

To those who cannot afford one of these stands, the only advice we can offer is to get the best they can for the amount of money they have to spend.

It would be impossible to give anything like a list of special cases in which the different styles of microscopes prove most useful: the reader whose attention is called to this point will have little difficulty in deciding the question for himself. We merely give the general rule, that where dissections of plants and animals are to be carried on, a simple microscope should in general be chosen, while the compound microscope furnished with good objectives, is indispensible whenever high powers are required for the *examination* of objects.

Having decided upon the *kind* of microscope that is needed, the next step is to determine the individual quality of the different instruments that may be offered to us. To do this thoroughly, it will in every case be found a good plan to take up, point by point, all those elements that are necessary or desirable in a microscope, and in this way subject the instrument to the most careful scrutiny. Unless a microscope is made specially to order, it will be difficult to find one that will combine all desirable features, but the plan we suggest certainly enables us to decide most readily and accurately as to the presence or absence of those points which are desirable for our purposes. The following are the chief points that demand attention:

Magnifying Power.—We place this first, because usually the first question in regard to a microscope that is asked by beginners is, "What is its magnifying power?" Now magnifying power, although an important element, is after all but a secondary consideration. A microscope magnifying a thousand diameters could easily be made and sold at a profit for five dollars, and a few cents expended in paper and paste will at any time double, or even treble, the magnifying power of an ordinary compound instrument. The proper question is not how much does a microscope magnify, but how much will it show. A magnifying power of one hundred diameters, obtained by the use of first-class objectives, will enable us to see more of the true structure of an object than could be reached by a magnifying power of five hundred, the lenses in the latter case being of inferior quality. But, although not the first consideration, magnifying power is a feature of sufficient importance to deserve careful deliberation, and without a knowledge of the powers required, and the mode in which they are expressed, the beginner will often encounter difficulty. Both these points being essential, therefore, before discussing the magnifying powers best suited to different purposes, it may be well to say a word in regard to the mode in which magnifying power is always expressed by scientific men.

When we look at a small object through a microscope, and see it magnified to twice its length, it is evident that its breadth is also magnified twice, and consequently its surface, no matter what the shape may be, is magnified four times. It might also be said that as we only take cognizance of bodies having a sensible thickness, this thickness must be magnified twice, and therefore the object is magnified twice four, or eight times. The latter, however, is a view which is never insisted upon, and even those who claim the most for their microscopes, never do more than express the magnifying power in surfaces. Scientific men are, however, agreed that to express a magnifying power in surfaces is to convey a wrong impression in regard to the assistance rendered by the instrument to the natural vision, for a careful study of the physiology of vision, teaches us that our power to appreciate and distinguish the features of any object depends upon the distances to which the characteristic points of that object are separated, and this can be measured only by linear, and not by superficial units. There are other considerations which lead to the same conclusion, but for the beginner it is sufficient to know that *all* scientific microscopists are agreed that when the magnifying power of a microscope is stated, it shall be stated in diameters, and not in areas. By common consent, then, ten times means ten diameters. And yet it is a very common thing for charlatans, and those who wish to deceive the public, to say that a microscope sold by them magnifies ten thousand times, or one hundred diameters, and as "ten thousand times" is much more readily appreciated by the popular mind than "one hundred diameters," the majority of those who read such statements suppose that they will be enabled to see ten thousand times more than they could see with the naked eye, which assuredly is not the case. In some instances these advertisers do not even state the diameters. We have now before us, clipped from a journal of deservedly good reputation, an advertisment which reads as follows, omitting what printers call the "display" arrangement of the words: "Microscopes constructed on scientific principles magnifying 10,000 times." The microscope in question, as we learned by personal examination, gives a magnifying power of about one hundred diameters. Carpenter speaking upon this point says: "The *superficial* magnifying power is of course estimated by *squaring* the linear; but this mode of statement is never adopted by scientific observers, although often employed to excite popular admiration, or attract customers, by those whose interest is concerned in doing so." We would, therefore, advise our readers to look with suspicion upon any concern advertising in this manner. Of course an advertisement claiming a magnifying power of "10,000 *areas* or 100 *diameters*" is unobjectionable, because both expressions are placed upon an equal footing. It must also be borne in mind that great though unintentional mistakes are often made by dealers in stating the power of the microscopes they offer for sale. Not long ago a friend told us that he had been offered a small microscope having a magnifying power of 500 diameters, for a moderate sum. We called to see it, taking the precaution to put a micrometer and a foot rule in our pocket. By actual measurement the highest magnifying power of this microscope was 45 diameters! Another instance occurs in the catalogue of a well-known and honorable business house, who offer a very neat and well made instrument, whose magnifying power is claimed to be 350 diameters. Careful measurement of several instruments, however, gave an average power of less than 200 diameters! Indeed it will in general be found that the magnifying power stated by dealers who do not devote their chief attention to microscopes, is greatly over estimated.

So much, then, being clearly understood in each case, the question naturally arises, What should be the magnifying powers possessed by microscopes intended for certain specified purposes? That a certain magnifying power is necessary, no matter what the quality of the lenses may be, is true beyond a doubt. Thus, for example, suppose we wish to see the lines on the *Pleurosigma Angulatum*, which lines are about the one fifty-thousandth of an inch apart; what magnifying power would be necessary?

With the best illumination, the average human eye can just clearly distinguish lines which are the two-hundredth of an inch apart. Some eyes, under favorable circumstances, can see lines placed as close together as 250 to the inch, but the average is as we have stated.* To be visible even to the best eyes, therefore, the lines on the *Angulatum*, must be magnified so that they will present the same appearance as lines spaced so as to give at the very most, say, 200 to the inch. This requires a magnifying power of 250 diameters, and with less than this they cannot be seen, no matter how good the objective may be. And when Dr. Frey says that they can be seen with a power of 80 or 100 times, while "weaker objectives, magnifying 40 or 50 times, should show something of the lines," he makes a statement that we cannot accept.

In order, therefore, that an object may be distinctly seen, it must be magnified to a certain extent, but the magnifying power absolutely necessary in any given case, will also depend upon whether the microscope is to be used for general purposes of investigation, or merely for the *recognition* of known forms. For the latter purpose a power of 100 may be sufficient, while for the former, on the same class of objects, a power of 500 would be the least that would be serviceable. The following are a few of the cases in which the power required can be stated approximately:

For medical purposes (except for pocket instruments, intended merely to enable the observer to recognize known forms) a power of 400 is needed, and the objective should be of really excellent quality.

Students of histology require a microscope with a wider range of power. Low powers are more useful to them than to the medical man, and if they push their researches in certain directions, there is no limit to the magnifying power needed.

---

*To test the statement in the text, place a glass micrometer, ruled 200 lines to the inch, on the stage of a microscope, and by means of the mirror throw a beam of light upon it, just as if for examination by transmitted light in the usual way. If we now look at the lines, not through the tube, but simply from one side, they will appear distinctly as well-defined lines. Try the same with a micrometer ruled 250 to the inch; some eyes will be able to distinguish the lines, but very many will fail to do so.

A good two-third, one-fifth, and one-tenth, giving magnifying powers of from 50 to 1000 diameters, will, in general, answer most requirements. It must be borne in mind, however, that *beginners* can hardly be expected to use a one-tenth inch objective to great advantage, and, therefore, the purchase of this item may safely be deferred.

For the study of botany, and the ordinary facts of vegetable physiology, a power of 300 is sufficient; but the very minute forms of vegetable life require a much higher power, and so do certain of the higher points in the physiology of plants.

For the detection of adulteration, Hassal recommends the inch and the quarter-inch objectives, giving a magnifying power with No. 1 and No. 2 eye-pieces, of from 60 to 350 diameters.

For ordinary purposes of instruction and amusement in the household, a microscope magnifying from 30 to 150 diameters will be found most satisfactory, and for these reasons: Such an instrument is easily managed; if well made it gives a power amply sufficient for all ordinary objects, and it need not be expensive. Moreover, while it is an easy matter to prepare objects so that they may be seen satisfactorily under low and medium powers, it requires great skill and long practice to enable the student to prepare objects so that they may be examined with profit under a high power. And finally, under a high power, but a very small portion of any ordinary object can be seen at once, and consequently many of those things that are best suited for popular examination can only be seen piecemeal— a very unsatisfactory mode of proceeding. Thus, under a power of 750 diameters, a fly's foot could not possibly be seen as a whole; we might examine a single claw or pad at a time, but not the whole foot, and consequently would find great difficulty in acquiring an idea of what the general structure of the foot is. To give the reader clearer ideas upon this point, we have just measured the diameters of the fields seen under French and American objectives, with the following results: With a magnifying power of 25 diameters, the field is about a quarter of an inch; with 50 diameters, it is one-eighth of an inch; with 100 diameters, one-sixteenth of an inch; with 500 diameters, one-eightieth of an inch; and with 1000 diameters, the one-hundred-and-fiftieth of an inch, a space which is ordinarily invisible to the naked eye. Consequently, when these high powers are used, it becomes very difficult for beginners to place the object properly under the microscope, for, as will be readily seen, unless it is adjusted with a variation less than the one-hundred-and-fiftieth of an inch, it cannot be seen at all.

The lowest powers that will show satisfactorily certain well-known objects, are about as follows: The scales, or so-called feathers on the wings of most butterflies can be very well seen with a power of 25 diameters; under the same power, the eye of a fly shows very distinctly the several smaller eyes, or *ocelli*, of which it is composed; the individual corpuscles or globules of the frog's blood can be distinguished with a power of about 35 diameters, human blood requiring 40 to 50; to show distinctly the form, etc., of these same corpuscles requires a power of 200 and upwards. The same may be said of starch granules. Human hair and wool may be seen very satisfactorily under a power of 100 diameters, the former appearing like a cord, a quarter of an inch thick. In order to show the peculiar characteristics of these fibres, however, the lenses must be good. Cotton and flax can be readily distinguished under a power of 80 diameters.

A question very frequently asked in regard to cheap microscopes is, Will they show the animalcules in water? And in almost all the advertisements of cheap microscopes, we are told that they will do this. Now, good well water does not contain animalcules that can be seen with ordinary microscopes. It is only in stagnant water that they are found, and many of them can be seen with the naked eye, without the use of any microscope whatever. Others require the use of microscopes having powers a hundred fold greater than that of the best microscopes in ordinary use. It is evident, therefore, that such statements are worthless as affording any indication of the character of a microscope. A microscope magnifying fifteen to twenty diameters will show objects that are perfectly invisible to the naked eye, and with fifty diameters, provided the definition is good, we can obtain a very interesting view of many of the most beautiful objects described in the books, and sometimes called animalcules, such as the *Volvox Globator*, the larger *Vorticelli*, etc., etc.

The Stand.—This should be firm and substantial, with the centre of gravity very low. Nothing detracts so much from the performance of an objective as tremor and vibration, and a large majority of the microscopes in market are very shaky, from the fact that they are made tall and showy in order to command a higher price. It is well, therefore, to bear in mind that size is no criterion of the value of a microscope. Instrument makers very properly give the size of their instruments, and it generally happens that the largest instruments by the same maker bear the highest prices. Other things being equal, however, small, compact instruments are altogether to be preferred. Some years ago the rage was for large, showy microscopes, which made a fine appearance in the office of the physician, and the study of the naturalist. It was found, however, that in this case efficiency was sacrificed to show, and all our best makers are now cutting down the sizes of their instruments, and making them steady, substantial, durable and easily operated.

There is, of course, a limit to the extent to which stands may be reduced in size without sacrificing their efficiency, and some makers seem to forget this. There are stands in market that are too small every way for anything but special classes of work. The bodies are too small to secure efficiency in the eye-pieces and objectives; the stage is too small to allow of the use of slides of proper size, and there is no room beneath the stage for the attachment of proper illuminating apparatus. All this is as inconvenient as the three-feet-high microscopes of the end of the last century.

The weight of the stand is a subject concerning which many seem to differ in opinion. One writer goes so far as to say that no stand weighing less than fifteen pounds can be steady enough for the performance of good work. It will be found, however, that a judicious distribution of the material, and a proper construction of the different parts, will more effectually resist the usual sources of unsteadiness than any increase of absolute weight. Of course, if it is merely desired to make the microscope steady, in the sense that an inkstand is steady—that is, not liable to be tipped over—weight is everything. But the stands that are most difficult to tip over are not those that resist vibrations most perfectly. For the latter a tripod with a small area of support is best; for the former a stand with a flat base resting over its whole surface on the table should be preferred.

It is obvious that the causes of unsteadiness are either vibrations transmitted from the floor, or movements caused by the hand in performing the necessary manipulations and adjustments. The first can never be stopped by weight, unless, indeed, we make the stand so heavy that its weight will impart rigidity to the table and floor, and this would require a good deal more than fifteen pounds, or even twice that. For the checking of vibrations transmitted from the floor, no device is better than the stand or table described in a subsequent section. So far as movements transmitted by the hand are concerned, if a stand of three or four pounds will not resist them, the observer should set himself about learning delicacy of movement before he proceeds any further.

All microscopes made in this country and in England are now constructed so that the body may be inclined to any angle, thus giving the power of using the microscope in any position—vertical, inclined or horizontal. The importance of this is easily seen when we consider that on the one hand, when liquids are to be examined, it is sometimes necessary, or at least desirable to use the microscope in a vertical position, though this is a very tiresome and inconvenient position, and one that is not calculated to enable the observer to obtain the best possible results; and on the other, it is equally necessary that the body of the microscope should be capable of assuming the horizontal position when the camera lucida is to be employed for making drawings, as will be hereafter explained. And yet Frey actually gives the preference to microscopes that do not incline, and which must always be used in a vertical position! This, of course, necessitates the complicated and expensive arrangement which he describes for adapting the camera lucida to the vertical instrument, a singular instance of prejudice against an obvious and successful improvement.

The Stage.—In every case, a large, roomy stage is of the utmost importance. One great objection to most French instruments is that the stages are too small. It should also be firm and substantial, so that its position in regard to the other parts of the stand cannot be varied by slight pressure.* The most important points connected with the stage are the means provided for holding and moving the object, and the facilities afforded for attaching accessory apparatus.

In the most complete stands, the object is held between *sliding* clips, which form a sort of clamp that is capable of being moved in two directions, at right angles to each other, by mechanical means, which generally consist of a screw for one direction and a rack and pinion for the other. This form, which is known as the *mechanical stage*, enables even a comparatively unskilled person to bring any part of the object into the desired position in the field of view, and this with the utmost precision. These mechanical stages may be said to be characteristic of the higher classes of English microscopes, and as they are expensive, they are not generally used. Neither are they absolutely necessary for ordinary work with low or medium powers, for with any objective lower than one-twelfth of an inch focus, the object can be moved by hand quite as readily as by the screws, and we hold it to be a well established rule in all manipulations connected with scientific work, that whenever any operation can be performed satisfactorily by means of the hands alone, all special contrivances should be dispensed with. For low and moderate powers, therefore, we prefer the plain stage, on which the object is moved by means of the hands alone. But when very high powers are used, and especially when delicate micrometrical or goniometrical measurements are to be made, a well-made mechanical stage becomes a necessity. For while it is easy enough to bring an object very near to a given point by means of the fingers alone, it is almost impossible to secure perfect accuracy. In the effort to attain this the mechanical stage is a great assistance, and therefore when Frey utters a wholesale condemnation of the

---

*At the same time, however, it must be borne in mind that no stage ever was made so firm that even a *slight* pressure would not affect it. If, therefore, the reader is determined not to rest content with anything short of a *perfectly* rigid stage, he will reject all the best microscopes in market.

English microscopes, and asserts that they are unpleasantly loaded with what he is pleased to call "screws and unessential appurtenances," it seems to us that he commits a great error. These costly and complex instruments are intended for the highest class of work, and the most powerful objectives; perfection of the work to be done, and not simplicity in the means by which it is to be done, is the end sought, and this can be attained only by the complex means employed.

We have never found any of the so-called lever stages that fulfilled the requirements of the highest class of work, and, therefore, if a mechanical stage is to be chosen at all, the best form should be procured.

A microscope fitted with a good mechanical stage leaves nothing to be desired, but when other forms are used, it is evident that the chief points to be attained are these: 1. The object should be held steadily, but at the same time perfect freedom of motion should be allowed. 2. It should be possible to remove instantly from the surface of the stage, everything in the shape of clips and holders, so that a clear field should be left for the adjustment of very large slides, plates, etc., or for the rotation of the object in relation to the light. 3. Even the simplest forms of the stage should be so constructed that it may be possible to pass *every* part of the object under the field of view, and this, without any risk of omitting even the smallest portion. This point is of special importance to physicians and naturalists. Thus, it not unfrequently happens that it is desirable to know whether or not certain forms are present in a given drop of liquid; unless we can subject every part of that drop to microscopical examination, we cannot be sure that the forms we are looking for are absent. There is always a risk of omitting some portion of the slide, and consequently doubt must always hang over the exhaustiveness of all our examinations. The only certain means of avoiding all risk of missing any portion of a given slide is to pass it across the field of view in successive parallel bands, just as a plowman plows a field. The process is clearly shown in the diagrams on the following page, Fig. 22, showing the mode in which the entire surface is *completely* covered with a series of parallel ribbons, the breadth of each of which is the diameter of the field of view, while Fig. 23 shows the hap-hazard way in which examinations are usually made, abundant room being left (as shown by the small crosses) for the escape of important features. Now, with ordinary clips, it is difficult to effect this,

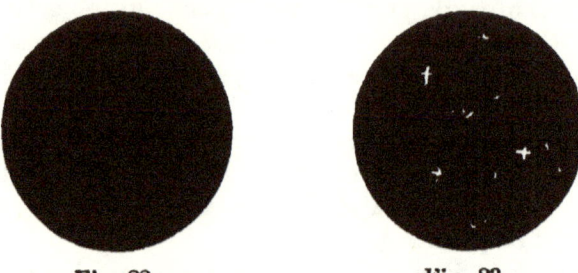

Fig. 22.   Fig. 23.

although it may be done by the aid of a plate of metal or vulcanite, a little thicker than the glass object-slide, and having a straight edge. The forward movement is made by pushing the vulcanite plate, while by sliding the object along the edge of this plate, we are enabled to examine a narrow strip, the width of the field of view, as shown in Fig. 22. A somewhat similar device is shown on the stage of Zentmayer's Histological Microscope, Plate VI. When slightly modified, this device also serves as a guide for the Maltwood finder.

In the simpler forms of the stage, the object is held in place by spring clips, which press it down, and under which it is moved. These clips are frequently screwed to the stage, which is a great mistake, as we are thus prevented from slipping them off, so as to leave the stage entirely clear. They should always be held in such a way that they may be instantly removed, and they should also be very thin and springy, otherwise it is impossible to move the object with sufficient delicacy.

The so-called glass stage, or Zentmayer stage, has come into extensive use, and is very much liked by some. As made by Zentmayer, it consists of a plate of glass, held against a brass support by means of a spring, which is pointed with ivory. The friction of the glass plate upon its metal support is thus easily adjusted, and may be either so reduced that the plate will respond to the slightest touch, or it may be so firmly clamped as to be practically immovable.

In some forms the glass plate is stationary, and the object-carrier moves over it, the points of contact being very small. Such a stage is seen in the microscope figured in Plate II.

Revolving Stage.—It is often desirable to rotate an object in the optic axis of the microscope, either for the purpose of measuring angles or changing the direction of the illumination in regard to the object. Means for effecting this with perfect accuracy have been applied both to the mechanical stage and the glass stage, though the latter is generally so constructed that rotation is impossible. In the large Ross stand (Pl. I), the stage rotates, and is graduated for measuring angles.

M. Nachet has devised a special form of the glass stage, in which provision is made for rotating it. In this form of the stage the object-carrier, F, is held to the glass plate, E, by means of two springs with ivory points, the springs being attached to the frame in which the glass plate, E, is set. Both the plate, E, and the object-carrier rotate in a light brass frame. In all these cases an attempt is made to secure coincidence of the centre of rotation with the optic axis of the instrument.

Fig. 24.

It will, however, be found that it is an impossibility to attain this object with any great degree of accuracy unless provision is made for occasionally adjusting the centre of rotation of the stage. No stage that ever was made will remain for any length of time so true that angles can be correctly measured by it, and therefore several devices have been suggested for securing accuracy without adjusting the stage, since when well-made an adjustable stage is expensive, and when poorly made it is worthless.

The best known of these devices is what is called the centering nose-piece. This is a kind of adapter which is screwed on the body and receives the objective. It is provided with centering arrangements, and the objective having been screwed into it, the latter may now be adjusted exactly over the centre of rotation. With common objectives this answers very well, but first-class objectives are apt to show the effect of being thrown out of centre.

Where rotation in regard to the illumination alone is required, several plans may be employed. One of the oldest is that found in the large microscopes of Hartnack and others, and recently adopted by Mr. Browning. This device consists in forming the stage in two pieces, the lower part being connected with the foot, and the means of illumination, while the upper

Fig. 25.

part, which rotates on the lower, is rigidly attached to the arm which carries the body. In this way the body, arm, stage and object may all be simultaneously rotated in relation to the illumination, and for ordinary purposes this answers very well.

When polarized light is used, however, it is obvious that it is impossible to rotate the object in relation to the polarized ray, without also rotating the analyzer, and, as every one that has worked much in this direction knows, it is often of great importance that both polarizer and analyzer should be kept stationary, while the object itself rotates between them.

The stage attached to the New Working Microscope of Mr. George Wale, and shown separately in Fig. 25, has a novel device for rotating the object. In this case the clips move round the stage. As ordinarily constructed they do not carry the object with them, but it would be easy to effect this by making each clip double, and clasping the object between the two clips.

The little diatom stage devised by the author, and described and figured in a subsequent paragraph, also affords very simple and convenient means for rotating many kinds of objects.

Stages for Special Purposes.—It may be safely asserted that there has never yet been constructed a stage which would suit the requirements of every worker with the microscope. Indeed, each investigator seems to require special modifications of his own. Thus, it will be found that the ordinary stage, with all its appurtenances, is too thick to admit the use of that very oblique illumination which is required by the worker on diatoms, while if the stage be made thin enough it loses the necessary rigidity. Some makers have sought to obviate this by supplying two stages—a stout one for common work, and a thin one for diatoms. A microscope now in our possession is furnished with an extra thin stage, which, by a very simple and ingenious device, can be instantly substituted for the heavy one. The microscope is said to have been made by Spencer or Tolles, and must be over twenty years old. Thin stages, on the same principle, called *Diatom Stages*, have been recently introduced by several makers, thus affording another illustration of the aphorism that history repeats itself.

The same object is also attained by means of the secondary stage, invented by Mr. Lewis Rutherfurd. This is simply a skeleton stage, which is placed on the ordinary stage, and is raised so far above it that the illumination may be applied between them. Rays of great obliquity may thus be passed through the object. Rutherfurd's skeleton stage forms also an admirable *safety stage*, since the object, being held against the *under side* of the skeleton stage, yields to the slightest pressure of the objective. Mr. Spencer has also taken advantage of this principle, and so formed the under side of the stage in some of his stands, that the object may be pressed against it by the clips, which for this purpose are pushed through from below upwards. In focussing, the objective is passed *through* the stage if necessary. Great obliquity, and perfect safety against breakage of the object by the objective, are secured. When the microscopist is using valuable slides, costing from ten to one hundred dollars, the latter feature is one of great importance.

In many microscopes, however—notably those of English manufacture—the under side of the stage is not flat and even, so that a slide cannot be laid against it. The following simple device obviates this difficulty: A rectangular plate of metal is pierced with a hole of the same size as the interior diameter of the sub-stage ring of the microscope, and in this hole is fastened a tube, which just fits this sub-stage ring. The plate is provided with two light spring clips, which hold the object against its under side, and it is easy to see that this simple contrivance which is shown in Figure 26, serves three very important functions: 1. It affords means for obtaining light of great obliquity, since in reality it forms a stage which has no thickness at all. 2. It serves as a perfect safety stage. 3. It enables us to rotate the object very nearly in the optic axis of the instrument.

Fig. 26.

The rotating clips employed in the New Working Microscope, also serve the same end, since they may be applied to the under side of the stage quite as well as to the upper one, a groove being provided for this purpose.

Sub-Stage.—The sub-stage is used chiefly for holding and adjusting illuminating apparatus beneath the stage, and may justly be regarded as one of the most important parts of the stand.

It forms a prominent feature in the New American Model, as well as in all first-class microscopes.

In its simplest form it consists simply of a short tube or ring, which is attached to the under side of the stage, and is fitted to receive polarizers, paraboloids, condensers, etc. It should be made removable, so that it may offer no obstacle to the employment of the most oblique illumination.

In the New American Model it is attached to a swinging arm, so that the illuminating apparatus, which it carries, may be placed at any angle with the optic axis of the microscope.

When a mere ring is used for receiving the accessory pieces of apparatus, the latter are adjusted by simply pushing them up or down, but a much better plan is to have the ring itself moveable, as is the case in the instruments shown in Plates III, IV, V, and VI. The accessory is then placed in the ring, and the latter may be slid up or down the carrying bar, so as to allow of proper adjustment. A still better plan is that shown in Plate I, where the distance of the sub-stage from the stage may be adjusted by means of a rack and pinion.

In any case the sub-stage itself, or the apparatus which it carries, should have facilities for accurately centering the various pieces of illuminating apparatus.

The Mirror.—The mirrors employed for illuminating microscopic objects are either plane or concave, and in the better class of instruments both kinds are provided, while the cheaper forms of the microscope have only the concave mirror. The plane mirror reflects the light just as it falls on it—that is to say, divergent rays (as from a lamp) remain divergent after reflection, and parallel rays (as sunlight or rays from the bull's-eye condenser) remain parallel. The concave mirror, on the other hand, causes parallel rays to converge and meet at a point, while other rays are rendered either less divergent, parallel or convergent, as the case may be. It is very important that the surface of the mirror should be accurately formed, and therefore in ' all good microscopes they are made of glass, which has been accurately ground and polished. Blown or cast glass will not answer. And as the quality and quantity of the light is greatly affected by the reflecting surface, the best mirrors are silvered with pure silver, instead of with the amalgam of tin and mercury, ordinarily used. The mirror should be so hung that it may throw a beam of great obliquity through the object. In many cases this is absolutely necessary, and even for ordinary work it is of great advantage, since it not only enables us to resolve lined objects, but to secure important changes in the illumination of common objects. A very fair dark ground illumination may be secured if the light is so oblique that none of it can enter the object-glass directly.

The mirror should not only be hung so as to swing to any angle, but it should be movable on the mirror-bar so that the rays which it reflects may be brought exactly to a focus on the object. This is done by sliding the mirror out or in, according as the rays are more or less divergent.

The concave mirror should be large, so that it may collect plenty of light. The plane mirror may be small without much loss. The concave mirror is frequently used for the illumination of opaque objects, as when large it concentrates the light very strongly. For this purpose it is either mounted on a separate stand, or the mirror-bar is so hung that it may be turned up over the stage, so as to reflect the light down upon the object.

The Body.—The only points connected with the body of the microscope which require consideration are its diameter and its length, and these must of necessity vary so much according to the purposes to which the microscope is to be applied, that no rule can be laid down. Pocket microscopes are of necessity small; microscopes intended for use with objectives of low power and large angles, must have a large diameter. And since the distance of the eye-piece from the objective affects the correction of the latter, it has been found necessary to adopt a standard length of body. This has been fixed at ten inches in this country and in England. On the continent of Europe, eight inches is the length that has been adopted, and most of the continental objectives are corrected for this length of body. Provided it is large enough to take the new broad-gauge screw, the diameter is not of very great importance in bodies of moderate length, but Beale tells us that in his long tubes, intended to produce great magnifying power, a diameter of two to two-and-a-half inches was found to be absolutely necessary to prevent the glare arising from internal reflection. An inch and a quarter is a good size for ordinary instruments. Since a very long body is inconvenient when the microscope is used in a vertical position, the best instruments are furnished with a

Draw-Tube, whereby the length of the body may be varied at pleasure. As explained in a former paragraph (page 20), when the distance between the eye-piece and the object-glass is increased, the magnifying power is increased also. The draw-tube, therefore, gives us the means of varying and adjusting the magnifying power of the microscope, and this is sometimes of great use. Thus, suppose it were required to draw an object to a scale magnified exactly one hundred diameters; it might be impossible to procure an eye-piece and an objective that, with a fixed length of body, would give exactly this amplification, but when we are able to vary the magnifying power by changing the length of the body, it is easy to get at it exactly. This, however, is but one of many advantages afforded by the draw-tube. If the objective be good, and the eye-piece not very high, an easy and very satisfactory way to increase the magnifying power of the microscope is to lengthen the body by means of an additional tube, which may even be made of smooth paper. But it must be borne in mind that any change in the distance between the eye-piece and the objective affects the corrections of the latter, just as a change in the thickness of the covering glass would do. Consequently, unless the objective has a considerable range of correction, it may be impossible to get good results when a very long draw-tube is used. On the other hand, the draw-tube may be used to good advantage as a means of correcting for covering glass when non-adjusting objectives are used. We have a one-fifth objective now before us, with which we can see clearly the lines on the *P. angulatum* on the balsam Probe Platte when the draw-tube is out, but when the tube is pushed in, the view is foggy and indistinct. This is due to a disturbance of the corrections.

The insides of all draw-tubes and bodies should be well blackened. When bright or white the glare greatly injures the defining power. When draw-tubes or long eye-pieces are so arranged that they rub against the inside of the tube in which they are inserted, they invariably make the latter bright by friction. They should, therefore, always slide in a collar.

It is always well to have the lower end of the draw-tube furnished with the Society screw, as by this means it is sometimes possible to use objectives of greater working distance than could otherwise be employed, and this arrangement also affords facilities for the use of amplifiers, erectors, etc.

Adjustments for Focussing.—In the cheaper forms of the microscope the adjustment is made directly by hand, one tube sliding within another. In a better class of instruments the objective is brought nearly into position by sliding the body through an outer tube, and then the final adjustment is made by means of a screw or other mechanical means. But in all the best microscopes, the coarse adjustment, as it is called, is made by means of a rack and pinion, while the fine adjustment is made in the manner just mentioned. Instead of a rack and pinion, a chain is sometimes employed, and the coarse adjustment is also made in some cases by screws of very wide pitch, and similar devices. Nothing, however, can equal a smoothly cut and well-fitted rack and pinion. It is sometimes alleged that the chain is more delicate, but this is not so. We have now in our possession a cheap, but well made microscope, the rack and pinion of which is so delicate, that with it we can focus an objective of an eighth of an inch focal distance with sufficient accuracy for all ordinary purposes.

For ordinary purposes, especially the work of the physician and medical student, the coarse adjustment may be more easily dispensed with than the fine one, but at the same time it must be remembered that any mode of adjustment in which the body is liable to turn round, is incompatible with the use of many important pieces of apparatus. Thus, for example, any turning of the body interferes with the use of the double nose-piece, the polariscope in its higher applications, Prof. Smith's opaque illuminator, etc. A rack and pinion, or its equivalent, should, therefore, always be chosen, especially as it does not add more than five or six dollars to the cost of the instrument.

Of devices for fine movements the name is legion. An old plan is to place the object upon a plate attached to the stage, and move it towards the objective by means of a fine screw. This is a cheap and convenient method. It has been objected to it that the object is "tilted," as it were, but this is imperceptible in practice, and causes no difficulty. The objection is, that when the object moves, many of the finer methods of illumination are disturbed. Another common plan is to make the nose-piece, which holds the objective, movable. This alters the length of the body, and changes the magnifying power every time a change is made in the focal adjustment. This change is too slight to be observable, but it is sufficient to interfere with delicate micrometric measurements.*

To avoid this difficulty, the entire body and its attachments, including the coarse movement, are carried by the fine adjustment. In its general features, this plan is a very old one, and at least a dozen modifications of it have been devised by different makers. As usually constructed, the body is *raised* by means of a lever, the long arm of which is acted upon by a delicate screw. A strong spring is arranged to *lower* the body, and as the spring maintains a continuous action, all lost motion is prevented. In the fine motion used by the Bausch & Lomb Optical Co., and which was invented by Mr. Gundlach, the body is suspended on two parallel springs, slides on carefully planed ways, and is moved by a fine screw.

Objectives of large aperture are so sensitive to slight variations in focal adjustment, that it is difficult to get a fine adjustment sufficiently delicate. Mr. Gundlach has recently attempted to increase this delicacy by using the well-known differential screw, and with very satisfactory results.

In judging of the quality of either a fine or coarse adjustment, the points to be observed are the delicacy and accuracy with which the objective may be moved to and from the stage, and

---

* It has been alleged that this increase or decrease of magnifying power is more apparent with the higher powers than with the lower powers. Indeed, it has been said that with high powers the change of magnifying power is quite perceptible. This, of course, is mere imagination, as any one of an arithmetical turn of mind can see. Indeed, the facts would seem to be rather the other way.

the freedom from twist or apparent displacement of the object. In many microscopes, when a high power is used, and the body is moved up or down for the purpose of adjusting the focus, the object is actually thrown out of the field of view. Such a microscope should be at once condemned.

Whatever be the nature of the fine or coarse adjustment, see that the body has sufficient range of motion to allow of the use of objectives of considerable working distance.

The Diaphragm.—Nothing tends so much to obscure our view of the finer points of structure in any object as to have them "drowned" in a superabundance of light, consequently in order to regulate the amount of light which passes through the object, a diaphragm is employed. As ordinarily constructed, it is simply a metal plate placed below the stage, and pierced with holes of various sizes, which may be brought exactly under the field of view, the small holes allowing but a small amount of light to pass, while the large ones admit a full stream. Considerable difference of opinion exists amongst microscopisis in regard to the proper position of the diaphragm. Thus Carpenter says (page 133) that unless placed half an inch below the object it is comparatively inoperative. Continental histologists, on the other hand, allege that it is useless unless placed close up under the object. Microscopes constructed according to both these plans are to be found in market. Where the microscope is furnished with a sub-stage, the distance of the diaphragm from the object is variable at will.

It is obvious that when the diaphragm is placed at a considerable distance below the object, the illumination is purified, as it were, from all cross rays. When the diaphragm is placed close to the object-slide, the illuminated field is contracted. The action in this case, however, is somewhat complex, owing to the influence of the slide in modifying the course of the rays.

Several very ingenious forms of Iris or graduating diaphragms have been devised, by which the size of the hole may be changed without interrupting the observation. They are exceedingly convenient, and present advantages which more than counterbalance the cost.

Objectives.—These are confessedly the most important parts connected with the microscope; they therefore deserve the greatest care in their selection. In a former section, we fully explained the general characteristics of the different kinds of objectives in market, and detailed the best methods of of testing them. A careful study of that chapter will, we hope, enable the beginner to avoid a glass that is absolutely bad, though we must acknowledge that all experienced microscopists are agreed that no amount of mere reading will enable a novice to pronounce a correct judgment upon the quality of an objective, unless its defects should be very glaring indeed. In this place we shall confine ourselves to a few hints in regard to those features which adapt objectives not only to special kinds of work, but to the skill of different classes of workers. For it is an undoubted fact that objectives which in the hands of skillful microscopists, and on certain classes of work, would give extraordinary results, would in other hands, and for other purposes, prove of far less value than lenses of what is commonly considered a greatly inferior grade.

We do not here propose to take part in what is called the "battle of the object-glasses," such a discussion being out of place in an elementary work like the present, but we think few will be hardy enough to deny that one who has a taste for such things, but has neither the money required to purchase a first class glass, nor the time necessary to acquire the requisite skill to use it, had better work with a cheap French triplet than not work at all. Moreover, it is astonishing how far patience, skill and experience will go to make up for a deficient instrument, while at the same time, it is unfortunately true that some who possess the very best glasses, and have done the most to throw ridicule upon all work done with inferior lenses, have never made a single contribution of the slightest importance to any department of microscopical science.

In a former chapter we discussed at length the different qualities of object-glasses, and showed how these various qualities might exist in very different degrees in different objectives. It is, of course, obvious that the extent to which any one quality should be sought in a particular glass, must depend altogether upon the kind of work that is to be done. To those who are addicted to what Holmes calls "fighting objectives," resolution will be the quality to be desired; others will prefer penetration, flatness of field, etc. In our estimation, for the purposes of ordinary scientific work, we would assign to these qualities values in the following order: 1. Defining power; 2. Freedom from aberration of form; 3–4. Resolution or Penetration; 5. Working distance; 6. Achromatism; 7. Flatness of field. The first quality that should be secured in every lens is undoubtedly defining power, and this whether its angular aperture be high or low. Achromatism we place low in the scale, because unless so marked as to injure the definition, a little color does no harm. Flatness of field we place last, because it will be found that perfect flatness of field is very seldom combined with first rate definition. Indeed, we have heard one of the most celebrated makers of objectives assert that the two qualities are to a certain extent antagonistic.

In giving advice in regard to the selection of an objective, one of the points concerning which it is most difficult to arrive at a decision, is that of angular aperture. Fortunately, however, experienced microscopists may safely be left to decide this question for themselves, and since those who have had *no* experience will find it difficult to use objectives of very wide aperture, it will certainly be prudent for them to choose those of moderate angle. Objectives of very high angle are worthless, unless the illumination is well managed, and the adjustment for thickness of cover properly regulated. On the other hand, a good non-adjusting lens will give very fair results, with but a moderate amount of skill on the part of the user. Almost all our best makers now produce objectives of moderate angle, which do not adjust for thickness of cover, but which have considerable resolving power. We have now before us a one-fifth which costs but fifteen dollars, and which will easily resolve the *Pleurosigma Angulatum* by central light. An important point for consideration will, of course, be, whether or not the glass is intended for original work, or merely for the study or examination of well known objects. The work of the physician is chiefly amongst well known objects, and may be very satisfactorily accomplished by means of good non-adjusting objectives, a great point in favor of such glasses being that work may be done with them more rapidly than with glasses that require greater care and skill. The same is true of the elementary studies of the botanist and histologist, carried on under the guidance of a competent teacher. And as in all such cases it is easy to find out the special thickness of glass for which the object-glass has been corrected, and to provide a supply of the proper thickness, the absence of a means of adjustment for cover thickness is not very important. But for all the higher class of studies, good glasses, with well-made adjustments for thickness of cover, are indispensable.*

Objectives of very low angular aperture, are, however, to be carefully avoided. There is a want of light, and an indistinctness which renders them worthless. It is generally said that the superiority of large angles is most marked in the objectives of high power, and that for low powers the common objectives do very well. In our judgment, however, the superiority of the low powers is quite as marked as that of the higher ones, and much more available to the beginner. It is true that the superiority of a well made one-sixth of high angle, over any triplet of whatever focal length, is immeasurable, but at the same time it is equally true that the view of an opaque object seen through an inch-and-a-half objective, carefully corrected, is as much superior to the same as seen through a common triplet, as it is possible to imagine. We have now before us a specimen of bone of very open structure, mounted as an opaque object. Seen through a first class inch-and-a-half objective, it presents almost a stereoscopic appearance, and the entire structure is easily made out. The view afforded by a very fair French triplet (No. 0) is so markedly inferior, that any person who should see the two would never again use a cheap objective, if he could afford to get a good one. Moreover, the objection which we have just urged against objectives of high power, and

---

*It is not long since a professional maker of microscopes, and one who seems to stand high in the favor of the medical profession, tried to persuade the author that the covering-glass exercised no influence on the action of the objective, and that a non-adjusting glass could be made with as great a resolving power, as one constructed so as to adjust for different thicknesses of covering glass! To such men, a famous microscopist used to apply the term "shopticians," and they deserve it.

wide angle, viz., that they are difficult to use by novices, does not hold in the case of low powers. A good inch, of comparatively high angle, is more easily used than a poor triplet.

A question which has considerably occupied the attention of microscopists, is the value of objectives of high power, and their efficiency as compared with those of lower denominations. That in many cases considerable amplification or magnifying power is absolutely necessary, admits of no doubt; but the question to be settled is: suppose that we wish a power of 2,000 diameters, would it be better to get this by means of a tenth of an inch objective, magnifying 100 times, and a half inch eye-piece magfying 20 times, or by a twentieth of an inch objective magnifying 200 times, and an inch eye-piece magnifying ten times ?

It is not very many years ago since one of our ablest American objective makers held that a lens of a quarter of an inch focus might be made to do anything that a lens of any power could be made to do, and the ground of this opinion was that the individual lenses of objectives as low as a fourth, could be made so much more perfect than the smaller lenses of higher powers, that this perfection more than counterbalanced the greater magnifying power of the objective of shorter focus. The reasoning here seems sound and obvious, but it has been found in practice that for everything except resolution, the limit to which the power of objectives may be carried, is far beyond a fourth. For resolution it has, we believe, been found that a well made tenth is capable of doing anything that any lens can do; for other kinds of work sixteenths and twenty-fifths, and even fiftieths and eightieths have been declared to possess advantages that are obvious. This, however, is one of those points upon which authorities differ; Beale, for example, favors high powers; Carpenter and Frey seem inclined to think that very high powers show nothing that cannot be seen by means of objectives of greater focal length.

French objectives of the numbers 1, 2, 3 and 4, if carefully selected, are capable of doing really serviceable work. A few years ago, some of the best known makers of American microscopes used nothing else, even in microscopes costing $150, but this course we can scarcely regard as judicious, for whenever the microscopist is prepared to expend $75 or more for a microscope, a large part of this sum should be laid out in the purchase of objectives of the better class, the one-inch and one-fourth, or the three-fourths and one-fifth being those that are usually selected by beginners.

French triplets are, however, going rapidly out of use, from the fortunate circumstance that objectives of low price and excellent quality are now produced by several makers of repute. It is well, however, for the reader to be on his guard against a fraud which has been but too common of late years. Some so-called opticians go so far as to add a little brass-work and engraving, and sell these French triplets as objectives of American make. We do not here refer to the mere operation of attaching the objective to an adapter, and fitting it in a brass box, for this adds greatly to the convenience with which such minute objectives may be handled and preserved, but to a sort of "making over," by which they are completely disguised and made to resemble the objectives of English and American makers. It is hardly necessary to characterize such a proceeding.

Eye-Pieces.—The eye-piece that is at present almost universally used is the Huyghenian, which, when well made, gives very excellent results. In the use of low powers, where a very flat and large field is desirable, the Huyghenian eye-piece fails, and the same is also true in regard to very high magnifying powers, where the enlargement is obtained in a great measure by means of the eye-piece. The extent to which the definition of really good objectives is deteriorated by the use of eye-pieces of great magnifying power, and the loss of light which they occasion, render them practically useless. For high powers, the solid eye-pieces of Mr. Tolles are vastly superior, while for low powers, where a large flat field is desired, Kelner's orthoscopic eye-piece presents important advantages.

Mr. Gundlach has recently brought out a new eye-piece, which he has named the *periscopic*, and for which a large field and excellent definition are claimed. They are much more expensive than the Huyghenian. We have not had an opportunity of examining them carefully.

In determining the quality of an eye-piece, attention is to be paid not only to its general excellence, but to its adaptability to the objectives that are to be used with it. In the higher departments of microscopy, the latter is a most important point, but one which is too frequently neglected. It does not, however, come within the scope assigned to the present work, and we, therefore, content ourselves with a few general hints.

The lenses composing the eye-piece, should be of homogeneous glass—that is, free from air-bubbles, specks and striæ, and the surfaces should be well polished. These points require attention, because we have in our possession a microscope in which— though it cost enough money to be free from such defects— they are glaringly apparent. On looking through the eye-piece at a strongly and evenly illuminated surface, the entire field of view—that is, the whole of the bright circle that is seen, should have the light evenly diffused over its surface, and the edges or border of this circle should be sharp and black.

Eye-pieces intended for first-class objectives should give a large field of view; but on the other hand, if French objectives be used, the field of view should be small, otherwise the definition will be poor. This is a point that is frequently overlooked, and we have seen very fair object-glasses condemned as worthless when used with a stand and eye-piece intended for objectives of an entirely different class. It is an easy thing to contract the field of view, by means of a round piece of thin sheet metal, having a hole of proper size in the centre. As previously explained, such a piece of metal is called a diaphragm, and should always be well blackened.

The magnifying power of every microscope depends upon three things: The focal length of the objective, the length of the body, and the eye-piece. Most microscopes are, therefore, furnished with several eye-pieces, whereby the magnifying power may be varied. There is, however, a limit to the extent to which this may be done. The image obtained by very *deep* eye-pieces, as they are called, is rarely satisfactory.

The different eye-pieces are generally denoted by letters—A, B, C, D, etc. A being the lowest, and B, C, D, etc., successively higher. Some makers use numbers—1, 2, 3, 4, etc. These letters and number, are, however, entirely arbitrary, in this point resembling the numbers assigned to objectives by continental makers. A great improvement upon this arbitrary and uncertain system would be to assign to each eye-piece its proper power expressed in inches. Thus, an eye-piece magnifying the same as a simple lens of two inches focus, should be called the two-inch eye-piece.

And here let us call attention to the terms *deep* and *shallow*, as applied to eye-pieces. By all authors of repute, a deep eye-piece is one of great magnifying power, while a shallow eye-piece is the reverse. See the Micrographic Dictionary, and the works of Carpenter, Beale, Lardner, Frey, etc., etc. It is, therefore, singular that Dr. Lankester, in his popular little work, "Half-Hours with the Microscope," should have committed the mistake of giving definitions exactly the opposite, upon the ground that eye-pieces of great magnifying power are always short, while low eye-pieces are always long. It is evident, however, that the terms are liable to give rise to confusion, and we prefer the words *high* and *low*—the meaning of which is so obvious as to require no explanation, as every body knows what high magnifying power is

While clearness of definition and resolving power are the most important qualities of every good microscope, magnifying power is also of considerable consequence, as explained in a former section. Therefore, every good microscope should be provided with at least one eye-piece of considerable power. It often happens that with the objectives and eye-pieces at hand, the amplification, as it is called, or, in other words, the extent to which the object is magnified, is not sufficiently great to enable us to make out its structure, while the objective has not by any means reached the limit of its defining power. In this case a high power eye-piece, which costs comparatively little, will greatly extend our power of successful examination.

ACCESSORY APPARATUS.

Every microscope should be accompanied with certain pieces of accessory apparatus, which are necessary for the convenient and thorough examination of objects, but which do not form part of the instrument itself. Some of these are intended for

128 SELECTION AND USE

Fig. 27.—FORCEPS AND FORCEPS CARRIER.

the better illumination of the object, and will be described in the section on "Light;" others are used for the procuring and preparation of objects, and will be described in the section devoted to that subject. The following are employed chiefly for holding and presenting objects that have not been "mounted:"

Stage Forceps.—This little instrument accompanies the oldest microscopes. It consists of a pair of very delicate forceps, such as those attached to the forceps-carrier in Fig. 27, which close by the spring of the jaws, and hold any object that may be placed in their grasp. They are opened by pressing on the pins which are seen at the sides. They are in general fastened to the microscope by being stuck into a hole in the stage, and the object may not only be moved backward and forward, but it can be turned round. The better class of forceps carry a small brass tube (shown in Fig. 27) which is filled with cork, and which serves to receive pins, etc., for holding insects, and other objects.

Forceps-Carrier.—However well made the forceps may be, it is almost impossible to slide, with sufficient delicacy, the rod through the tube that holds it. Consequently, it is exceedingly difficult to bring into the field of view, the exact part of the object, that we may wish to examine. To avoid this difficulty, the author, instead of inserting the pin of the forceps in the stage, provides a special forceps-carrier like that shown in Fig 27. This consists simply of a metal plate, the size of an ordinary slide, and having a hole in one end to receive the pin of the forceps. A large hole is pierced through the centre, to allow the passage of light from the mirror when that is needed. This plate is placed on the stage like a common slide, and it can be moved with as great delicacy as any ordinary object. The mode of using it is too obvious to require further explanation. We have found it exceedingly convenient.

Object-Holder.—The importance of being able to present an object to the light in all directions is well-known to every microscopist. Many years ago we devised an object-holder for effecting this, the construction of which is very simple and inexpensive. It consists of a slip of metal, the size of an ordinary slide—three inches by one—having a hole in the centre

Fig. 28.—OBJECT-HOLDER.

and a short pillar rising from one end, as shown in the engraving, Fig. 28, which gives a sectional elevation of the instrument. Through this pillar runs a wire, carrying at one end a milled head by which it may be turned, and at the other a ring which holds a perforated block. This perforated block has a milled collar on the lower end, so that it can be readily turned in the ring that carries it. The hole passing through the block is just the size of a stout pin, so that a disk of card or leather, with a pin through it, will be held steadily when the pin is inserted in the hole. The object to be examined is attached to the surface of the card, by means of balsam or mucilage, and it is obvious that by the combined rotations that may be produced by the two milled heads mentioned, it may be exposed to the action of the light in any desired manner.

The changes which are produced in some objects when the light is made to fall on then in different directions are very marked. Thus, for example, the mineral known as *specular iron ore*, when illuminated by light falling on it in one direction, is brilliant in the extreme, while when the light falls in other directions it is dead and lustreless. And as it is not always convenient to change the position of the lamp, it is a great advantage to be able to turn the object round. The simple contrivance just described enables us to do this perfectly.

A more perfect arrangement, intended for the same purpose, has been devised by Mr. Beck, of London. Mr. Beck's is, however, more expensive than ours.

Plain Slides.—The common plain slides serve very well for examining ordinary deposits in liquids. This is particularly the case where inanimate objects, vegetables and minerals are to be examined. Active animals require some contrivance for keeping them still.

The Concave Slide, as it is called, is simply a thick slide with a cup-like hollow ground in the centre. Such slides are cheap, and very convenient. A drop of water placed in one of these concaves, and covered with a thin glass, may be examined easily and thoroughly with moderate power. It is sometimes desirable to employ a cell with a perfectly flat bottom of very thin glass. Such cells may be easily and conveniently made out of a slide of metal, or preferably of vulcanite, through which a hole the size of the proposed cell has been pierced. A piece of thin glass may then be cemented to the under side of the slide, so as to form a water-tight cup. The hole in our slides is round, and has, on the under side, a seat or rebate, a little larger than the hole itself. In this rebate a round glass cover fits, so as to leave the under side of the slide perfectly smooth. Such cells are very convenient, as they are easily cleaned, and are not difficult to repair when the thin glass gets broken. The liquid is also easily covered by means of a thin glass cover, and when full, considerable inclination may be given to the slide before the liquid shows a tendency to run out. Various other devices of a simple kind may be contrived by the microscopist for similar purposes.

Watch-Glasses.—Dr. Beale recommends small flat watch-glasses for holding liquids that are to be examined, and we have found them very excellent. The best kind for this purpose are those known as *lunette glasses*, which are nearly flat on the bottom. They are awkward things to manipulate, however, unless some means is provided for holding them steady, and moving them about on the stage. We use for this purpose a strip of wood, three inches long, and so wide that we can easily bore in it a hole, about one-eighth of an inch less in diameter than the watch-glass, of which the smallest size should be chosen. The thickness of the strip should be such that when laid on any flat surface, the watch-glass will not come in contact with it. Glasses held in this way are very convenient.

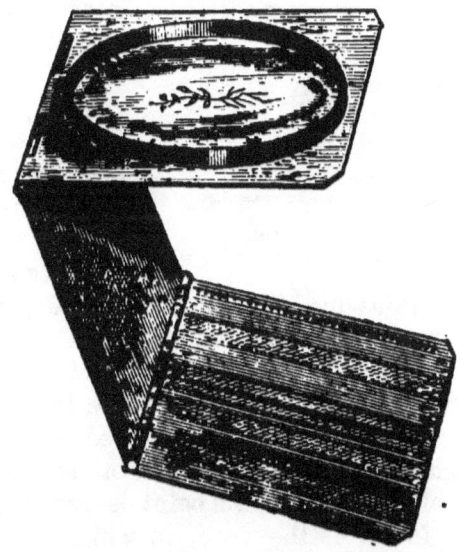

Fig. 29.—WATCH-GLASS HOLDER.

Watch-glasses are very convenient for examining a "dip" from a pond or stream, but for this purpose they require a holder. The little instrument shown in the cut is formed of three pieces of bright tin, which are hinged together. In the upper piece is cut a hole just large enough to receive a watch-glass. A ring of metal of proper height surrounds this hole, and forms a perfect protection to the glass when the instrument is carried in the pocket. The lower slip of tin may be adjusted to any angle, and by turning towards the proper direction, the light of any bright cloud may be reflected up through the liquid. All the joints are made stiff enough to remain in position when once adjusted. A watch-glass arranged in this manner holds a liberal supply of liquid, so that an entire "dip" may be readily examined at once. We have found this little contrivance far superior to more expensive arrangements. It packs into small compass, and is safely carried.

Animalcule Cage.—This forms a very excellent means for holding animalcules that are too active to allow of observation on slides, or in watch-glasses. A good idea of its construction may be obtained from the engraving, where it will be seen to consist of a plate of metal, three by one inches, to the centre of which is fixed a short tube. In the upper end of this tube is fastened a beveled piece of glass, and a second tube fits over the first, and has a thin glass cover secured in its upper end. The animalcule is securely held between the two pieces of glass, and the lower glass being beveled on the edge, a drop of liquid placed on it is held between the two glasses by capillary attraction, and cannot spread over the inside of the cage. This point is generally neglected in the cheaper forms of the cage, in which the lower glass is simply a plain disc burnished into the upper end of the inner tube. The consequence is that when the two glasses are brought together the liquid flows over the entire inside of the cage, and the objects are liable to be floated out and lost. As it is important that the distance of the two glasses from each other should be easily and accurately regulated, the outer tube should be slit, so as to make it springy. In this way it may be made to move with a soft and equable motion.

Fig. 30.—ANIMALCULE CAGE.

The Zoophyte Trough.—This little piece of apparatus is almost indispensable to those who desire to watch the growth and development of the larger animalcules and small aquatic plants. Several forms are in common use, the most complete being that shown in Fig. 31. The trough itself is simply a glass tank, to which is fitted a slip of thin plate glass that acts as a division, and enables the observer to keep the objects close up to the front plate. The distance of the dividing plate from the front plate is regulated by an ivory wedge, and the dividing plate is kept firmly up to its place by means of a spring. This contrivance enables us to regulate the thickness or width of the tank, so that the interior of the vessel may be made so large that it can be easily cleaned.

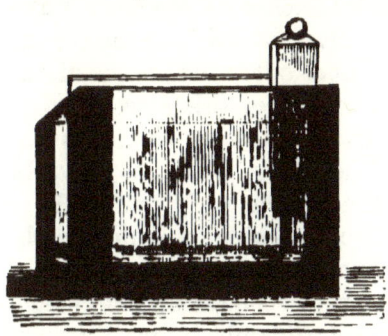

Fig. 31.—ZOOPHYTE TROUGH.

A smaller and simpler form of the Zoophyte trough is shown in Fig. 32. It consists of a simple glass box, open at the top. The back of the box is formed of a stoutish piece of plate glass, to which is cemented three glass strips, forming the bottom and ends. The front is formed of glass as thin as is compatible with durability, and is also cemented to the end pieces. The width of the trough from front to back is generally from an eighth to a quarter of an inch. When the trough is filled with water, and living animals are placed in it, their changes and movements may be very readily watched.

Fig. 32.—ZOOPHYTE TROUGH.

Small troughs, such as that just described, are not difficult to make, though the very low price at which they are sold (60 cents to $1.00) renders it scarcely worth the while of ordinary microscopists to construct them for themselves. Where this is desirable, however, the best method of making them is as follows : Select a piece of plate glass, of the thickness of an ordinary slide, and cut it about three inches by one and a quarter. Then select another piece of glass, as thick as the trough is to be deep (from front to back), and cut it to the size of the outside of the trough. From the bottom of this piece of glass cut a strip a quarter of an inch wide, and from the sides also cut strips of the same width. The centre piece may now be thrown aside, and the ends of the bottom strip will make a tight joint with the side strips. The three strips should then be cemented to the large plate, and over them should be cemented a piece of the thin glass used for covers. The strongest cement is marine glue, but it is somewhat difficult to use by those who have had no experience. Prof. Starr, who is well known for his success in keeping and exhibiting living microscopic objects, uses old Canada balsam, and we have seen a large variety of microscopic animals and vegetables which had been kept for months in a healthy condition in such troughs or cages.

Walmsley's Zoophyte Trough.—A serious objection to the troughs which we have just described is the difficulty of cleaning them, and of repairing them when broken. To avoid these difficulties, Mr. Walmsley has devised the little piece of

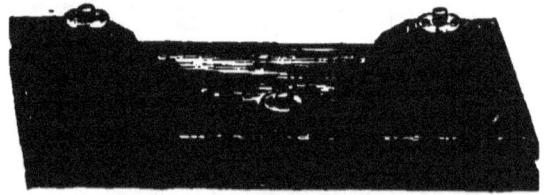

Fig. 33.—ZOOPHYTE TROUGH.

apparatus shown in Fig. 33. This trough consists of two glass plates, which are separated by a semi-ring of vulcanized india-rubber, against which they are squeezed so firmly as to be watertight, by means of two vulcanite plates, held together by screws with milled nuts. The front plate may be made of thick or thin glass, as desired, while the depth of fluid employed may be regulated by the thickness or number of semi-rings of rubber placed between the glass plates.

By means of the three screws with milled nuts, the trough may be taken to pieces in a few seconds, and as easily put together. In this way it is easy to clean the inside of the glass plates, to replace broken ones, etc., etc.

The Weber Slide.—This ingenious device consists of a common slide, rather thicker than usual, in the centre of which an annular groove has been ground, as shown in Fig. 34. The central part of the cell is left nearly the full original height of the glass—just enough being taken off to allow of a thin layer of liquid between it and the cover-glass. Any liquid containing minute forms of animal or vegetable life having been laid on the top of the central elevation, will be held there by capillary attraction as soon as the cover is laid on, and if the latter be cemented round the edges, an air-tight aquarium on a minute scale is formed, in which, if the proper balance of animal and vegetable life is present, the objects may be kept in good condition for a long time. We have kept one of these slides for weeks with desmids, diatoms, and minute forms of animal life, all in good condition. The proper cement for attaching the cover to these slides is beeswax softened with oil.

Fig. 34.—THE WEBER SLIDE.

The Weber slide is a very handy and convenient piece of apparatus, but it is difficult to obtain. We have, therefore, used the following form, which anyone can make for himself.

The Cell Trough.—The simplest trough in which living objects may be kept for some time, is constructed out of an ordinary cell and thin cover, as shown in Fig. 35. If we have a liquid containing some very minute objects which we wish to keep for some time in a condition suitable for examination, we place a drop on the centre of a thin cover-glass, which must be larger than the cell. A very small cover is then placed over the liquid, for the purpose of forming a layer of equal depth throughout, and if there should be any danger of crushing the objects, a few fibres of hair, silk, cotton, etc., will keep the two thin glasses sufficiently apart. The edge of the cell having been lightly smeared with a soft mixture of beeswax and

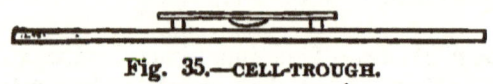

Fig. 35.—CELL-TROUGH.

oil, and the interior corner having been moistened with pure water by means of a camel-hair pencil, the inverted cell is placed on the large cover, which at once adheres, and thus the cell is converted into a veritable Wardian case. Owing to the moist atmosphere, there is no danger of the liquid under examination drying up, and as the apparatus is very cheap, several may be fitted up and used for watching the life history of any particular subject.

The Compressorium.—The animalcule cage, shown in Figure 30 is open to the objection that it is difficult to adjust the pressure with sufficient delicacy, and we are apt either to crush the animal or leave it too free in its movements. These difficulties may be avoided by the use of a well-made *Compressorium*, of which there are several kinds in use.

This little instrument also serves another important purpose. In the examination of certain objects, it is frequently necessary to flatten, and even to crush them, in order to render their structure visible, and this the compressorium enables us to accomplish. The most powerful instrument of this kind consists of a metal plate, in the centre of which is fixed the disc of glass upon which the object is laid. A second disc of glass, fastened in a ring which is hung at the end of a lever, by means of two pivots, is pressed against the first by means of a screw, which tilts the lever. In this way a very strong pressure may be exerted, while, owing to the free movement of the ring on the pivots, the plates of glass always remain parallel to each other.

Where very great pressure is not required, a different form of the instrument may be used. Instead of being forced down by a screw and lever, the upper glass disc is fastened to a thin plate of metal, which may be raised by a screw, but when the screw is withdrawn the "spring" of the plate carries it down and gives the pressure.

A compressorium, in which the pressure is caused by the *weight* of the upper plate, is shown in Fig. 36. There are two plates of metal, each with a hole in the centre, to receive the glass discs. At one end the upper plate has two pins, which fit into two holes in the lower plate, and serve to prevent all side movements. A screw passes through the other end of the upper plate, and serves to separate the two. A drop of water containing an animalcule having been placed on the thin glass attached to the lower plate, the upper plate, with the screw projecting sufficiently from the under side, is laid on it. Then by turning the screw, we can bring the two plates together to any required degree of nearness, and with the utmost delicacy.

Fig. 36.—THE GRAVITY COMPRESSORIUM.

Any minute animal may thus be firmly grasped, without crushing it, while the compressing power exerted by the mere weight of the metal plate is in almost all cases sufficient, even for the complete flattening out of small worms, etc. Even such creatures as the larva of the common gnat or mosquito may be completely crushed by the weight of a plate less than the eighth of an inch thick; and, where greater force is required, it is of course easy to apply the pressure of the finger. In the latter case, no danger of exerting too great a pressure need be incurred, as the projecting screw prevents all that. The want of parallelism between the plates does not prove a serious objection, as it is so very slight that it is hardly perceptible in the short distances ordinarily under observation. Where, however, it is desirable to avoid this defect, screws may be substituted for the pins, and the points may be made to work in holes bored half through the lower plate.

Where animalcule cages are not accessible, a small animal may be held between a common slide and a thin cover. To prevent crushing it, a hair or even a thread may be placed between the cover and the glass. A German author recommends the use of fine gauze or netting, in the meshes of which an animalcule may be held very conveniently. Acting on this idea, we took a thin metal plate, and bored it full of holes of various sizes. An animalcule placed in one of these holes may be kept in the field of view for any length of time, and exhibited to those who desire to see it, but it cannot be kept quiet for scientific examination. We like a piece of fine wire-gauze, better than cotton or linen netting.

Growing Slides.—Where it is desirable to keep the same living object for a considerable time, so as to watch its changes, it is necessary to use what is called a *growing slide*, by which it may be regularly supplied with air and moisture. A large num-

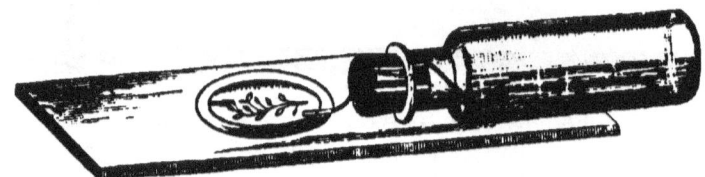

Fig. 37.—GROWING SLIDE.

ber of complicated devices have been described for this purpose, but the following simple contrivance answers the end very well; we have used it for years. To one end of a common slide with a concave centre, cement a small bottle, as shown in the figure. This is easily done by means of a little marine glue. The glue, cut in small pieces, should be laid on the slide at the point where the bottle is to be attached; the slide is then to be gradually heated until the glue is softened, when the bottle is laid on and moved back and forth until it has been thoroughly imbedded in the cement. The bottle is filled with water and corked, the upper side of the cork having two notches cut in it, one for the entrance of air, and the other for the passage of a loose cotton thread. The object is placed in the concavity, covered with a piece of thin glass, and the end of the thread is carried under the cover by means of a small notch cut in the slide with a file. The bottle must be filled with very pure water, otherwise the salts, etc., contained in it, become concentrated under the thin cover, owing to the evaporation, and destroy the object.

Frog Plate.—The circulation of the blood in the capillaries of living animals may be observed in the web of the frog's foot, the tail of a small fish or water-lizard, the larvæ of many insects, the ear of a young mouse and the wing of the bat. The tongue of the frog is also a favorite subject with some, and dissections of the living animal have also been made, and the circulation observed in the parts thus displayed. Except, however, for important investigations, we have no right thus to inflict torture and destroy life, and, moreover, the obvious cruelty of the means employed, will to most minds destroy nearly all the pleasure arising from the beauty of the exhibition. Fortunately the circulation of the blood in the foot of the frog may be witnessed without subjecting the animal to any pain. For this purpose the web of the hind foot is spread out over a piece of glass, which is held in a *frog-plate*, as it is called, to which the little animal is attached. The frog-plates usually sold, however, do not lie conveniently on the stage of a small microscope; they are apt to tip up, and there is no means of attaching them firmly to the stage, so that it is impossible to incline the microscope. The annexed engravings represent a frog-plate, in which these difficulties are avoided. As seen in the figure, it is of the usual form, and has a large opening, into which is burnished a piece of thinnish plate glass upon which the web of the foot is laid. Around this opening is bored a number of small holes, through which threads, tied to the frog's toes, are passed and held firmly by small wooden pins. A series of holes are also bored on each side and cut out at the edge, so that it is unnecessary to pass the twine *through* the holes, as it may be readily slipped *into* them. The frog may be enclosed in a bag, one foot being left out, but a simpler and better plan is to swathe him in a strip of muslin two inches wide and eight to twelve inches long. The muslin is dipped in water, and the

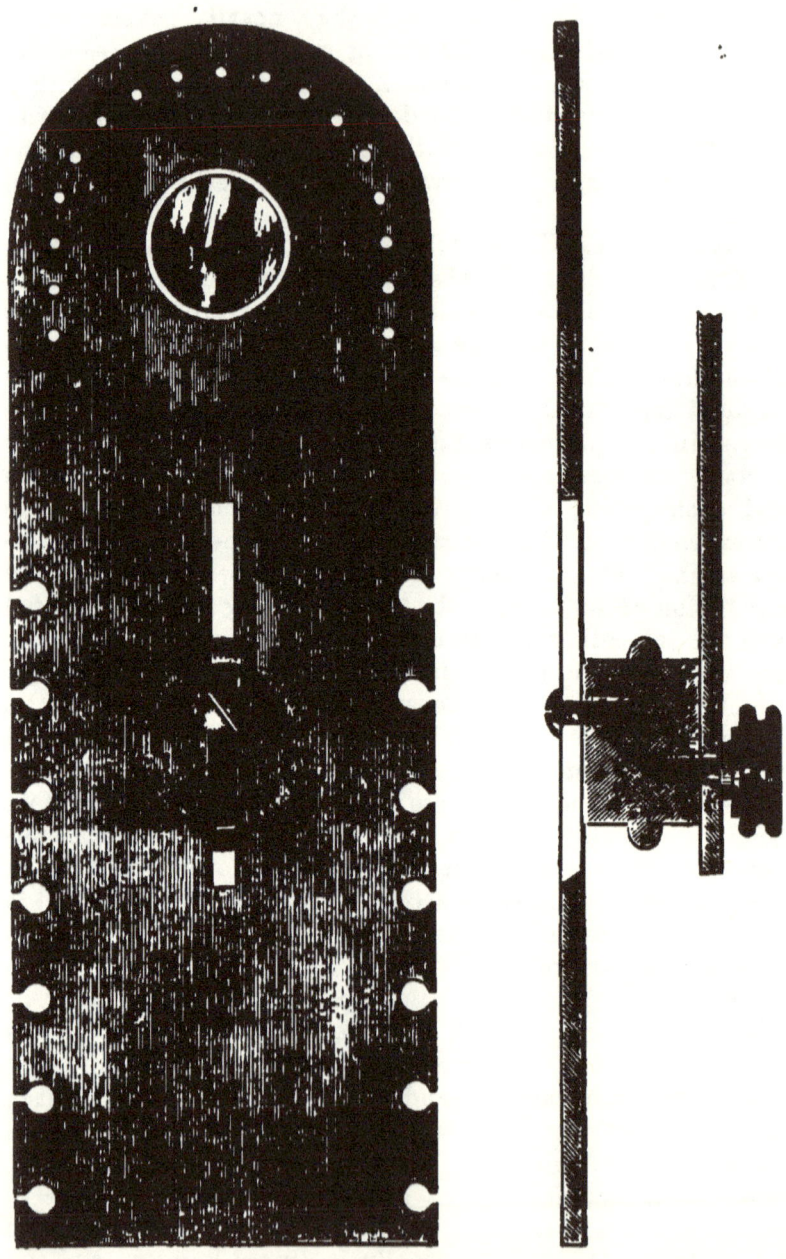

Fig. 38. FROG PLATE, PLAN AND SECTION. Fig. 39.

frog rolled up in it and laid on the plate, where he is held by a few turns of light packing twine passed into the slits in the side of the plate and carried from one to the other and over the animal. Small frogs are best for this purpose, but when too small they are not easily handled. The position of the animal on the plate is so arranged that the foot may be spread over the glass plate that fills the large opening.

The plate is attached to the stage as follows: A cylindrical brass block (Fig. 40) is provided—this block having a milled belt, which renders it more easily turned. The upper surface of this block receives a screw which passes through a slot of considerable length, cut in the frog plate, thus allowing a wide range of motion on the part of the latter; the under surface of the block receives a second screw, which serves to secure it to the stage of the microscope, as shown in Fig. 39. The holes for these screws are not in the same line, their axes being about a quarter of an inch apart, and the consequence is that when the brass block is rotated on the stage, the screw that passes through the plate acts like a crank in relation to the plate, and moves it longitudinally, provided it (the plate) is kept from rotating with the block. The upper screw is inserted with sufficient tightness to keep the plate from shaking, but is left so loose that the plate can be readily moved back and forth. Hence, while the plate is attached to the stage in such a way that it can not tip up or fall off, it may readily be moved in two directions, one the arc of a comparatively large circle, and the other a longitudinal motion at right angles to this.

Fig. 40.

This frog plate forms in fact a sort of mechanical stage which admits of very delicate movements being very steadily made. Where this plate is used, the microscope may be inclined to any angle, and no jerking or starting of the animal can displace the portion of the foot that is under observation. Different parts of the same foot and different corresponding parts of different feet are more or less suited to purposes of observation, according as they are more or less transparent and more or less fully supplied with vessels. It is therefore of great advantage to be able to select that part which answers our purpose most perfectly, and this plate affords peculiar facilities for effecting this.

Table.—The table used for supporting the microscope should be firm and substantial, so that all shake and vibration may be avoided. Those who use very high powers, and desire to avoid vibration as much as possible, will find that a barrel or box, filled with sand, and resting on three feet, makes the best support. Some years ago, having some rather delicate investigations to make, we constructed a table in this way, and found the results very gratifying. Our table was arranged as follows: a common barrel, cut down a little, and filled with sand, was supported on three stout blocks nailed to the bottom. The table proper was made of plank, nearly square, and it entirely covered the top of the barrel. It was supported by a + shaped piece of wood, which was fastened to the centre of the table, and descended into the sand. With such a table, walking on the floor, and the passage of heavy teams in the street, produce no vibration, though, on an ordinary table, they render work with high powers almost impossible.

Where several persons wish to look through the same microscope, it is very awkward if each one has to get up and go to the instrument. At the same time it is of course impossible to move the microscope without moving the arrangement for illumination also. This difficulty has been avoided by means of revolving tables, around which the observers sit, each one in turn examining the object, as the microscope is passed round to him. This is a very excellent, but a somewhat expensive arrangement. The same end may be attained by placing the microscope, lamp, etc., on a smooth board of suitable size and shape, and passing this board to each observer in turn. The board, carrying microscope, lamp, etc., may be made to slide quite easily, and if placed on three feet, it is tolerably steady. Such a support, however, is not to be chosen where the microscope is used for scientific investigations.

Double Nose-Piece.—This is one of the most useful accessories that the microscopist can possess. The result to be obtained, and the method of accomplishing it are obvious. The nose-piece screws on to the nose, or lower end of the body of the microscope, and is fitted to receive two objectives of different powers, either one of which may be brought into action by simply turning the nose-piece. In this way a low power may be used for finding objects and examining them as a whole, while the details may, without trouble, be subjected to an object-glass of much higher power. Two forms of the nose-piece are in use. The older form is straight, as in Fig. 41; the later form is bent, as in Fig. 42. The latter form is altogether the most convenient. Nose-pieces capable of receiving three or four objectives have been constructed, and a very old microscope, at one time in our possession, had a nose-piece with eight objectives! The modern nose-piece, so arranged as to be capable of carrying the best objectives, is the invention of Mr. Brookes.

Fig. 41.—STRAIGHT NOSE-PIECE.

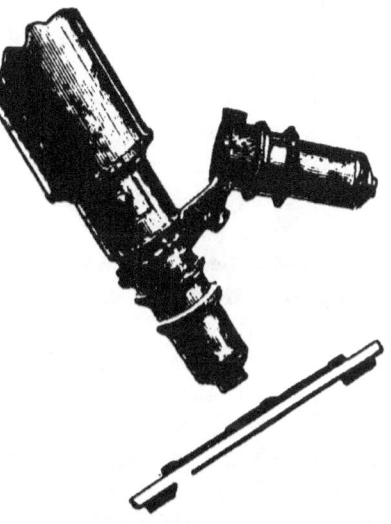

Fig. 42.—BENT NOSE-PIECE.

ILLUMINATION—SOURCES OF LIGHT.

Sun Light.—It is generally acknowledged that the best light for microscopical purposes is that of the sun; not direct sunlight, however, for this is altogether too intense, but sun light reflected from a white wall, or a light fleecy cloud. Sunlight is something which we cannot command at will, and, therefore, the microscopist can do nothing more than select the location of the room which he occupies. In general a room with a northern aspect is to be preferred; if there should also be windows looking towards the east or west, so much the better, provided they can be completely darkened when not in use, as cross lights produce a bad effect.

Artificial Light.—While *good* daylight is the best source of illumination, *poor* daylight is one of the worst, and we have frequently, during the day, obtained by the use of lamps and candles, results which could not possibly be secured by natural daylight. At the present time, gas-light, lamp-light and candle light are the most available means of artificial illumination. Candles are rarely used except when the microscopist is traveling, or in a peculiar situation, but a good candle gives very fair results, especially if the flame be protected from currents of air, which may easily be done by extemporizing a shade out of a piece of glass tube or small lamp chimney. Wax, paraffine or sperm candles should be chosen, as they give a clear, white flame. Common tallow candles give a dull yellow flame of inferior quality. Gas-light, as obtained from the ordinary, flat, unprotected burner, is not sufficiently steady; it flickers and changes, and for microscopy this is the worst fault that an artificial light can have. Where gas is employed it is, therefore, necessary to use an argand burner, with a glass chimney. Light obtained in this way is in general very excellent. But the most convenient, as well as the best means of illumination, is a good lamp, of which the ordinary student's lamp is, on the whole, perhaps the best kind. It gives a pure, steady and intense light; it is easily regulated, both as regards brightness, and also position, and consequently direction, and it may easily be procured almost anywhere. In default of a good student's lamp, any of the ordinary lamps with circular, or flat wicks, may be made to answer. Where a large quantity of light is required, as in the illumination of large opaque objects, the circular, hollow wick, from the superior brightness and whiteness of the light, is always to be preferred. But where a small light of great intensity is needed, the common flat wick, turned edgewise to the mirror, answers very well. It is a curious fact that flame is transparent to light, and, therefore, the greater the depth of flame, the more intense is the light. This is easily tested by looking at the flame of a common hand lamp sidewise and edgewise. In the latter case the eye receives the light from the entire flame concentrated to a mere band.

Several varieties of lamps have been devised specially for the use of microscopists, and some of them are very excellent, the most perfect being that devised by Dr. Drysdale and Rev. W. H. Dallinger, and described in the *Monthly Microscopical Journal* for April, 1876.

It is hardly necessary to say that all kinds of oil have been displaced by the mineral oils ordinarily called kerosene.

Very intense light, such as that from burning magnesium, the calcium light, the Bude light and others, have been tried, but without material advantage. Many years ago, we arranged a common kerosene lamp, so that the air surrounding the flame could be enriched with a supply of pure oxygen when necessary. Dr. Beale describes the same thing in his work, but does not seem to regard it as of any advantage. When used as a source of direct light, however, we found that it more nearly resembled sunlight than any other artificial source of illumination. A large diaphragm or shade, with an aperture of moderate size, was placed close to the light, which was placed at some distance from the microscope, and the rays passed directly through the object, not being reflected from a mirror. The results in some cases were well worth the trouble incurred. It is probable that in some cases very excellent results could be obtained from the electric light if properly arranged. This, however, is a department of microscopy which is certainly not suited to beginners, and we, therefore, dismiss it.

The rays of light, from whatever source obtained, are either *parallel, convergent* or *divergent;* and in the illumination of transparent objects the character of the light, as depending upon these features, is of marked importance. This subject, and the action of lenses and mirrors in changing the relative direction of the rays, should be carefully studied by the student, who will find it fully discussed in any work on optics. The general principles may be best explained by a few experimental illustrations.

Take a piece of cardboard about six inches square, and in it punch a hole about half an inch in diameter. If this card be held in front of a wall upon which the sun is shining strongly, we will see the shadow of the card and a round spot of light exactly the size of the hole. If the card be now moved away from the wall, the shadow and the bright spot will still remain of the same size, showing clearly that the rays proceeding from the sun are sensibly parallel. The same holds true of a bright cloud or a white wall placed at a great distance; but when the wall or other reflecting object is very near, the rays no longer possess this character to the same extent.

If in the first experiment the wall be illuminated by a candle instead of by the sun, it will be found that as the card is moved from the wall the shadow and the spot become *larger*, showing that the rays are *divergent* instead of parallel. The same effect is produced by fixing both the lamp and the card on a stand and moving them away from the wall.

Convergent rays, that is rays that tend to meet at a point, can be obtained only by passing parallel or divergent rays through a lens, or reflecting them from a concave mirror. By carefully arranging a large convex lens in the path of rays that are divergent, it is easy to render them parallel. They are known to be parallel when the bright spot which they make on a fixed surface, after passing through a hole, is not varied in size by changing the position of the hole.

The variations which are produced in the appearances of objects when they are viewed by light possessing these different characteristics can only be learned by practice, and the young microscopist should experiment in every conceivable way.

Whatever be the source of light employed, most objects may be viewed by means of any one of several very different methods. Thus, an object, if transparent, may be viewed by *transmitted* light, that is, by light reflected from the mirror, and passing *through* the object. If opaque, it may be viewed by *reflected* light, in which case the light that passes to the eye through the microscope is reflected from the *surface* of the object.

ILLUMINATION OF OPAQUE OBJECTS.

Diffused Light.—This term is applied to ordinary daylight or lamp-light, allowed to fall on the object without the intervention of any special means of concentration. That diffused light may be available for the illumination of objects, it is necessary that the objectives be good. Objects which, with ordinary triplets of low angular aperture, are entirely invisible, become beautifully distinct when a better class of objectives is used. Under favorable circumstances the view obtained in this way of any well marked object is very pleasant.

Bulls-Eye Condenser.—This is a large lens of comparatively short focus, which is made to condense the light on the object in the same way that the common burning-glass acts, but with effects greatly less marked, since the light is so much less intense. In some cases the condensing lens is attached to the microscope, and in some special cases this is very convenient, but where there is only one condenser, it should be mounted on a stand, as shown in Fig. 43, so that it may be placed at any height and turned in any direction. Placed between the object and the lamp, it collects the rays of the latter to a focus which brightly illuminates any object upon which it may fall. Opaque objects, which by diffused light are barely visible under the microscope, become very distinct and clearly defined when thus illuminated, and many of them, such as the wings of insects and certain minerals, appear in the most gorgeous colors, which, however, are perfectly natural, and are not the result of chromatic defects in the lenses.

Fig. 43.—BULLS-EYE CONDENSER.

In viewing an opaque object by reflected light, it is evident that we are enabled to judge of the irregularities of the surface largely by means of the shadows cast by the prominences. By raising or lowering the lamp, and also the condenser, the direction and extent of these shadows may be greatly varied. Hence one of the advantages of the students' lamp.

An important use of the condensing lens is to change the direction or character of the rays employed. Thus, when a lamp is in use the rays are divergent, and the easiest way to render them parallel is to pass them through a condensing lens. To effect this the distance of the lens from the lamp must be exactly the same as that at which it brings parallel rays to a focus. In other words, the lens must be at a distance from the lamp which is exactly equal to its focal distance for parallel rays.

Condensing lenses are made of all sizes, and some of them are quite expensive, but we have frequently obtained wonderfully fine results by means of a cheap lens of small size, but good form. A condensing lens is, perhaps, the most important accessory that can accompany a microscope.

Side Reflector.—This is a small silvered concave mirror, which is used to throw the light on the object for the same purpose as the condensing lens. The results which it gives are slightly different, and it is a most valuable means of illumination. It has not been so generally introduced as it deserves to be, and few microscopes are furnished with it unless to special order. It should always be used in combination with a bulls-eye condenser, as light of much greater intensity is thus obtained.

The Lieberkuhn.—This was one of the first instruments used for illuminating opaque objects. It consists of a small, concave, spherical mirror, through the centre of which the objective passes, the focus of the mirror and objective coinciding. The object must be small, and is generally mounted on a small circular disc of leather or card, which stops out the central rays, while the light which passes round it strikes against the concave mirror, and is reflected back again upon the object.

The Lieberkuhn gives very brilliant effects with many objects, and if well managed it enables us to obtain very satisfactory views, especially with powers which are too high to admit the use of the side reflector, the parabola, or the bulls-eye. The great objection, however, is the fact that the light falls almost vertically, thus obliterating all the shadows produced by elevations on the object. For "show" objects the Lieberkuhn is unequalled in its effects, and there is no doubt that in certain investigations it may be made to do good service.

The Parabolic Reflector.—This accessory was first made by Messrs. Beck for Mr. Sorby, who employed it to examine the microscopical structure of iron and steel. As ordinarily constructed, it consists of a parabolic mirror attached to the end of a rod furnished with universal joints, so that it may be placed in any position as regards the object and the illumination. It answers admirably for condensing the light on the surface of objects, and by throwing the rays in any particular direction across the surface, the observer is enabled, by means of the shadows, to determine the nature of irregularities upon some objects in a very satisfactory manner. In this it resembles the ordinary side reflector, which, however, is formed to a spherical instead of a parabolic curve. Like the side reflector, this illuminator should always be made to receive parallel rays, and condense them upon the object. To obtain parallel rays, place the lamp in the focus of the bulls-eye condenser.

Fig. 44.—PARABOLIC REFLECTOR.

The side and the parabolic reflectors cannot be used with objectives which have a short working distance, since the rays from the lamp must reach the reflector from the opposite side of the objective.

Since many stands have no conveniences for attaching this accessory, some opticians furnish it with an adapter, whereby it may be fastened between the objective and the nose-piece. Such a contrivance, however, must have originated in a want of knowledge of the principles which control this method of illumination. It is evident that the *object* should always be in the focus of the reflector; if, in adjusting the focus of the objective, we move the reflector, we must, of course, destroy the proper relation of the latter to the object.

Objectives with Tapered Fronts.—When the objective has a very broad front and a short working distance, as is the case with most objectives of high angles, it is impossible to illuminate the object satisfactorily with the bulls-eye condenser. To avoid this difficulty, several makers, notably Mr. Swift, of London, have narrowed the brass work of their fronts to the last limit, so as not to interfere with the illumination of opaque objects. Mr. Tolles has, however, gone a step further, and has allowed the glass of his front lenses to project beyond the brass work, so that the bull's-eye may be used with comparatively high powers. We have a one-quarter constructed on this principle, which allows of the clearest illumination, and shows the *P. angulatum* as an opaque object so well that the markings are sharp and well defined. These lenses are moderate in price, very easily used, and give very satisfactory results.

Smith's Vertical Illuminator.—This admirable device is due to Prof. Hamilton L. Smith, of Hobart College, Geneva, N. Y., and is intended for use with objectives of such high power, that the Lieberkuhn, condensing lens, side reflector, etc., cannot be employed. Several different arrangements have been suggested. The first was a small annular silver reflector, placed just above the back lenses of the objective, and forming an angle of 45° with the optic axis of the microscope. A hole in the side of the brass mounting of the objective admitted the light, which was thus thrown down through the lenses on to the object, and back again to the eye. We have used such an arrangement with most satisfactory results. For example, with a one-fourth inch objective, thus fitted, it is easy to view the *P. angulatum* as an opaque object, and bring out its markings. The illuminator, as thus constructed, may be either a separate reflector which may be screwed into the nose-piece of any microscope, and which is furnished at its lower end with the Society screw, into which the objective is inserted, or it may be a permanent part of the particular objective employed, and be specially adapted thereto. In our own experience, the best results have been obtained by the latter arrangement.

Instead of the silver reflector, Mr. R. Beck uses a thin glass plate (an ordinary cover-glass), which is inserted into an adapter which fits between the nose-piece and the objective. The thin glass is supported by a small pin with a milled head, by which it may be turned so as to present its surface at the best angle for reflecting downward the light admitted through a suitable aperture.

All forms of the vertical illuminator give their best results when used with immersion objectives, as has been very fully shown by Mr. Geo. W. Morehouse, of Wayland, N. Y., who uses with success objectives as high as the one-tenth. The markings on the most difficult tests—even the 19th band of Nobert's plate—are shown clearly and well by this arrangement.

In using the vertical illuminator, success will depend greatly upon the management of the illumination. The size of the aperture which admits the light to the reflector should be carefully regulated and diaphragmed down, if necessary, and the rays should be rendered parallel by means of the bulls-eye condenser.

Tolles' Vertical Illuminator.—So far as we have been able to find, Prof. H. L. Smith was the first to illuminate the object by light passed down through the objective, and the different forms which have been introduced, such as Beck's, Powell & Lealand's, etc., are mere modifications of his original plan. To Mr. Tolles, however, is due the invention of a modification which exhibits considerable originality. He inserts, above the front lens, a small prism, which is so constructed that the light passes in freely, and is then totally reflected downwards. In this way the rays pass down through only one lens of the system, instead of through all of them. Mr. W. A. Rogers has used this illuminator with very satisfactory results in the examination of fine rulings on metal, incident to his investigation of the comparative value of various standard linear measures.

ILLUMINATION OF TRANSPARENT OBJECTS.

The different methods which have been devised for viewing transparent objects are quite as numerous as those available for opaque ones, and require quite as much tact and study. A skilful worker, who thoroughly understands the points essential to good, or rather to appropriate and efficient illumination, will attain results wonderfully superior to those achieved by persons ignorant of the subject, and this, too, although the latter may be working with far superior instruments. This is seen every season at our microscopical exhibitions and conversaziones, and although the work done on these occasions is chiefly for show, the same principle holds good in regard to work done in the direction of study and investigation.

Direct and Reflected Light.—When the microscope is so arranged that the light from a lamp or other self-luminous body shall pass directly through the object and into the microscope without being first reflected from the mirror, the illumination is said to be *direct*, in distinction from light which has been first reflected from a mirror or other surface. Light from a cloud or a white wall can scarcely be regarded as direct. Direct light gives results which are appreciably different from those produced by reflected light, since light always suffers a change in character by reflection. These two kinds of illumination may be either axial or oblique, and in the case of both reflected and direct light, if the source of light be very distant, the rays will be sensibly parallel, but if the source of light be very near, the rays will be divergent, and, consequently, under such circumstances, the illumination must in part be more or less oblique.

Axial or Central Light.—When the mirror, either plane or concave, is placed directly in the axis of the microscope, and reflects the light through the tube, the illumination is said to be *axial* or *central*. The same term also applies to direct light, when the direction in which the rays pass through the object coincides with the optical axis of the instrument.

The rays must, of course, be parallel. If either divergent or convergent, some of the rays will be oblique. Purely axial or central illumination can be obtained only by passing the light through a very small hole placed some distance below the stage.

Oblique Light.—Many objects fail to show their peculiarities when illuminated by parallel rays of light passing through them in the direction of the optic axis of the microscope, but are seen very clearly when the light is sent through them obliquely. To secure illumination by oblique light reflected from the mirror, the latter must be so suspended that it can be turned to one side, and thus send a beam of light through the object at an acute angle. Where direct light is employed, the necessary degree of obliquity may be obtained by adjusting the position of the lamp—a device to which we have resorted when compelled to use a stand in which the mirror did not swing to one side. In this way, also, oblique light may be employed to illuminate objects viewed through a pocket lens, and very interesting effects obtained. For the resolution of fine markings upon diatoms, etc., oblique illumination is a necessity. When the angular aperture of the objective is low, and the light is very oblique, the objects appear light on a dark ground—in fact a sort of dark ground illumination is obtained.

The Achromatic Condenser.—The earlier forms of the achromatic condenser consisted simply of an achromatic lens, similar to an object-glass, so arranged that by means of it the light from the mirror could be brought to a focus on the object. With some objects, even this simple contrivance gave very fine results. It was soon found, however, that great advantage was derived from cutting off portions of the pencil of rays transmitted by the condenser, and by means of the proper diaphragms, central, peripheral and one-sided or oblique illumination was obtained. First-class achromatic condensers became, therefore, quite complicated and expensive. Several cheaper but very efficient forms are now made by opticians, a favorite being the Webster condenser, shown in Fig. 45.

Of this accessory Carpenter gives the following very practical description: "In its present form the arrrangement of the lenses strongly resembles that used in the Kellner Eye-piece; the field-glass of the latter serving as a condenser to receive the cone of rays reflected upwards from the mirror, and to make it converge upon a smaller achromatic combination, which consists of a double-convex lens of crown, with a plano-convex lens of flint, the plane side of the latter being next the object. These lenses are of large size and deep curvature; so that when their central part is stopped out, the rays transmitted from their peripheral portion meet at a wide angle of convergence, and have the effect of those transmitted through the peripheral portion of the ordinary achromatic condenser. When, on the other hand, this combination is used with a diaphragm that allows only the central rays to pass, these rays meet at a small angle; and the illumination thus given is very suitable for objects viewed with low powers. Again, by stopping out the central portion of the combination, and removing the condenser to a short distance beneath the object, the effect of a black ground illumination can be very satisfactorily obtained with objectives of moderate angular aperture. Further, by stopping out not only the central, but also a great part of the peripheral rays, so as only to allow the light to enter from a small portion or portions of the margin, oblique illumination can be most effectively obtained."

Fig. 45.—WEBSTER CONDENSER.

The Wenham Reflex Illuminator.—This is generally conceded to be the most perfect device for illuminating balsam-mounted objects when viewed by objectives of very high angles. It is shown in section in Figure 46, where a is a cylinder of glass half an inch long, and four-tenths in diameter, the lower convex surface of which is polished to a radius of four-tenths. The top is flat and polished. Starting from the bottom edge, the cylinder is worked off to a polished face at an angle of 64°. Close beneath the cylinder is set a plano-convex lens of 1¼ inch focus. Parallel rays, f, f, f, sent through the lens, after leaving the lower convex surface of the cylinder, would be refracted to the point, h, if continued in solid glass, but by impinging on the inclined polished surface (which is far within the angle of total reflection), they are thrown on the flat segmental top; here they would be totally reflected and beaten down again to a point outside the cylinder, but if an

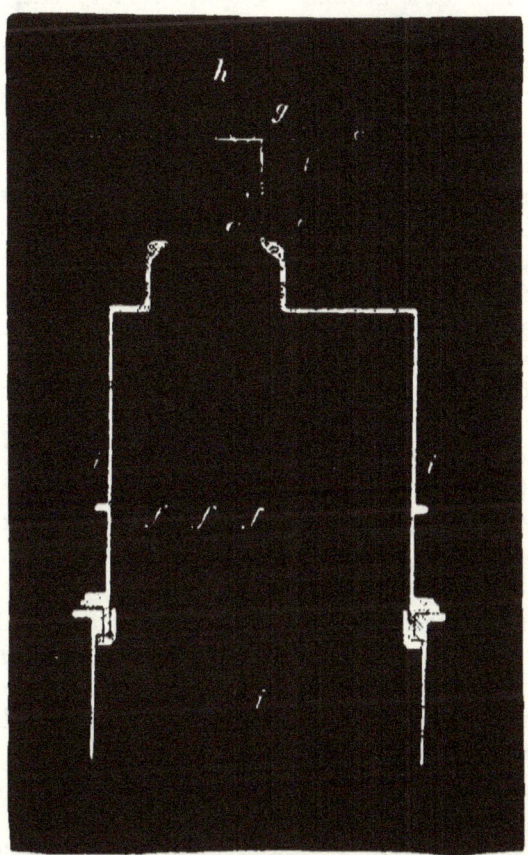

Fig. 46.

object-slide, c, be laid over the flat top with an intervening film of water, the rays will proceed on to the point, g, if the glass slide be thick enough. As shown in the engraving, however, the slide is of the usual thickness, and the point, g, lies above it; therefore, if the upper surface of the slide is clean and polished, the rays will be totally reflected therefrom, and will be sent to the point, *b*, outside the cylinder. If, however, any insect scales, diatoms, or thin flat objects should be in contact with the upper surface of the slide, the rays will be enabled to pass through, and the objects will be brilliantly lighted up on a dark ground. Objects seen in this way show many points of their structure with remarkable clearness. Speaking of the *Amphipleura pellucida*, Mr. Wenham tells us that it assumed a substantial appearance not seen in any other way, and at once displayed its striæ with an ⅛th that had never resolved them before.

It is very evident that the results which we have just described will only take place when a stratum of air lies above the slide, and the objects which we wish to view must be in contact with the slide, and not mounted on the cover, as is usually the case. But if the objects be mounted in balsam, the light will pass through to the upper surface of the cover, whence it will be totally reflected down, and the objects will be invisible, or, if sufficiently substantial, will appear on a black ground with *dry* objectives. But if we use an immersion objective, the light will no longer be totally reflected at the surface of the cover, but will pass through, and will be taken up by the objective provided the latter has sufficient angular aperture.

Used under these latter conditions, the reflex illuminator constitutes a means of obtaining oblique illumination of great purity and force, and the instrument is now a general favorite for this purpose, for which it was first used by Mr. Samuel Wells, of Boston.

To use the reflex illuminator successfully demands great care and some experience, but those who will carefully study its construction and mode of action, will find no difficulty in getting good results. First of all, then, we must remember that the reflex acts as a condenser, and consequently it is necessary to use but a moderate amount of light, which should be as intense as possible. This is best obtained from a small hand lamp. Secondly, we must use parallel rays, or the points to which the light is brought to a focus will not be those which accord with the other features of the instrument. Parallel rays may be either the light from a bright cloud thrown up by the plane mirror; divergent rays from a lamp made parallel with the concave mirror; or divergent rays from a lamp made parallel with a bulls-eye condenser, and thrown up by the plane mirror; or a combination of these last. Thirdly, we must remember that the instrument has two centres, arising from the fact that the optic axis is bent by internal reflection from the polished facet of the cylinder. Hence, we have the centre of the lens below the cylinder, to which the illumination must be adjusted, and we have another centre at which the rays are brought to a focus, and which must be made to coincide with the optic axis of the microscope. This centre is generally marked by the maker on the small side piece, e, and it should be brought exactly to the centre of the field of view of the objective, a low power—say a half inch or two-thirds—being used for this purpose, in the first place.

It is, of course, obvious that by adjusting the other conditions of the instrument, the points which we have laid down may be varied. Thus, for example, divergent rays may be used; but in that case the focus of the rays will not be at the point, g, unless the flat top of the cylinder is depressed a little, which may be easily done if a tenacious liquid like glycerine be used as the connecting medium.

We think that if the reader will bear these points in mind, and will work over this accessory faithfully for a few hours, he will attain results which will abundantly compensate him for the labor spent.

The reader must always bear in mind that where totally reflecting surfaces are used, as in paraboloids, reflex illuminators, etc., they must be kept scrupulously clean or they lose their effect.

The Wenham Prism.—This simple and ingenious little device was first described by Mr. Wenham in a paper read before the Royal Microscopical Society, March 26, 1856. At that time immersion objectives were unknown, or at least were not in use, and the effect of the prism was to produce a very brilliant dark-ground illumination; but, as with the Reflex Illuminator, the introduction of immersion objectives of wide angle has greatly enlarged the scope of usefulness of this little piece of apparatus.

The Wenham prism consists of a small right-angled prism of crown glass, which is "patched" on to the under side of the slide by means of a little glycerine, oil of cloves, or any similar fluid. In the figure, *b* is the slide and cover, and *a* is the prism. Rays of light, as shown by the dotted lines, if sent through the face of the prism, pass straight to the upper surface of the cover, and if a dry objective be used, they are reflected down again on to the underlying objects in balsam, which appear brilliantly illuminated, as if beneath a speculum. An immersion object-glass prevents the covering glass from acting as a speculum, and light emerges beyond what would otherwise be the critical angle, thus affording very oblique illumination, which, with suitable objectives, enables us to resolve the most difficult tests.

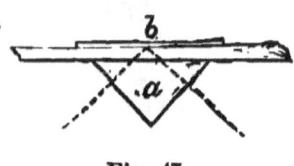

Fig. 47.

THE WENHAM PRISM.

If the prism is used with dry mounted objects, total reflection, instead of occurring from the cover, takes place from the upper surface of the slide itself, and all is total obscurity except where some object, such as a butterfly's scale or a diatom, is in intimate contact with the slide, and then these objects allow the transmission of light, and appear curiously distinct in a jet-black field.

This illuminator requires no fitting to adapt it to the microscope. It is merely stuck on the under surface of the slide with a little glycerine; the slide is then placed on the stage, the object found, and the position of the prism adjusted by the finger.

It has been objected to this method of attaching it, that when the microscope is inclined, the prism is apt to slide down. This will not occur if the quantity of liquid used be very small. It is not difficult, however, to arrange a very thin plate of metal with a square hole in the centre, the metal which originally filled the hole being bent down so as to form an ear or clip at each side of the opening. These clips grasp the prism, which, being cemented into this frame, may be laid on the stage; over it is placed the slide. If the metal plate be fastened to the stage by any contrivance, the object-slide may be moved about at will without disturbing the prism.

As we have already stated, the Wenham prism has a right angle and two angles of 45° each. Prisms for the same purpose have been made with unequal angles at the base, and with other than a right angle at the apex, and this is sometimes advantageous.

It is, of course, obvious that the Wenham prism transmits the rays with their direction unaltered. If we wish to condense them, this must be done previously by means of mirrors or lenses. Two illuminators, which combine the effects of the condenser and the prism, have been devised by Mr. Wenham, and we will now describe them.

The Hemispherical Illuminator.—Instead of a prism, Mr. Wenham has used a hemispherical lens, patched on to the slide in the same manner as that described for the prism. This lens concentrates the rays on the object, and as rays from any direction will always enter the lens at right angles to some part of its surface, more light and greater obliquity can be obtained by it than by the prism. This device was described by Mr. Wenham in the same paper in which he first described the right-angled prism, but we believe it was first applied by Mr. Tolles as an oblique illuminator for balsam-mounted objects seen with immersion lenses.

The "Half-Button."—A still more efficient illuminator, and one which is complete in itself, is shown in the engravings, Fig. 48 being a side view, Fig. 49 a section, and Fig. 50 a perspective view of this little contrivance. It consists of a semicircular disc of glass of one-quarter of an inch radius; the edge is rounded and well polished to a transverse radius of one-tenth of an inch, for the reason that the focus of a spherical surface on crown glass falls within its substance to nearly three times the radius, consequently the line of light will be in the most concentrated position at one-twentieth of an inch above the centre of the semi-disc, which distance is sufficient to reach objects mounted on slides of the usual thickness. The "half-button," as it has been called, is connected to the under side of the slide by means of water, glycerine, or oil of cloves, its sides being grasped by a simple kind of open clip attached to the sub-stage. This illuminator is complete in itself, and requires no supplementary condensing lens; the obliquity is

Figs. 48.   49.   50.

simply obtained by swinging the ordinary mirror sideways, and by this means *Amphipleura pellucida*, mounted in balsam, can be at once resolved.

The Woodward Illuminator.—This method of mounting and arranging a right-angled prism for the illumination of balsam-mounted objects, was described by Col. Dr. Woodward in a paper read before the Royal Microscopical Society, June 6, 1877. It consists of a prism of glass, the apex of which has been truncated. This prism is cemented to the truncated apex of a similar prism of brass, the long side of the glass prism being upward, and connected with the under surface of the object-slide by suitable liquid (glycerine, oil of cloves, etc.) The homologous side of the brass prism is downwards, and slides in a holder which is supported by the sub-stage. To this brass prism are attached two arms, which serve to support a thin screen at some distance below the stage. The screen is parallel to that face of the glass prism that receives the light, and is pierced with a pin-hole, which permits the passage of a minute beam of sunlight. With this apparatus, Col. Dr. Woodward secured very fine results.

Tolles' Illuminating Traverse Lens.—The most perfect arrangement for allowing a beam of light to reach, without refraction, a suitably immersed object, is the *illuminating traverse lens* of Mr. Tolles. The engraving, Fig. 51, and the description, which is in Mr. Tolles' own words, are from the *Journal of the Royal Microscopical Society*.

The device is represented in the annexed figure, where P is the basilar plate of the whole traverse system, having a circular groove and track, in which the carriage, C, moves. On a projecting arm, A, of the carriage, C, are mounted whatever appliances are to be used to modify or direct the light upon the traverse lens, T, in the direction of the object at the centre of the system.

In the figure the concave lens, N, is shown in position on the arm. Thus situated, the interior convex and concave surfaces being of no effect, the two exterior plane surfaces of *the traverse*

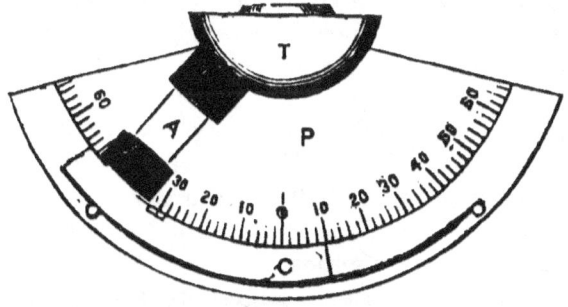

Fig. 51.—TOLLE'S ILLUMINATING TRAVERSE LENS.

system constitute it a prism, and every slightest movement of this concave facet lens on the traverse lens, T, would *would give a different prism* to infinite variety. In this arrangement, the concave mirror can be used in the ordinary manner and condense light enough upon the object for all ordinary purposes. The full interior aperture of a dry objective would be reached at the very convenient obliquity of 41°, i.e., at less than the critical angle, or angle of total internal reflection between crown-glass and air. L is a double-convex condensing lens, that may be placed at about its principal focal distance from the object.

For a condenser, with the size of apparatus as drawn in the figure, a simple lens of 1¼ inch focus, and about ten degrees (10°) of aperture is convenient, and if the lens is movable along the arm, A, it can be focussed readily on the object, the position being fixed by inspection, This would be well for parallel rays. If diverging rays are used, another lens of two or three inches focus, mounted on the arm, A, will conveniently take up the rays from the radiant at the distance of the focus of this supplementary lens.

The plate, P, is graduated on its circular edge, as in the figure, to two degrees, and the arm, A, has a swing of seventy degrees of arc each way from the axis of the microscope. An index-line is marked on the bevelled edge of the carriage 10° from the axis of the condenser, which must be added to or subtracted from the real obliquity of the illuminating rays.

It is obvious that any observation made and duly recorded as to its conditions, as of obliquity of incidence of illuminating pencil or ray, form of the pencil or beam, focal length and distance of the condenser, such observation could be successfully repeated. The record of the obliquity of the most oblique rays reaching the object directly and giving view of it at the eye-piece with luminous field, would express the "balsam" aperture, or more correctly, the half interior aperture of the objective when the front lens of the objective and the traverse system are of glass of similar refraction.

Having thus the "balsam" angle, we readily calculate or learn the corresponding angle for glycerine or water, or any medium of which we have the index of refraction. A corresponding notation, perhaps for air, might be engraved in juxtaposition on the basilar plate.

The Spot Lens.—This is a plano-convex lens of very high curvature (it is generally hemispherical), so mounted that its distance from the object may be adjusted in such a way that the rays which pass through it, may be brought to a focus on the object. The central rays are stopped out by means of a black spot (hence the name), so that the object is illuminated wholly by rays which are of too great obliquity to enter the object-glass, except when their direction is changed by the object. The latter, therefore, appears brilliantly illuminated on a dark ground, and in many cases features which could not otherwise be seen are shown very distinctly.

The larger diatoms, insect scales, and similar objects are peculiarly suited to this method of illumination, and some of them are very beautiful as "show" objects.

The Parabolic Illuminator.—This is an instrument intended to accomplish the same end as the spot lens, but in a far more efficient manner. It consists of a block of glass, the outer form of which is a parabola with a cup-shaped depression cut in the upper end. It is mounted in a brass fitting, which slides up and down in the sub-stage of the microscope, and thus may be readily adjusted, so as to throw the light properly upon the object. The results obtained by means of the parabolic illuminator are wonderfully beautiful.

Fig. 52.—THE PARABOLIC ILLUMINATOR.

Polarized Light.—The micro polariscope consists of two distinct parts, a *polarizer* and an *analyzer*, each of which is now generally formed of a Nichol prism properly mounted. A

Fig. 53.—POLARIZER.

Fig. 54 —ANALYZER.

common method of mounting the polarizer is shown in Fig. 53. As there shown, the lower ring is intended to slip into the ring of the sub-stage, the rack and pinion of which enables us to place the end of the prism at a proper distance from the object. When the microscope is not provided with a sub-stage, the polarizer is turned upside down, and the brass fitting slipped into a ring, which is attached to the under side of the stage. The milled ring, which is shown uppermost in the figure, enables us to rotate the prism in both cases.

The analyzer may be arranged in either one of two ways. It may be slipped over the eye-piece, or it may be mounted in a brass tube, the upper end of which has an external Society screw that attaches it to the body, while the lower end of the tube has an internal Society screw for receiving the objective. Fig. 54 shows the latter arrangement.

Polarized light, except for the mere beauty of its effects, has not received the attention that it deserves. In some departments of scientific investigation, especially mineralogy and geology, its use has afforded very satisfactory and brilliant results. As regards its applications to medicine and physiology, Dr. Frey says: "The examination of tissues by polarized light has a high scientific value, as, by this means, molecular relations become evident, which by investigation with ordinary light, remain entirely concealed. The interpretation of what is seen, is in many cases difficult, and generally lies within the province of optics, with which the medical observer is usually but little familiar."

To detail the method of using it, and the special features which it discloses, would, however, far transcend the limits of this work, and we must, therefore, refer the reader to some special treatise on the subject.

HOW TO USE THE MICROSCOPE.

The remarks which we are now about to offer, are intended for the merest beginners—for those, in fact, who have never used a microscope at all; and therefore they may, perhaps, to some, appear childishly simple. And yet we have seen not only teachers, but professors in colleges, who might have derived some benefit even from these simple hints. We remember on one occasion seeing a professor of botany attempt to examine a minute plant with a common pocket magnifier with three lenses. In the first place he turned the instrument wrong side up, so that, although he could *see* through it, the results attained were very inferior to what they would have been if the instrument had been properly used; in the second place he wore his hat in such a way as to cut off nearly all the light, and in the third place he did not know how to hold his hands so as to obtain the requisite degree of steadiness. If he had given a few minutes *thought* to the subject, he could no doubt have corrected his bad methods, but then he evidently had never considered it worthy of earnest thought, although it formed the very foundation of his powers of observation.

Simple Hand Magnifiers.—These are perhaps the most important of all optical instruments, and yet we rarely find a person who can use them efficiently. There are but three points that require attention, viz: The proper position of the magnifier itself, the perfection of the illumination, and the steadiness with which the instrument is held at the exact focal distance from the object. Many magnifiers are so constructed that it is impossible to place them in a wrong position; the side which should go next the eye, and the side which should go next the object are so well marked that no mistake can be made. The greatest liability to error exists where two or three lenses of different powers are fixed in the same frame and used together. This forms one of the most common and useful of our magnifiers, and the rule is always to *place the lens of greatest power nearest to the object.* Plano-convex lenses should be placed with the plane or flat side next the object.

Hand magnifiers are, in the majority of cases, used for examining opaque objects, and one of the most important conditions for perfect vision is that the object be well illuminated. First of all, then, see that the light falls full and direct on the object; then place the magnifier as nearly in focus as can be done without actually looking through the lens, and, *after* this, approach the eye to the magnifier. The errors most commonly committed are: Turning the object away from the light; cutting off the light by the projecting brim of a hat or cap; shading the object by the hand or the lens itself; attempting to examine an object in a room that is not sufficiently lighted.

Having secured a proper position for the magnifier and a good illumination, the next step is to devise some means for holding the lens steadily in focus during the examination. This is most readily effected by resting the hand that holds the lens upon the hand that holds the object. Lens and object then move together, and the focussing remains unchanged.

Compound Microscopes.—We presume that the instrument in hand is a very simple one, and that the magnifying power to be used is not very great. No person should attempt to use high powers and complicated instruments until he has served an apprenticeship by using a microscope of simple construction, and objectives of considerable length of focus.

Let the beginner commence by examining some transparent object already mounted. To do this, set the microscope on a firm table, in front of a window by day, or before a lamp at night. Direct sunlight is to be avoided, the light from a white cloud being usually preferred to any other source of illumination. At night use a gaslight that does not flicker, such as an argand burner, or a good kerosene lamp, the German student lamp being very well suited to this purpose. Good results may, however, be obtained from any of the ordinary lamps, especially those with a circular wick, which are now so common. Very fair work may also be done by means of a good candle. This subject has, however, already been discussed at greater length in another section.

If the microscope be a cheap French one, the objectives will be found attached to the body, there seldom being any special provision made for holding them. But with all American and English microscopes, and the better class of instruments from the continent of Europe, special boxes are provided for holding the objectives. These boxes are usually made of brass, and are indispensable to the microscopist that endeavors to take good care of his instrument. Where the objective is kept in a separate box, the body of the microscope must be raised to a sufficient height, and the objective screwed into its place. In doing this be very careful not to let the objective fall and strike against the stage. We have seen more than one good lens spoiled through such an accident.

When the objective has been properly secured in its place, move the body of the microscope up or down until the front lens—that is, the lens which is nearest to the object, is about a quarter of an inch above the stage. Then turn the mirror until the light from the window or lamp is reflected through the microscope, so that when looking through it a bright circle of light is seen.

Place on the stage some mounted object of large size, such as a fly's wing or section of wood. If a low power objective be used, say one magnifying less than 100 diameters, move the body of the microscope up, so as to increase the distance between the objective and the object. At the same time keep your eye at the eye-piece and watch closely. At a certain point the object will be seen with great distinctness; it is then in focus, and is ready for examination. Always begin with low powers. One of the greatest risks that the beginner runs is that of breaking the objective by forcing it down on the object. To avoid this with high powers, bring the objective down almost into contact with the slide; when doing this do not look *through* the microscope, but watch the objective, and stop whenever it is sufficiently near the object. Then apply the eye to the eye-piece, slowly raise the body, and watch for the coming of the object into focus. This is the only safe method with high powers.

Before attempting to place an object on the stage, or to remove one from it, see that the objective is raised at least half an inch above the stage. By attempting to introduce a new slide without raising the objective, when using high powers, you run great risk of injuring both the object and the objective. And in removing objects from the stage, never lift them up; always *slide them off*. In lifting them up, great danger is incurred of bringing them into contact with the objective, and thus doing irreparable injury. Sliding entirely prevents this.

Where the microscope is not provided with mechanical means for adjusting the focus, such as a screw or rack and pinion, a great deal may be accomplished by special methods of manipulation. Thus if, instead of pushing the body directly through the collar, it be moved with a slightly twisting motion, the focus may be adjusted with considerable delicacy, and when the microscope is not provided with a fine movement, a great deal may be done by means of a slight pressure of the fingers on the stage. Few stages are sufficiently rigid to resist even the slightest pressure.

The chief points which the beginner should endeavor to study are the variations which are made in the appearance of the object by means of slight changes in the focussing and the mode of illumination. Experienced microscopists constantly keep their fingers on the fine adjustment of the microscope, and watch the different appearances which are produced by a change in the mode of illumination. Swinging the mirror to one side, so as to send the light through the object in an oblique direction, or, where the mirror cannot be turned to one side, merely turning it on the trunnions which support it, will often produce most important effects.

From what has previously been said in regard to the necessity for clear and brilliant sources of illumination, the young microscopist may, perhaps, be led to suppose that the field of view cannot be too brilliantly illuminated. Such, however, is far from being the case. With ordinary powers (those below 500 diameters) it is almost always necessary to moderate the light, even of a flat-wicked lamp, and still more that of a students' lamp. The finer details of an object cannot possibly be made out if the illumination be too strong; they are "drowned out," and the whole object becomes what artists and engravers call *flat*. The light may be regulated by the diaphragm which has been previously described. Where the microscope is not furnished with a diaphragm, increasing the distance of the lamp from the instrument is the best mode of lessening the intensity of the light.

Very bright light is exceedingly trying to the eyes, and therefore the student will find it advantageous to use lights of moderate intensity, and to increase their efficiency in every possible way. This may be done to a very great extent by judicious management—chiefly by excluding from the eye all *unnecessary* light. In a room very brilliantly lighted with a number of powerful argand burners, it would be impossible to secure the proper illumination of a microscopic object by means of a candle, for the eye, accustomed to the bright light, would fail to be impressed by the weaker one. Extinguish the bright lights, give the eye a short time for rest, and the candle will answer very well. The principle thus illustrated finds a practical application in the use of pasteboard shades surrounding the eye-piece, and excluding from the eye all light except that which passes through the microscope. Such a shade is easily made and adapted to any microscope, and is of great service. We have also in our own practice carried out the same principle by means of extra diaphragms to our eye-pieces, thus cutting off all the light which passes through the microscope, except that which actually serves to illuminate the object.

It will also be found of great importance to secure perfect purity in the special illumination employed. Thus, if we are examining an object by transmitted light, it always detracts from the clearness and beauty of the image if light is reflected from its surface. It is, therefore, of advantage to shade the object by means of a small tin, brass or pasteboard shade, attached to the stage so as to prevent any light from the lamp from falling *on* the object.

A difficulty which frequently occurs to young microscopists consists in the almost impossibility of securing a field of view equally illuminated in all parts. Assuming that the mirror is in proper position, and that there is nothing to shade any part, it will in general be found that the difficulty arises from the fact that the mirror throws images of the lamp, etc., upon the object. Sometimes this is very distinctly seen; the shape of the flame can be clearly distinguished, and the metal portions of the lamp appear as dark shades. The cause is that the lamp is at the exact distance at which the mirror forms an image of it on the upper surface of the slide, just as a lens, held in front of a white wall, will throw an inverted image of a lamp or candle on the wall, provided the relative distances of the wall, lens and candle are properly adjusted. The remedy is very simple; move the lamp either towards the microscope or away from it, as may be most convenient.

As previously stated, the character of the illumination afforded by a mirror, and by a white surface placed at a short distance from the object, are appreciably different. A very pleasant method of illuminating transparent objects consists in the use of a plate of plaster of paris. Its whiteness is probably as pure as that of any other substance, and it is easily procured. The plate we use was cast in the cover of an old tin box, half an inch deep and three inches in diameter. A flat surface was secured by casting it upon a board. If cast on glass or metal, the surface is glazed and shiny, which is bad. Instead of plaster, fine white paper or cardboard may be used. Such surfaces must not be glazed, and they should be kept scrupulously clean.

The light is also sometimes modified by passing it through ground or colored glass—blue being a special favorite. Such light-modifiers, as they are called, produce a pleasant and equable illumination, which is a great relief to the eyes, but, except for the resolution of finely lined objects, we have not found them otherwise of any special advantage. When it is desired to obtain the greatest resolving power that a lens is capable of affording, the *blue cell*, as it is called, is probably the most efficient accessory. This is simply a glass tank, somewhat like a zoophyte trough, filled with a solution of oxide of copper in liquor ammoniæ. The solution is prepared by adding liquor ammoniæ to a saturated solution of sulphate of copper, until the precipitate which is first formed is re-dissolved. The intensity of the blue may be regulated, either by diluting the solution, or by varying the thickness of the layer of liquid.

When it is desired to examine anything by light *reflected from* it, instead of light *transmitted through* it, the object should be placed before a dead-black surface, such as the dark part of the diaphragm, or a blackened card, and at such a distance from it that the surface of the background is not in focus. Then, place the condensing lens in relation to the lamp, so that a bright spot of light will fall on the object, and on bringing it into focus it will be clearly seen. Low powers only can be satisfactorily used for the examination of opaque objects by beginners.

The beginner should commence with the simplest mounted objects, and afterwards, when a little skill in the manipulation of the instrument has been acquired, he should proceed to the examination of such simple unmounted objects as are easily prepared. The latter course will prove altogether the most valuable and instructive, for he who confines himself to the examination of mounted objects only can never hope to become a microscopist. After a time, when a little skill has been acquired in the *preparation* of objects, the student may proceed to preserve and mount them. Most young people try to *mount* before they have learned to *prepare* objects, and the consequence is that they soon find themselves in possession of a large collection of very poor slides.

On the Use of Objectives of Large Apertures.—
When the first edition of this book was issued, wide-angled objectives were far from common. The "Battle of the Object-Glasses" was at its height, and objectives capable of resolving the *Amphipleura pellucida*, or Nobert's nineteenth band, by simple lamplight, were comparatively scarce. During the intervening years the opticians have been hard at work, and have turned out objectives of a high class to such an extent that almost every microscopical society numbers amongst its members those who have glasses of high balsam apertures. It is an unfortunate fact, however, that thus far the text-books are entirely innocent of any directions for using these glasses. We have now before us a treatise of over 400 pages, which left the author's hands as late as the middle of 1880, and which does not contain a single direction for the use of the cover correction! As a justification of such omission, it has been alleged that objectives of large aperture require no more care and skill than others. From this position we most emphatically dissent, and if evidence were wanting we could cite the case of a prominent officer of one of our microscopical societies, and one who claims to be an expert in the use of the microscope, who thought it a great feat to show No. 18 of the Probe Platte with a ⅛ objective, which undoubtedly was capable of resolving No. 20 handsomely if properly handled! The forthcoming work of Prof. J. Edwards Smith will probably be the first text-book that will have treated this department thoroughly, and students are anxiously looking forward to its appearance.

Instruction in the proper methods of handling first-class objectives is best obtained from a living teacher. It will be found one of the most difficult things to learn from a book. One reason for this is that until he has become expert, or has seen the objects in the hands of some one who is expert, the student does not know what appearance to look for. The consequence is, that he is all the time working in the dark. But after he has seen the Amphipleura or the Saxonica well shown by some one who knows how to handle a good objective, he has a standard of excellence to go by, and it will be very strange if, after a few trials, he does not surpass the work of his teacher. Then, as soon as he has learned to bring out what he knows to be the best results on difficult diatoms, he knows when his lenses are doing good work in his hands, and, so far as his instrument is concerned, he feels confident that he can apply it to any class of objects and get views that are trustworthy.

To get the best results from modern objectives of wide angle of aperture, there are two things that must be carefully attended to—the illumination of the object, and the adjustment of the correction for the thickness of cover-glass. Of delicacy in focussing, which, by the way, is a most important point, it is unnecessary to speak.

As regards illumination, the three great points that must be secured are *purity*, *intensity*, and *suitability*. By purity we mean that the light must be wholly of a certain degree of obliquity, for these wide-angle lenses gather in so many rays, that a diffused light, which does not affect low-angled objectives, greatly injures the working qualities of those of high angle. Thus, for example, if we are working by central light, it is necessary to shut out all the direct rays from the lamp, which would enter at every sort of angle, and produce confusion. A narrow pencil, produced by sending a beam of parallel rays of intense light through a small hole placed some distance below the stage, will give central illumination, which will give very different results from that obtained by a dull, diffused light, such as may be obtained from the flat side of the wick of a lamp, falling on a large mirror and reflected upward.

When oblique illumination is used, great care should be taken to prevent rays of different degrees of obliquity from falling on the object. A large, concave mirror fills a large portion of the arc through which it swings, and its upper and lower edges reflect rays which fall upon the object with very different degrees of obliquity. Where very oblique rays are used, but a small proportion of them enter the glass slide, unless they are "guided" through by some such contrivance as the Reflex Illuminator, Tolles' Traverse Lens, etc. Rays of less obliquity enter much more freely, and although less in quantity than the others in the first place, they drown them out. In the exclusion of these rays consists in a great degree the value of many of the "illuminators" in common use, and the same effect may be secured to a considerable extent by means of a simple screen. This fact has been made very apparent by Prof. J. E. Smith, who, by the use of a simple "oblique diaphragm," as it is called, has secured results which were previously supposed to demand much more complicated and expensive arrangements. This oblique diaphragm, or screen, consists of a plate of very thin metal secured to the under surface of the stage. The stage then forms the upper surface of a >, and the metal plate the lower one. The angle may be adjusted at will by simply bending the plate, and it is evident that all rays from below will be entirely excluded. A piece of the thin iron known as ferrotype plate is the cheapest and best material for this purpose. Its surface should be dead black.

The same result is obtained by the use of a conical diaphragm fitted to the sub-stage.

When such objects as difficult tests are viewed by oblique light, it will be found that there is a certain angle of illumination at which the objective will generally perform best, and this must be found by careful experiment. The higher the angle of aperture of the objective, the greater may be the angle at which the object is illuminated, but it will be found that many objectives fail to work up to the full angle claimed for them by their makers.

Such are the general principles to which the student must pay attention in regard to the matter of illumination, but in addition there are numerous minor details, a knowledge and appreciation of which can only be acquired by practice. The finer objectives are so sensitive to the slightest changes, that the least movement of the mirror or lamp influences the result in a very marked degree.

The other important point to be attended to is the cover-correction. This will be found to demand great patience and attention. The older authorities give fixed rules for regulating the cover-adjustment, but as it unfortunately happens that this adjustment varies not only with the thickness of the cover-glass, but with the depth to which the object is sunk in the mounting medium (and this is not always the same), and the angle of illumination, it will be seen that each object requires special attention in regard to these points. In addition to this, it will be found that each objective has its own special characteristics, which must be carefully studied by the owner if he would command success.

The difficulty of giving any rules which will enable the student to put the "finer touches" on this kind of work, is well set forth by Dr. Blackham in a recent article,* from which we quote as follows:

"It will probably be expected that something should be said here in reference to the *adjustment* of the objective for different cover-glasses, etc., by means of the screw collar, but on this point, unfortunately, but little can be said, though, of course, it is a most important one, and the better the objective, and the wider its angle, the more important is accurate adjustment. Every wide-angled immersion objective that is worth having, is a separate work of art, and, as such, has an individuality with which the worker must become acquainted, and which he must learn to turn to his advantage.

"None of these lenses which I have seen are perfectly achromatic, and each has a special wave length at which it does its best. In Tolles', and Bausch & Lomb's, and I believe in Spencer's lenses, this is between the blue and the green, but the exact shade differs with different lenses, and must be found by experiment. My plan is to adjust roughly by means of the tint of the field, then to bring an object into the field (if we are at work on the Probe Platte, one of the easier diatoms, say *Pleurosigma angulatum*), and focus on it and arrange the illumination as accurately as possible, and then with the finger and thumb of the left hand, turn the correction collar of the objective backwards and forwards, keeping the object in focus all the time by means of the forefinger of the right hand on the milled head of the fine adjustment, until the best effect is obtained. An occasional slight change in the position of the mirror is often needed.

"In all these manipulations, deliberation and care are needed, and the patience of the beginner will often be sorely taxed, but let him remember that nothing worth having, can be gotten without trouble."

American Journal of Microscopy for February, 1880.

Care of the Microscope.—A microscope, when not in use, should always be kept well covered, either in its case or under a suitable cover. There is no more convenient mode of keeping a microscope than to stand it upon a cloth mat, and cover it with a glass shade. It is thus kept free from dust and vapors, and is always ready for use; but when it is kept in its case, and especially if it has to be screwed together, interesting, valuable, or even important objects, will often fail to be examined, simply because too much time and labor are necessary to prepare for the operation.

A good microscope should be so carefully protected, that it shall rarely require to be cleaned or dusted, as this wears off the lacquer, and exposes the metal, which, when thus uncovered, soon begins to tarnish. When dusting or cleaning becomes absolutely necessary, chamois leather, or a very fine old linen or silk handkerchief is most suitable. Never use coarse cloths, or those that have been lying about exposed to dust and dirt.

The lenses should be kept in their boxes when not in use, and when they are attached to the microscope, great care should be taken to keep them from coming into contact with liquids. In order to prevent the latter accident as far as possible, never examine liquids unless when they are covered with thin glass. In the pursuit of micro-chemical studies, the microscopist has frequently to deal with liquids that corrode metals, and even glass. In well-appointed laboratories *inverted* microscopes are used in such cases, but with ordinary instruments, special means must be employed. The object should be laid on a large piece of thin plate glass, and the brass work of the objective should be coated with oil. The rest of the metal work may be protected with oiled silk or thin india-rubber.

When liquids which corrode glass are used, the front of the objective should be protected by means of a very thin leaf of the best mica, which may be attached either by glycerine or balsam.

These, however, are exceptional precautions. In ordinary work it is sufficient to see that the lenses and metal work are kept free from stains and finger marks.

Never touch with the fingers the surface of any lenses, either eye-pieces or objectives, as this will be certain to soil them. Use soft camel-hair brushes to remove particles of dust, etc. Where dirt adheres more strongly, use fine linen *slightly* moistened with alcohol, and wipe dry with very fine chamois leather. Remember, that alcohol, if used profusely, will attack the lacquer of the brass-work, and even dissolve the cement which holds the lenses together. When objectives are smeared with balsam, the best cleansing agent is said to be kerosene oil. The piece of leather used for wiping lenses should be free from dust, and is best kept in a small box by itself, and used for nothing else. It must be remembered that the glass of which objectives are made is easily scratched, being soft when compared with particles of sand and grit; consequently, when frequently wiped it soon loses that exquisite polish upon which its excellence of performance so much depends. What, then, are we to think of the directions given by the author of a popular work on the microscope, in which we are told to use a piece of leather, slightly impregnated with brick dust!! No better method of destroying an objective could possibly be devised. Therefore, see that in wiping, the *slightest* possible pressure is used, lest any particle of grit should make a scratch.

The exposed parts of all microscopes, as well as the objectives and their cases, are lacquered, to protect them from being soiled by handling, but the interior of the boxes which hold the object-glasses are rarely so protected, and the black coating of the interior of bodies, draw-tubes, etc., is frequently not very firmly attached. Therefore, never touch them with the fingers.

After taking an objective out of its box, either screw on the cover of the box, or place the latter with its open end down. Do not stand it mouth up, so that it may catch all the dust.

When exhibiting the microscope to others, great care is necessary to keep meddlesome fingers from soiling the glasses. Some people are never content when merely allowed to look at things: they insist upon handling them, and feeling them. To the young microscopist, we would say that if any of your friends insist upon handling your objectives, eye-pieces, etc., put up the instrument and pack it away. A microscope carefully used is as good after fifty years as when first made, but we have seen an instrument suffer more injury in half an hour at the hands of a thoughtless and dirty person, than it would have sustained in twenty years in the hands of a careful microscopist.

COLLECTING OBJECTS.

Those who are engaged in special studies and researches require no directions for *collecting* objects; but to those who use the microscope for purposes of general instruction or amusement, a few hints may not be out of place. Almost every text-book on botany, physiology, mineralogy and kindred subjects, will not only indicate a long list of objects, but will give directions for procuring them. Plants yield a very large variety of interesting subjects. Thus the cuticles of the leaves and flowers; cellular tissue as shown by dissections, and by cross and longitudinal sections; hairs, pollen, seeds, etc., all deserve careful microscopical examination. Insects furnish an almost unlimited field, and their wings, feet, eyes, mouth, scales, spiracles, hairs, etc., are all worthy of careful preparation and examination.

It is, however, amongst the more minute forms of animal and vegetable life, as found in pools and running streams, that the most interesting objects are to be found, and the number and variety of these is so great that several large volumes would be required to describe them. Even the ponderous works of Ehrenberg and Pritchard do not begin to exhaust the subject, and, therefore, it will be obvious, that even if we were to devote the whole of the present volume to this department, we could but skim the surface. Thus far we have had to depend chiefly upon foreign works for descriptions of these organisms, but it is fortunate that while the higher classes of plants and animals which inhabit Europe, and are described in European works, are entirely different from their congeners on this continent, the same does not hold true in regard to the lower forms. We have found localities which teemed with the *Volvox Globator* and various species of *Closterium, Staurastrum, Pediastrum,* etc. Hydras are to be found in great abundance, and so nearly like the described European species that the beginner will find it difficult to detect the difference. We have repeatedly found the *Stephanoceras, Melicerta* and other beautiful microscopic objects, and as for the more common ones, such as the *Vorticelli,* or wheel animalcules and *Entomostraca*, or water fleas, they are to be found in every pool.

Every young microscopist that is desirous of pursuing his studies in this direction, is met at the outset by two difficulties; the first is to obtain the objects, the second is to find out what they are after he has got them. The first is by no means a difficult task, but the second will often puzzle more experienced students than those whom we expect to be readers of this book. We know of but two ways to accomplish it; one is the laborious plan of searching for them in the "Micrographic Dictionary," or the books of Carpenter or Pritchard; the other is to obtain the desired information from some well-informed friend.

The objects which are of most interest to the microscopist are not difficult to obtain, if we know where to look for them, but they are not to be found everywhere. Many stagnant pools will be found to yield but a scanty supply, while others, which, perhaps, to the uninitiated present a less promising appearance, will yield a rich harvest. Beginners are very apt to entertain the popular notion, that *every* drop of water teems with animalcules, and that when placed under the microscope, it will appear to be literally filled with living things. This idea is fostered by popular writers who describe a drop of water as a globe filled with life, and by lecturers who exhibit pictures and enlarged images of what they call "a drop of water," but which is in reality a considerable quantity of that liquid which has been artificially supplied with inhabitants. Clear well water is almost free from microscopic organisms, and the same is true of the water from clear brooks, which flow swiftly over a pebbly bottom. Ordinary rain water, as found in cisterns having free communication with the air, usually contains large numbers of the larvæ of gnats and mosquitoes, and when exposed to the light it is almost always rich in wheel animalcules, and some of the lower forms of vegetable life. The water supplied to our cities is in general very rich in microscopic vegetables. Thus in the Croton water, which is comparatively pure, we have found a large number of very beautiful species, amongst them the exquisite *Monachinus*. The best way to secure a supply of the animal and vegetable inhabitants of city water, is to pass a considerable quantity of it through a filter, the surface of which will then furnish a large amount of valuable matter.

But it is not in such fields that the microscopist will find his best hunting grounds. Along the edges of quiet pools of clear water is the best place for the finer vegetable forms, such as the *Volvox Globator*, *Closterium*, etc. If the water is much contaminated with dead animal matter or with sewage, nothing will be found but the coarser organisms and animalcules, such as *Paramecium*. The same is true of small pools found in woods, or very much shaded with trees, and filled with dead leaves. Such places are, however, the favorite haunts of the larvæ of insects, and also of frogs and Tritons. The size of the pools is not of much consequence. We remember on one occasion to have found by the roadside in Centre County, Pennsylvania, a little pool which was almost filled with the larvæ of Tritons. The gills, which were beautifully developed, would have formed a splendid object under the microscope, but when we returned next day, for the purpose of securing some, the water had dried up, and the larvæ were all gone.

The little pools formed in boggy ground by the footsteps of cattle will often be found to contain large quantities of one or two species of desmids or diatoms. It will not do to look for these objects in similar pools formed in ordinary soft land, and temporarily filled with rain water. The ground must be naturally and constantly wet, so that the pools are always kept filled by the infiltration of water from the surrounding soil. Such pools, however small, usually contain a large number of specimens, and it is in such places that one is most likely to find a supply of *one* variety unmixed with any others.

While many of the most interesting objects will be found swimming freely about in the water, others of great beauty are always attached to floating weeds, sticks, etc. We have generally been most successful in discovering specimens of this kind when we have placed the gathering in a large glass jar, and allowed it to stand quiet for some time. The water will then settle, and the objects of which the microscopist is in search will have time to expand, when they may be seen in a form resembling light mould, or down, attached to the surfaces of the solid matters.

The surface of the mud at the bottom of ponds of clear water, is frequently very rich in microscopic vegetable organisms. These minute plants seem to seek the light, and to rise through the mud which would otherwise cover them, so that by carefully scraping the surface of the bottom, we are enabled to procure them in large numbers.

It must, of course, be borne in mind, that while some species are found in fresh water, others are *marine*, that is, they live only in sea-water. The best locations for finding marine forms are: 1, the pools of clear water, found in salt marshes; 2, the surface of the mud at the bottoms of harbors and quiet coves; 3, the waters of the ocean itself, as well as that of the bays and coves connected with it.

The apparatus required for capturing these various objects, is neither bulky nor expensive. For larvæ and the larger animalcules, the most useful implement is a small net. Ours consists of a ring of brass wire (iron wire would rust and destroy the net) about six inches in diameter, soldered to a tin tube or ferrule, which fits tightly on the end of a walking cane. To the ring is attached a bag of any light, gauzy material, which possesses the two qualities of letting water out rapidly, and keeping small objects in. With this net it is easy to capture anything from a small fish or a frog to the very smallest larva, and it is very portable, since an ordinary walking cane forms a sort of universal handle for this and other implements. Next to the net, we find the most useful articles to be bottles. They should be of clear glass, so that any object contained in them may be readily examined by means of a pocket lens. For this reason we prefer what are called homœopathic phials of large size (half ounce and quarter ounce), and we generally carry a dozen or two when out on a tramp. A fair sample of the contents of a small pool is easily obtained by gently lowering the phial, mouth downwards, under the water, and bringing it cautiously to the place which is supposed to be richest in specimens. The phial is then turned mouth upward, the air rushes out and the objects are carried into the bottle by the force of the inrushing current of water. For small, shallow pools, the phial is most conveniently held in the hand, but when the water is deep a handle is required, and for this we use the holder shown in

Fig. 55, which is made to fit on the end of the walking stick. It consists of a ferrule having a semi-cylindrical piece soldered at

Fig. 55.

right angles to it. The ferrule fits the cane, and the bottle is fastened to the cross piece by means of a rubber ring—the method of arranging the latter being easily understood from the engraving. A dozen or more bottles of proper size may be taken along, and they are so easily attached to the holder that there is no necessity for transferring a "dip" to another bottle. The contents are most easily carried in the bottle in which they were first obtained.

When the water is too deep for a walking cane, a fishing rod or any long pole may be used, and where these prove too short, as in harbors, etc., a bottle may be lowered and raised properly by means of strings. For this purpose the bottle must be heavily loaded with lead round the neck, and two strings must be attached to it, one fastened to the neck and the other to the bottom. It is by the latter that the bottle must be lowered, but it must be raised by the other. If properly managed it will descend mouth downwards, but the tension of the string attached to the neck will invert it, and when raised by this string it will bring up its contents very perfectly.

For scraping the surface of the mud at the bottom of shallow pools, we use the spoon shown in Fig. 56. It is simply a ring of tin five inches in diameter and one inch deep. The lower edge is "wired" as the tinsmiths call it, and there is a ferrule soldered to the side so that it may be fixed to the same cane that is used for the net. Over the bottom is stretched a piece of some

Fig. 56.

thin fabric, such as thin muslin, gauze or tarletan, which is held in place by a rubber band that slips over the wire ring on the lower edge It is best to make one side of the ring somewhat flat, so as to adapt it better to the flat surface of the mud. When the pieces of cloth get soiled, they are easily replaced, and, indeed, in some cases it is not a bad plan to carry the mud home in the wet cloths, a dozen or more of which, with their contents, may be easily packed in a tin box of small size. One of the boxes used by school children for lunch boxes answers very well, but any tin box with a lid or cover will answer. As it is important that a record should be kept of the locality from which the dip was taken, we carry a few slips of parchment paper, one of which is pinned to each cloth, after the necessary memoranda have been written upon it with a hard pencil. On returning home, the contents of each cloth may be transferred to a separate bottle. This plan saves the carrying of numerous bottles, and the water required to fill them.

An exceedingly covenient traveling companion for those who are fond of collecting, is shown in the accompanying engraving, Fig. 57. The main part forms a very convenient walking cane of ordinary appearance. Like many fishing rods, however, it is hollow, and contains a second rod by which it may be extended to twice its length. This enables the user to reach the bottom of any ordinary pond, and to reach as far as is necessary from

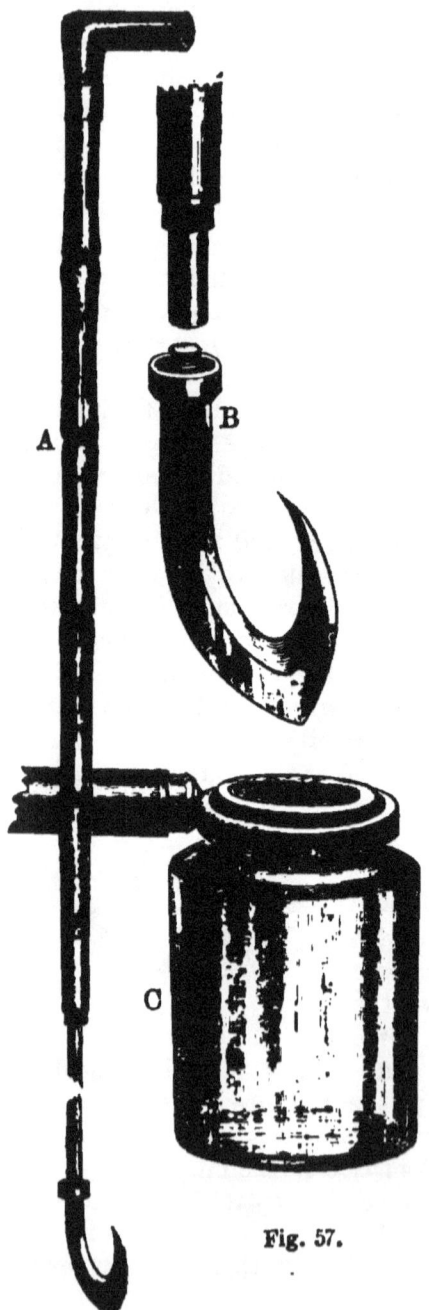

Fig. 57.

the shore. Accompanying the cane, A, are the hooked knife, B, and the ring and bottle, C. These are made with a double screw, so that they may be attached either to the end of the cane itself, or to the inner rod, and in this way we can have either a short and stout handle, or a longer and more slender one, as circumstances may require. The bottle is made so as to screw into the brass ring, and the same screw enables us to fit a wooden cap on it, which thus encloses the contents tightly. The hook is made of fine steel, and has a sharp cutting edge, as seen in the engraving, so that it is easy to cut off a piece of weed, drag it out of the water and secure it.

Those who carry such a cane do not attract attention by any unusual paraphernalia, and at the same time they are at all times ready to secure any valuable material that may present itself. Several bottles may be carried in the pocket, and screwed into the ring as required.

The collector who desires to make a thorough examination of the microscopic flora and fauna of any pool or stream, must not rest content with infinitesimal quantities of material. It is not necessary, however, to lug home a gallon of water for the sake of the objects contained in it, and so fully have microscopists been impressed with this idea, that the devices which have been prepared for straining out the valuable portions are almost endless. The best and simplest that we have seen is a modification of an

Fig. 58.—WATER-STRAINER.

arrangement, designed, we believe, by Mr. Highley, and figured in Beale's work on the microscope. It consists, as shown in the engraving (see Fig. 58), of a bag or net of some light material, to the bottom of which is attached, by means of twine, or a strong rubber ring, a wide-mouthed bottle. Any quantity of water may be poured into the bag, and all the objects which it contains will roll down the sides of the bag and fall into the bottle, while the fluid escapes through the sides. Delicate objects are consequently not exposed to pressure, rubbing, or any other violence, as they would be in an ordinary filter or bag, and the whole affair is so simple that any one can make it.

A slight modification of this arrangement will be found admirably adapted to the microscopic examination of the water supplied to cities. The bag may be attached to any faucet, and and all the water that is used in the household may be caused to pass through it. In this case, if the bag be made of some tolerably stout material, it may be firmly tied to the faucet, and then all the water that is consumed will be very thoroughly purified.

Another very excellent device is the bottle invented by Mr. Wright, of which a modified form is shown in Fig. 59. The mouth of the bottle is closed by means of a cork in which two funnels are inserted. One of these funnels is placed in the bottle, mouth down; the other projects above the cork, as shown in the engraving. The mouth of the funnel that is in the bottle is covered with muslin or flannel, held in place by a rubber band, which is prevented by a wire ring from slipping along the conical surface of the funnel. When water is poured into the other funnel, it passes into the bottle until the latter is full, and then it flows out of the first funnel, and is carried off by means of a short piece of rubber tubing. Meanwhile, all solid particles are held back by the filter, and as the latter is horizontal and with the filtering

Fig. 59.

surface downwards, most objects of interest fall away from it, and may be found in the water. A single bottle of this description is sufficient, as the cork is easily removed, so that the water may be poured into other bottles. As ordinarily made and sold, Wright's collecting bottle is an expensive piece of apparatus, costing four or five dollars, but as shown in the engraving it may be made for a few cents by any tinsmith.

Where it is desirable to keep the specimens thus obtained so that they may be examined, and their life-history studied, bottles and jars of almost any kind may be used, but those which we have found most convenient are what are known as "quinine" bottles, and may be had at most druggists. For ordinary objects they are just about the right size, and as they are made of tolerably clear glass it is easy to examine the objects through the sides of the bottle. A dozen or two of these little aquaria occupy very little space, and are easily handled. Great care must in general be taken to exclude from the vessels containing the finer organisms, such predatory animalcules as devour them. Water fleas, the larvæ of insects, etc., will soon make away with the finer specimens. On this account great difficulty is found in keeping the *Volvox Globator*, since it is greedily devoured by various rotifers, and these are exceedingly difficult to exclude. We have succeeded best in this case by partially filling a bottle with well-filtered water taken from the same pool as the specimens, and transferring the objects to it singly so as to avoid transferring their enemies too. For this purpose the dipping tube should be used. Some authors caution us against mixing the inhabitants of different pools, on the ground that being strangers to each other they will fight. This is more fanciful than accurate, though it has a basis of truth. It is not the circumstance that they are strangers that causes the difficulty, but the fact that the one is the natural prey of the other. The same thing occurs between inhabitants of the same pool. It must be remembered, however, that very slight changes in the conditions in which they are placed will often cause the destruction of these objects. Thus, we have seen some very fine gatherings totally destroyed by being removed from soft, boggy water to clear, hard well water. Therefore, in transferring either animals or vegetables to an aquariun, it is well to supply them with the same water, mud, etc., in which they were originally found. It will sometimes, however, be well to filter the water so as to remove all such inhabitants as are apt to eat up the others. Water, may be filtered through paper, or where filtering paper is inaccessible, the neck of a funnel may be loosely plugged with cotton. Even this does not quite free it from noxious eggs or germs, and we have sometimes boiled it in the flask in which the objects were to be kept. The mouth of the flask was then plugged with loose cotton, and when the water was cold, the objects we wished to preserve were introduced.

When floating freely in these diminutive aquaria, many objects are as difficult to find and capture as would be a small fish in a large pond. The microscopist, therefore, requires special means for capturing them, and placing them on a slide. For this purpose nothing serves so well as what are known as dipping or fishing tubes. These are simply glass tubes of different diameters (from one tenth to one quarter of an inch), and of any convenient length. They are used by closing the upper end with the finger, bringing the lower end near the object (under the water), and then removing the fingers from the upper end. The water, in seeking to find its own level in the tube rushes in with great force and carries the object with it. By again placing the finger on the upper end of the tube, the latter may be lifted from the bottle, and the water with it, and by a little dexterous management it is easy to cause the object to flow out on a slide without allowing too much water to go with it. These tubes are made straight, curved, and with one end drawn to a point, but for most purposes the straight tube answers best as it is most easily kept clean. We prefer to grind the ends rather than to make them smooth by fusion, as the latter process generally contracts the opening, and renders the tube difficult to clean. The best plan, however, is to heat the upper end strongly before the blowpipe, and turn the edge outward like the mouth of a test-tube. It is then easily closed, and the tube is very strong. The lower end should be ground.

PREPARATION, PRESERVATION AND MOUNTING OF OBJECTS.

These three operations are so frequently applied as a single process to objects, that many writers have failed to make a sufficient distinction between them. By keeping the proper distinction clearly in mind, however, the student will not only save much valuable time, but he will secure vastly better results. Except by those who are more anxious to increase the number of objects in their cabinet than the amount of knowledge which they possess, a very large proportion of the objects examined will never be preserved or mounted at all. This however, should not prevent the utmost care being given to the process of preparing them for thorough examination. On the other hand it often happens that objects which have been carefully prepared and mounted, spoil because they have not been subjected to a proper preserving process. Hence the importance of treating these operations separately and fully.

The Preparation and Examination of Objects.— It is a common but very erroneous idea that the only thing that is necessary in order to examine any object under the microscope, is simply to place it on the stage, and get it into focus. With the exception of mounted objects, a very few transparent objects—such as the wings of insects—and some things that are viewed by reflected light, every substance requires to undergo careful preparation before it can be fit for profitable examination. A good example of the necessity for such preparation is seen in the common potato, a piece of which when simply placed on the stage of the microscope, and brought into focus, appears as a glistening mass, and reveals nothing of its true structure. If we now cut from this lump, by means of a very sharp knife, an exceedingly thin slice, place it on a plate of glass, moisten it with a little spirit and water, or better still, glycerine and water, and place over it a thin glass cover, it will disclose to us a most wonderful and beautiful structure. The entire mass will be seen to be composed of cells, these cells being filled with granules of starch of various sizes.

The operation which we have thus briefly described as applicable to the potato, is required for a great many other materials; for whenever a substance is to be examined under any except the very lowest powers, it is absolutely necessary to obtain it in pieces as thin as possible, so that the light may readily pass through them, and it is in general requisite to increase their transparency either by immersing them in a fluid, or by some other means. In preparing objects for the microscope, our aim is in general to examine either the ultimate structure of the substance under investigation, or the arrangement of its different parts; and the processes which are most available for this purpose may be classed under three heads: 1, Mechanical, such as section-cutting, dissection and injection; 2, Chemical, such as the use of iodine for detecting starch; of alcohol for hardening certain structures; of coloring substances for staining germinal matter, etc.; 3, Optical, such as the action whereby certain liquids change the transparency of some objects. Of some of these processes, such as injection, staining and the extended use of chemical tests, elaborate descriptions would be required in order to enable the student to carry them out with success, and we must refer him to the works of Beale and Frey, which are very complete on these points.

Thin sections of any soft substance are easily made with a very sharp knife—a good razor being probably the best available instrument. For work in the higher departments of microscopy, and for the preparation of fine objects *for sale*, special instruments known as section-cutters are employed, but for the ordinary work of investigation, they are not absolutely necessary though very convenient. Using a good sharp razor, it is an easy matter to shave off any soft substance a wedge shaped piece, the edge of which thins off to nothing, and which presents in its different parts all varieties of thickness, so as to afford a perfect opportunity to study the object under examination. In this way, which is known as the "free-hand" method, suitable sections of most animal and vegetable substances may easily be prepared, and the student will be surprised at the dexterity which a little care and practice will confer.

For cutting sections of very soft tissues a special knife, known as Valentin's knife, has been invented. It consists of two blades so arranged in one handle that their distance from each other may be easily regulated. When a cut is made with this double-bladed knife, a thin slice of the tissue passes between the blades, and constitutes the section. It is an instrument, however, which will hardly be used by beginners. Sections of substances of greater consistence, such as wood and soft bones, are most easily made in a regular section cutter. The patterns according to which these instruments are constructed are very various, but they all act on the principle of raising above the surface of a brass table, by means of a fine screw, the substance to be cut, and then passing a very sharp razor or knife over the table so as to shave off the projecting part of the object. The table is usually of brass, ground and polished. This gives rise to two serious defects. The metal is too soft in the first place, so that it is impossible to press with sufficient force on the razor without cutting into the table, and secondly, when any soft metal has been ground on a grindstone or emery wheel, the surface becomes so impregnated with gritty matter, that it very rapidly destroys the edge of the cutting tool. We avoid these difficulties by fitting to our section cutter a stout plate of hardened steel, the surface of which has been highly polished by means of buff leather. Quekett describes a cutting machine in which the difficulties we have mentioned are obviated by fixing the knife in a frame so that it is raised above the table, and does not touch the metal. Its edge is thus preserved from injury, and the blade itself cannot be affected by variations in the pressure exerted. Dr. Curtis, of this city, has adopted the same principle in his section cutter, the details of which are admirably carried out.

In making sections of wood and similar substances, the specimen is first well soaked in dilute alcohol, and is then fastened securely into the tube of the section cutter, either by wedges or by casting wax or paraffin around it. The process of raising it by means of the screw and passing the knife over it, is simple enough, and can easily be learned.

With the ordinary cutting machine, success in making thin sections seems to depend upon the perfect sharpness of the cutting edge, the thorough moistening of the knife and section, and the rigidity of the blade. The latter point frequently fails to receive the attention that it deserves. Where a thin, flexible blade is used, a moderate change in the amount of pressure employed will make a great difference in the thickness of the section, even so far as to double it. When the blade is stiff, a change in the degree of pressure has but little effect.

Soft substances must first be hardened either by immersion in alcohol or other means, and in general must be supported by being surrounded with melted wax or paraffin. Where the specimen is very slender (such as a hair) it must be carefully supported between firm and rigid clamps. Corks and similar yielding substances, which are recommended in most books, never give a cross section accurately taken at right angles. The same is true of the plan so much recommended for obtaining sections of hair, viz.: to pass the razor over the face shortly after shaving. We get sections it is true, but they are all oblique. The best way to get true sections is to imbed the substances in glue, gum, paraffin, wax or some such material.

Sections of bone are prepared by sawing off a thin slice in the first place, and cementing it to a slide by means of thick or old balsam; one side is then filed or ground flat, and polished on buff leather, after which the section is transferred to another slide so as to expose the other side, which is then filed down and polished as before. Great care must be taken so as to hit just the right thickness, and the operation of cementing to the slide must be performed expeditiously, so that the balsam may not saturate the section, and render it too transparent, as when this occurs certain very important features become invisible.

Very hard substances require special apparatus, and considerable skill. Still it is astonishing what may be accomplished by means of good files, whetstones and grindstones in the way of preparing thin and transparent sections even of such substances as rocks and stones.

In order to acquire correct ideas in regard to the structure of objects, of which sections are examined, the student should familiarize himself with the geometrical forms produced by cutting cylinders, cones, spheroids, etc., in various directions. Thus a cylindrical vessel, cut square across, shows a circle; when cut obliquely it shows an oval (ellipse) of greater or less length, and when cut longitudinally it shows two lines which have no apparent connection with each other. The truth is, however, that we should never deduce the form of vessels from sections alone. In every case it is necessary to examine carefully *dissected* preparations as well as sections.

The soft parts of animals and vegetables are frequently prepared for examination by careful dissection, that is to say the different parts are separated from each other, and freed from extraneous matter by means of knives, scissors, forceps, needles, camel hair pencils, etc. The knives used by the microscopist are similar to the scalpels ordinarily employed by anatomists, but smaller, and unless very finely tempered and well-sharpened, they are worthless. The knives sent out with low priced microscopes are in general the veriest trash, and the same is true of the needles. There are three kinds of scissors which the microscopist will find useful—plain, straight scissors, elbow scissors, and curved scissors. They must be small, sharp and well made. But the most useful, as well as the simplest instruments for dissecting are a pair of needles, or, rather, a needle and a very fine spatula. The needles used are those ordinarily employed by seamstresses; they should be fixed in a light wooden handle and carefully polished. The latter is a most important point, for it will be found that ordinary needles are too rough for delicate work, as may be easily seen by examining them under the microscope. For microscopical purposes needles are made both straight and curved—the latter being a very useful form. In order to bend a needle, it must first be heated in the flame of a candle, then bent by proper pliers, after which it must be carefully re-tempered. There is little danger of getting it too hard, provided it is not burned. After being hardened it must be carefully re-polished. The handles should be light and smooth. Ordinary penholders make good handles and cost but a trifle, but in case of need any piece of straight-grained, light wood will answer. Universal handles, handles with ferrules, handles wound with thread, etc,, look as if they were not common articles, and are purchased by many, but no working microscopist would give them table-room. All the so-called universal handles in market are too clumsy and heavy.

In using needles or knives for dissection, they are generally used in pairs, that in the right hand being used for teasing or cutting, while the one in the left hand is used for holding the object firmly in its place. For the latter purpose, however, we prefer a very narrow spatula, curved and highly polished. Curved needles, with the curve placed flat, answer very well, however.

For the removal of loose matter, and for arranging parts which have been dissected out, there is nothing more useful than good camel hair pencils. Indeed, they are indispensable, and with needles and pencils—two of the simplest and cheapest articles—it is possible to do almost everything.

During the process of dissection the object must be supported upon a glass plate or a dissecting pan, according to its size. Some of the finest preparations have been worked up on ordinary slides three inches long by one wide, and as it is almost always necessary to have the object covered with liquid, a single drop suffices in this case. But where larger objects are to be dissected, ordinary slides are not large enough, and besides there is no provision made for holding a sufficient quantity of liquid. Various kinds of dissecting dishes or pans have therefore been devised. Those used by the author are exceedingly simple and cheap, and are shown in Fig. 60. We use three kinds, two with opaque bottoms, and one in which the bottom is transparent. The latter is used for objects which are transparent, and is precisely like the others, except that a portion of the metal bottom is cut away and a piece of plate glass cemented over the aperture.

Fig. 60.

Those used for opaque objects are simply oblong tin dishes, each two inches long, one and a quarter wide and half an inch deep. The bottom plate extends on each side, so as to form rests for the fingers, by which the pan may be kept steady. Into this pan is poured a mixture of equal parts of resin and beeswax, softened if necessary with a little lard. It should be just so soft that a pin may be easily stuck into it, and this affords us the means of pinning out the different parts of a dissection as we progress. In one dish the wax is colored black with lampblack, and this forms a wonderfully effective back ground for most objects; the wax in the other pan is white, chalk or sulphate of baryta being substituted for lampblack. The pan with a transparent bottom is of precisely the same size, except that the depth is but half as much—the extra depth in the other pan being filled with wax. A quarter of an inch is a sufficient depth of liquid for most objects, and when the sides of the pan are higher than necessary they interfere with the use of knives and needles.

Dissections may also be carried on in watch-glasses, though they are not quite as convenient as pans with perfectly flat bottoms. The kind known as *lunette* glasses should be chosen, as they are flat in the centre. When a watch-glass is used for this purpose, it is necessary to cement it into a hole cut in a thin piece of wood about four inches long, and of a width which is rather greater than the diameter of the glass.

Most of this work is, of course, done under a simple microscope. The Excelsior, when screwed to a larger base, as described on page 42, answers very well. Larger and more expensive dissecting microscopes are supplied by most opticians.

In addition to these general methods, which are applicable to a great variety of subjects, there are a few special processes which must be adopted in particular cases. In some instances, as when the line of investigation is a new one, the microscopist must work out his own processes, but the following special cases will probably prove interesting to beginners.

It frequently happens that the objects for which the microscopist is searching are found mixed with coarser materials, and in this case it will be found possible to effect a separation by the process known as *elutriation* or washing. Mix the matter thoroughly with water in a tall jar and allow it to settle. In a short time—say one minute—the very coarse particles will have fallen to the bottom, and if the liquid be now poured off and allowed to settle, the finer portion will be found in the second vessel. By graduating the time and carrying the process out to its full extent, a wonderfully perfect separation may be effected. Diatomaceous earth may frequently be treated in this way to advantage.

In some cases separation must be effected by burning, or the action of chemical agents. Guano and various organic matters yield interesting residues after everything soluble has been washed away and everything combustible has been burnt either with fire or nitric acid. So too the siliceous cuticles of plants may be procured by destroying all the other parts by chemical means. The best way is to heat them in nitric acid, and add to the hot liquid a small quantity of powdered chlorate of potash. The quantities used must be very small, and great care must be exercised.

It is frequently necessary to separate a small quantity of deposit from a large amount of liquid, filtering being inadmissible. For this purpose use a conical glass or a large test tube, allow plenty of time for the deposit to settle, and give occasionally a slight stir, so as to detach the particles from the sides of the vessel. Then pass a large dipping tube (one quarter of an inch in diameter) to the bottom, the upper end of the tube being closed with the finger. On withdrawing the finger the liquid and deposit rush in. Have ready a small ball of soft cement (resin and beeswax equal parts, softened with oil) and with it close the upper end of the tube, which may now be withdrawn, carrying the liquid with it. Place the tube in a vertical position, with its lower end on a slide or in a watchglass, and support it either by means of the ring of a small retort stand or by a simple wire having a ring (horizontal) at the upper end, and a small piece of board for a foot. Beale directs us to *cork* the tube, but this is difficult unless the tube is made specially for the purpose with a mouth like that of a test tube. Tubes made in this way are, however, the most convenient, and a good velvet cork closes them perfectly.

There is a class of insect preparations, which are quite interesting, though they are not as instructive as inferior preparations made by the process of dissection. We refer to the whole insects found in most collections. They are prepared by soaking the insect in liquor potassæ, which may be had from any druggist; this renders the internal organs soluble and the outer horny skeleton transparent. The viscera are then expelled by pressure with a camel hair pencil, the insect well washed in pure water, soaked first in alcohol, and then in turpentine, and finally mounted in balsam. The points requiring attention are these: Soaking just the right length of time in the potash, for if the insect remains too long in this liquid it will be destroyed;

allowing plenty of time for the alcohol to displace the water, and for the turpentine to displace the alcohol; and manipulating the insect with great care, so as not to break any of the parts. The eyes of insects are prepared by macerating them in very weak potash, and, while still soft, pressing them between two slips of glass. If allowed to harden before being pressed they will split at the edges. The handsomest preparations of eyes are obtained by taking a thin slice from a large eye, such as that of a dragon fly, and treating it as directed.

The feet of insects are in general easily prepared. Moderate soaking in potash, careful washing in water, thorough soaking in alcohol and turpentine, and careful management in properly displaying them on the slide, are the secrets of success. The student who wishes to make a careful study of these objects, however, should place them in glycerine, after soaking them in potash and thoroughly washing them. They should of course be deposited in a cell filled with liquid, and then covered with thin glass, and examined. The so-called tongues, etc., of insects require no potash, being sufficiently transparent without it, and after being soaked successively in alcohol and turpentine, they may be mounted in balsam. When wanted for examination merely, immerse them in dilute glycerine, and if the student can succeed in mounting them in cells, in glycerine or some of the gelatinous media hereafter described, they will show their structure to far better advantage than in balsam.

In determining the character of what is brought into view by the processes detailed, great aid will be derived from the use of chemical tests. Thus, in the case of the potato, previously described, most persons who had read anything at all upon such subjects, would recognize the starch granules. All starch granules, however, are not of the same form as those found in the potato; indeed, some would hardly be recognized at all, except by those having considerable experience. But if a little of the tincture of iodine be brought into contact with them, they at once become deeply blue. This subject is too extensive to be discussed here, but those who desire to become proficient in the use of the microscope cannot safely neglect it.

In most cases after an object has been carefully brought into proper mechanical condition, in one of the ways we have described, it is necessary to immerse it in some suitable medium, so as to render it clear and transparent. The action of such media may be very well illustrated by the following experiment: Take a short piece of black human hair, place it on a slide, bring it into focus and examine it. It will appear as a dark cord with a light line running down the centre, and from this circumstance has arisen the erroneous popular idea in regard to the tubular structure of hair. Apply a drop of glycerine diluted with an equal bulk of water, and again examine it. The appearance will have entirely changed, having become clearer and more definite, so that the structure of the hair is more easily made out. This effect depends upon the refracting power of the liquid used. The following liquids are usually employed for this purpose, their efficiency being in direct ratio to their index of refraction, which we append to each. Water, 1.336; glacial acetic acid, 1.38; alcohol, 1.372; vitreous humour, 1,340; sea-water, 1.343; equal parts of glycerine and water, 1.40; pure glycerine, 1.475; oil of turpentine, 1.478; Canada balsam, 1.532—1.549; bisulphide of carbon, 1.678; oil of annis, 1.811. Alcohol and water, and solutions of various salts in water are also very useful. When a pure article of glycerine is not available, a solution of white sugar may be used with good results.

Great care must be exercised lest the fluid that is added should change the form or structure of the object. Upon this subject the remarks of Frey are very judicious. He says: "Theory requires that each constituent of the body should be examined in a fluid medium which resembles in respect to quality and quantity, the fluid which saturates the living tissue. Naturally this requirement cannot be completely fulfilled in practice; our aim should be to approach it as nearly as possible. Saliva, vitreous humour, amniotic liquor, serum and diluted albumen are generally recommended as suitable media for the investigation of delicate changeable tissues, and, in certain cases, they accomplish their object in a satisfactory manner. But do not expect them to suffice for every case. Not unfrequently one and the same tissue of different species of animals reacts differently with the same fluid medium, as may be seen with the blood corpuscles. M. Schultze has communicated to us an important and readily proved observation of Landolt's, that animal fluids may be preserved from decomposition for a long time by the addition of a small piece of camphor."

Schultze recommends as a neutral fluid, suitable for most tissues, a liquid which he calls "Iod-serum." It consists of the amniotic fluid of the calf, to which has been added a concentrated tincture of iodine or a strong solution of iodine in the proportion of six drops to the ounce. The color of the solution is at first wine yellow, but after a few hours it becomes paler; this paleness afterwards increases, and the subsequent addition of a few drops of the iodine solution becomes necessary. As the amniotic fluid is not always attainable, a good substitute may be prepared by mixing 1 ounce white of egg, 9 ounces water, and 40 grains chloride of sodium, with the proper proportion of tincture of iodine.

During the entire process of preparation, the greatest attention must be paid to cleanliness. Particles of dust, which to the unassisted vision are invisible, become offensively prominent under the microscope. To exclude these, and to protect the objects, it is important that the latter should be kept carefully covered when not actually undergoing some operation. Small bell glasses are recommended for this purpose by Dr. Carpenter, and they answer admirably. We prefer, however, as being cheaper and less bulky, watch glasses to which a handle has been cemented as shown in Fig. 61. The handle may be a little knob, turned out of a piece of wood, or where this is not convenient a small cork will answer. A little sealing wax serves for a cement, the watch glass being heated before the wax is applied. Flat plates of glass answer well to cover the dissecting pans previously described.

Fig. 61

When a number of objects are to be protected for some time, we place them on a piece of plate glass eight inches square, cover each with a watch-glass cover, and protect the whole by means of a bell jar with ground edges. The latter fits closely to the plate glass and excludes everything, while the small covers protect the individual specimens when the large cover is raised for the purpose of getting at them.

Singular mistakes have arisen from the fact that foreign

bodies which have accidentally found their way into a preparation have been mistaken for part of the specimen. The only way to avoid similar errors is to exclude all such intruders by means of proper covers, and to become familiar with them so that they may be instantly recognized when present. Dr. Beale gives the following list as those that are most apt to find their way into the preparations of the microscopist: Oil globules; milk; starch from the potato, wheat and rice; bread crumbs; feathers; worsted; fibres of flax, cotton and silk of different colors; human hair, cat's hair and hair from blankets; the scales of butterflies and moths, particularly those from the common clothes moth; fibres of wood, fragments of tea leaves, hairs from plants, vegetable cellular tissue and spiral vessels; particles of sand. The curious circumstances under which such bodies will find their way into a specimen was recently illustrated in the author's experience. In a liquid submitted for examination, and said to be pure, he found foreign matter. It proved to be brick dust, used to clean the tin funnel with which the vessel was filled, and which had been washed in by the passage of the fluid. The student can have no better exercise than to examine these intruders and familiarize himself with their appearance.

Preservative Processes.—The object of all preservative processes is to prevent any change either in the structure or composition of the object. An object may be most perfectly prepared and beautifully mounted, but if it be not so treated as to preserve it from change, the labor thus expended is wasted, as regards the preservation of a permanent record. And yet how many objects there are that we would like to keep for future examination and comparison, or to show to friends. This department of the treatment of objects is, therefore, of great importance, and success in it can only be obtained through a thorough understanding of the principles involved.

There are four methods in common use for the preservation of perishable animal and vegetable substances: 1, Constant exposure to temperature considerably below the freezing point of water; 2, the perfect exclusion of air; 3, reduction to a state of complete dryness; and 4, the employment of certain anti-septic compound. The third and fourth are the methods usually employed in microscopy, but the same principles which render the second method so successful in the preservation of canned fruits and meats, deserve the attention of the microscopist.

Drying, as a preservative process, can be applied to but few specimens, chiefly transparent insect preparations, and opaque objects. Blood and similar matters are also sometimes preserved by drying. Such preparations are so easily dried that no special directions are needed. Warming them over a lamp, or preferably on a water-bath, before applying the thin glass cover (as directed in the section on mounting objects) is almost always sufficient. Where the specimen is liable to be injured by heat it may be dried by placing it over sulphuric acid, and covering both acid and preparation with a bell jar having ground edges and resting on a perfectly flat plate of glass. The acid soon absorbs all the moisture and renders the object perfectly dry. Where a cell is used for an opaque object, and dryness is essential, great care must be taken to make the cell impervious to air, otherwise dampness will be sure to penetrate, and if the object be of animal or vegetable origin, fungi will be very apt to grow on it. We have found cells of cardboard peculiarly liable to this defect, and such cells should always be thoroughly saturated, and coated with varnish, such as gold size or Canada balsam.

The great dependence of the microscopist, however, is in the employment of certain preservative media, of the most important of which, the following is a list:

CANADA BALSAM.—Of all the media employed for the mounting and preservation of objects, Canada balsam is undoubtedly the most generally useful, and it is probable that more objects are mounted in this material than in all the other media put together. As a *preservative* it is perfect, and its action in rendering many objects transparent and clear is often of great value. Frey tells us that "several sorts of Canada balsam occur in commerce. To be good it should be of thick consistence, nearly colorless, and thoroughly transparent." One difficulty, however, is that much of the Canada balsam that is sold is factitious, being made of cheap resins dissolved in impure turpentine. Such balsam soon becomes cloudy, and is very apt to crack. Balsam that is too highly colored may be bleached by exposure to sunlight—a process applied by most opticians to the balsam used by them for cementing the lenses of achromatic combinations. Balsam when new is quite fluid, too much so, indeed, for the mounting of most objects. On the other hand, old balsam is thick, and is apt to crack. Microscopists generally keep balsam in wide-mouthed bottles, and take out what is wanted by means of a glass rod. As the process of evaporation, which makes balsam thick and viscid, goes on more slowly in narrow-mouthed bottles, we prefer the latter, and transfer the balsam to the glass slide by means of a fine wire with a small loop at the end. The wire is passed through a cork, or preferably a wooden stopper, and descends to such a depth as to be just below the surface of the balsam. As the latter is used up, the wire is pushed down, and if cemented in its place by the balsam, a little heat soon frees it. The latter remark applies also to the wooden stopper, which is very apt to stick in the neck of the bottle. A very slight exposure to the flame of a spirit lamp is sufficient to loosen it.

SOLUTION OF BALSAM.—When the objects that are to be preserved in balsam would be injured by the heat necessary to melt it, it is advisable to use a solution of balsam in ether or chloroform. The balsam used for making the solution should be old and thick. This solution is frequently sold with the label, " Balsam for use without heat."

COLOPHONY.—Thiersch recommends a solution of resin or colophony in absolute alcohol. The advantage which this material presents is that the preparation may be placed in it directly from the absolute alcohol, without becoming cloudy, and without prejudice to the durability of the specimen. He advises the microscopist to prepare the colophony himself from Venice turpentine, which is done by dissolving it in an equal volume of ether, filtering it through paper, and evaporating, until, when cold, it breaks with a conchoidal fracture. The material that remains is then to be dissolved in absolute alcohol until it is of a syrupy consistence.

Damar Medium.—Gum damar has been recently introduced amongst the materials used by microscopists, and with some it has found great favor. Carpenter speaks highly of it. Diatoms are said to show better in it than in balsam, and for delicate physiological preparations, especially transparent injections, it is very excellent. It is thus prepared: Half an ounce of gum damar is dissolved in one ounce of oil of turpentine, and half an ounce of gum mastic in two ounces of chloroform. The solutions are filtered and mixed.

Ordinary damar varnish, such as is used by painters, is sometimes sold for microscopical purposes, but it does not give satisfactory results.

Preparations which have been preserved and mounted in balsam or damar are very durable, while those that are mounted in fluids are a source of continual annoyance and loss.

Many microscopists, therefore, exclude from their cabinets all preparations mounted in liquid on the ground that sooner or later they will become worthless. And many of our best dealers refuse to have anything to do with them. Nevertheless, as Frey well says, "the natural condition of the tissues is completely represented only when mounted in a moist condition. This method permits of the most accurate recognition of delicate textural relations, pale cells and fibres, etc., and should not be omitted with any tissue in the production of histological collections."

Glycerine.—At the head of the list of preservative media for moist preparations stands glycerine. "Its strong refractive power, its property of combining with water, and of attracting the same from the atmosphere, render it an invaluable medium for mounting animal tissues containing water. It may be truly said, that what Canada balsam is to dry tissues, glycerine is to moist ones."—(Frey.) Much of the glycerine in market is very impure, and although the impurities do not show themselves very strongly at first, they soon become manifest by the darkening of the liquid, (owing probably to the presence of lead), and the formation of a cloudy precipitate. Dr. Beale strongly recommends Price's glycerine, and we have found it very excellent.

When employed as a preservative, glycerine is used either pure or diluted, according to circumstances. Equal parts of glycerine and water form a very excellent medium for most objects. It is alleged, however, that fungi are very apt to grow in glycerine and its solutions. We are inclined to believe that this may be avoided by adopting the precaution detailed at the end of this section. We have now before us specimens that were mounted in pure glycerine and water, eighteen years ago, and they are still quite perfect. If, however, there should be any danger in this direction, the addition of a little camphor will prevent the evil. Glycerine exerts a powerfully solvent action on many salts, particularly salts of lime, such as the carbonate, and hence it is employed for preventing scale in the boilers of steam-engines. This property renders it dangerous to use it for the preservation of structures containing compounds of lime.

GLYCERINE JELLY.—The original directions given by Lawrance are as follows: "Take any quantity of Nelson's gelatine, (any good gelatine will answer, however,) and let it soak for two or three hours in cold water; pour off the superfluous water, and heat the soaked gelatine until melted. To each fluid ounce of the gelatine add one drachm of alcohol, and mix well; then add a fluid drachm of the white of an egg. Mix well while the gelatine is fluid but cool. Now boil until the albumen coagulates, and the gelatine is quite clear. Filter through fine flannel, and to each fluid ounce of the clarified gelatine add six fluid drachms of Price's pure glycerine, and mix well. For the six fluid drachms of glycerine a mixture of two parts of glycerine to four of camphor water may be substituted."

Glycerine jelly is a very excellent medium, and is easily used. At ordinary temperatures it is quite solid, but when slightly heated it melts, and may be used like balsam, directions for mounting in which will be found in the next section. Objects that are to be mounted in glycerine jelly should be soaked until thoroughly saturated with a mixture of 7 parts glycerine, 6 parts water, and 1 part alcohol. It is also well, after immersing them in the melted jelly, to place the slide for a short time on a water bath heated to about 125° Fah. The jelly then penetrates every part of the preparation.

When intended for use in very warm climates the proportion of the gelatine to the other ingredients should be increased.

HANTZSCH'S FLUID.—Very beautiful preparations of delicate vegetable forms have been prepared with this liquid, even the coloring matter being left unaltered. It consists of 3 parts of pure alcohol, 2 parts of distilled water and one part of glycerine. The object, placed in a cell, is covered with a drop of this liquid, and then set aside under a bell-glass. The alcohol and water soon evaporate, so that the glycerine alone is left, and another drop of the liquid is then to be added, and a second evaporation permitted; the process being repeated if necessary, until enough glycerine is left to fill the cell, which is then to be covered and closed in the usual manner. We have used this liquid with gratifying success. It is easily prepared, is not difficult to use, and it gives very excellent results.

GLYCERINE AND GUM.—Of this medium Carpenter says: "For many objects that would be injured by the small amount of heat required to melt Deane's gelatine or glycerine jelly, the glycerine and gum medium of Mr. Farrants will be found very useful. This is made by dissolving 4 parts by weight of picked gum arabic in 4 parts of cold distilled water, and adding 2 parts of glycerine. The solution must be made without the aid of heat, the mixture being occasionally stirred, but not shaken, whilst it is proceeding: after it has been completed, the liquid should be strained (if not perfectly free from impurity) through fine cambric previously well washed out by a current of clear cold water; and it should be kept in a bottle closed with a glass stopper or cap (not with cork), containing a small piece of camphor. The great advantage of this medium is that it can be used cold, and yet soon viscifies without cracking; it is well suited to preserve delicate animal as well as vegetable tissues, and in most cases it increases their transparency.

DEANE'S GELATINE.—Before the introduction of glycerine jelly, Deane's gelatine was a favorite medium, and we still use it with success. Take gelatine, 1 ounce; honey, 5 ounces; water, 5 ounces; rectified spirit, ¼ ounce; creosote, 6 drops. Soak the gelatine in water until soft, and then add it to the honey, which has been previously raised to a boiling heat in another vessel. Then boil the mixture, and when it has cooled somewhat add the creosote mixed with the spirit. Lastly, filter through fine flannel. When required for use, the bottle containing the mixture must be slightly warmed, and a drop placed on the preparation upon the glass slide, which should also be warmed a little. Next, the glass cover, after having been breathed upon, is to be laid on with the usual precautions. The edges may be covered with a coating of Brunswick black. Care must be taken that the surface of the drop does not become dry before the application of the glass cover; and the inclusion of air-bubbles must be carefully avoided.

ALCOHOL.—Mixed with water in various proportions, alcohol forms one of our best preservative liquids, for both animal and vegetable substances. The chief objection to it is the difficulty with which it is retained in the cell.

THWAITE'S FLUID.—Take water, 16 ounces; alcohol, 1 ounce; creosote, sufficient to saturate the spirit; chalk, as much as may be necessary. Mix the creosote and spirit, stir in the chalk with the aid of a pestle and mortar, and let the water be added gradually. Next add an equal quantity of water saturated with camphor. Allow the mixture to stand for a few days and filter. Used for preserving desmidiæ, and also animal substances.

BEALE'S LIQUID.—Creosote, 3 drachms; wood naphtha, 6 ounces; distilled water, 64 ounces; chalk, as much as necessary. Mix the naphtha and creosote, then add as much prepared chalk as may be sufficient to form a thick, smooth paste; afterwards add, very gradually, a small quantity of the water, which must be well mixed with the other ingredients in a mortar. Add two or three small lumps of camphor, and allow the mixture to stand in a lightly covered vessel for a fortnight or three weeks with occasional stirring. The almost clear supernatant fluid may then be poured off and filtered if necessary. It should be kept in well-corked or stoppered bottles.

GOADBY'S FLUIDS.—Goadby used two distinct fluids, designated by letters A and B, the difference being that alum was a constituent of one and not of the other. Of both fluids there were several degrees of strength, which were designated by numbers. A fluid, as usually employed (A2), consisted of rock salt, 4 ounces; alum, 2 ounces; corrosive sublimate, 4 grains; boiling water, 2 quarts. To make the B fluid take rock salt, 8 ounces; corrosive sublimate, 2 grains; boiling water, 1 quart.

PACINI'S FLUID.—Take corrosive sublimate, 1 part; pure chloride of sodium (common salt), 2 parts; glycerine, 13 parts; distilled water, 113 parts. This mixture is allowed to stand for at least two months. After that time it is prepared for use by mixing one part of it with three parts of distilled water, and filtering it through filtering paper. This fluid is very strongly recommended by Frey. It is used for blood globules, nerves and ganglia, the retina, cancer cells, and especially delicate proteinous tissues.

CASTOR OIL.—This is used for preserving certain crystals. The best cold-drawn castor oil answers the purpose.

There are a few general rules which we have found essential to the successful use of these media, but which are often neglected, the result being the ultimate destruction of the specimens. One of the most important points is the use of an abundance of the medium (we are now talking of *preserving*, not *mounting*) and the *gradual* saturation of the object with it. A piece of fresh muscle, simply mounted in a shallow cell with a drop or two of Goadby's fluid, will spoil in a very short time. The same object, properly treated, may be preserved indefinitely. The proper course is to completely immerse the object in a considerable quantity of the liquid, and if necessary change the liquid several times until the substance to be preserved has been thoroughly subjected to the action of the medium. For this purpose the quantity contained in ordinary cells is altogether too little; small cups, basins, large watch-glasses, etc., are needed. It must be remembered that the substance acted upon generally absorbs certain constituents of the preserving fluid, and hence the latter is left either very weak or there is an unequal distribution of the constituents as regards the substance itself and the surrounding fluid. Moreover the fluids contained in many objects are displaced by the preserving medium, and tend to dilute the latter. In most cases, therefore, where the preserving medium is a liquid, the desired result is best attained by soaking the substance in the fluid for several days before mounting, changing the liquid two or three times, and finally mounting in fresh fluid of regular strength. We would lay great stress upon this point, having seen many fine preparations spoiled by pursuing a different course. The late Dr. Goadby, whose skill in this department was well known, always insisted upon this course, and during a somewhat extended intercourse with him, and observation of his methods and processes, we became fully convinced of its importance.

With many preservative liquids, it is well to begin with a diluted article, and gradually increase the strength at each change of fluid until the proper strength has been reached. This course is specially recommended with glycerine and saline solutions.

Another point which demands attention is the entire exclusion of air, especially of oxygen. Now air adheres with great tenacity to most surfaces, such as those of glass or metal, and it dissolves to a considerable extent in all watery solutions. To get rid of it, the surface of the cell and cover should be either well warmed, and then allowed to cool just before being filled, or washed with alcohol (after which it may be dried). To expel the air from the liquids, they should be boiled, and to prevent the absorbtion of a fresh dose of air, they should be kept well stoppered. But as air *will* find access to the liquids so as ultimately to saturate them, it is necessary to boil the fluids at frequent intervals, so as to get rid of this element. Without strict attention to these points it is almost impossible to preserve animal substances for any length of time in saline fluids.

Mounting Objects.—For the purpose of conveniently exhibiting and comparing objects, and arranging them in cabinets where they can be at all times accessible, it is necessary to *mount* them securely in such a manner that they may be easily handled. For purposes of mere examination and study, mounting is unnecessary, but when the objects are to be kept for future reference it is indispensable. It is true that where the specimens are large they might be kept in bottles in a preservative fluid, and taken out when wanted. This would be very inconvenient, however, and with very minute or delicate objects it would be almost impracticable.

There are three modes in which objects are mounted: 1. Dry, the object being simply attached to the slide and suitably protected. 2. In balsam, the object being immersed in Canada balsam, damar medium, copal varnish, or some similar material. 3. In fluid, the object being mounted in some of the preservative liquids previously described. Specimens may be mounted in any of these ways, so as to be viewed either as transparent or opaque objects, and the instruments and materials required are neither numerous nor expensive. With those named in the following list almost any *ordinary* object may be neatly put up, though it is of course to be expected that occasions will frequently arise when *special* instruments and methods, which are not described by any author, will be needed. Experience alone can enable the microscopist to treat such cases successfully.

SLIDES.—Most objects are mounted between two pieces of glass, one of which is called the *slide* and the other the *cover*. As it is convenient to have these slides all the same size, so that they may be easily arranged in cabinets, the Microscopical Society of London has adopted a slide three inches long by one inch wide as the standard size for use amongst their members, and this size has been generally adopted by microscopists throughout the world. All the best slides that are found in market are of this size, and the microscopist who fails to adopt it will be subject to great inconvenience when he desires to exchange objects with others who are pursuing similar studies. Several other sizes are employed by the French, most of them being quite small ($2\frac{1}{8}$ by $\frac{7}{8}$ and $2\frac{1}{8}$ by $\frac{5}{8}$), but as these small slides are the only ones that can be used with some French microscopes—the stages of which are too small to take a slide 3 by 1— they are usually kept in stock by dealers in microscopic apparatus. Small slides have this advantage, that they cost less, and take up less room in a cabinet. Large slides look best, and afford more room for descriptive labels, which is an important point. But since slides 3 by 1 have been adopted by common consent, the microscopist who mounts specimens, or who buys objects mounted on slides of a different size, commits a mistake for which the advantages offered by the small slides are but a slight compensation. The only exceptions to this rule are where the objects are too large to be mounted securely on a slide of standard size, or where a large number are to be prepared for the purpose of illustrating some special series of investigations. It is to be presumed that such a series will never be broken up and separated, and as it will in all probability be assigned to its own cabinet, it is sometimes of advantage to have it upon slides of a size other than that in common use. As the objects composing such a series will probably be numbered and catalogued, there is no necessity for extended descriptions on the labels, and therefore slides of half the usual size (1¼ by 1) will serve very well. The cabinet may thus be reduced in bulk by one-half. We have a special cabinet, illustrative of textile fibres, mounted upon slides of small size, and find it quite convenient.

The glass from which slides are cut should be free from airbubbles, scratches and that wavy appearance which is due either to inequalities in the surface or to irregularities in the composition of the glass itself. Ordinary window glass is entirely unfit for the purpose. The most suitable kind is plate glass, the surface of which has been ground and polished, so as to be perfectly even and smooth. Glass of this kind is used for looking-glasses and by photographers, and when other material could not be had, we have made very excellent slides out of broken looking-glasses and photographer's plates, though it is difficult to get the latter thin enough. Slides of good glass are, however, manufactured in quantity and sold at a reasonable price, so that under ordinary circumstances it will hardly pay the microscopist to cut out his own slides. Moreover the slides sold by the dealers have the edges neatly ground, an operation which the microscopist will find tedious and troublesome.

As procured from the manufacturers, the slides are always dirty, never having been washed after the process of grinding and polishing the edges. If this dirt were soft it would not matter so much, but it is in general hard and gritty—being in fact the grinding sand—and the consequence is that the surfaces of the slides are very apt to be scratched and injured. There is but one firm that exports slides to this country, and they are very careless in this respect. Out of a gross of slides it is often difficult to find two dozen that are not so scratched as to be worthless for the finest class of work. Having procured the slides, however, the first thing to do is to clean and assort them. They should be cleaned by being rinsed in water containing a little washing soda; the dirt being removed if necessary by the use of an old nail brush or tooth brush. Until this has been done they should not be wiped with cloth or leather, for by so doing the particles of sand are dragged along the surface, making a deep mark. They should then be washed in pure water, carefully wiped with a soft cloth, and assorted for thickness and quality. It is in general best to sort them into three classes—thick, medium and thin—the latter being used for test and other very delicate objects. Elaborate instruments have been devised for measuring the thickness of the slides, so as to assort them accurately, but they are entirely unnecessary; the eye is a sufficiently accurate guide. To determine their quality, they must be examined under the microscope, and as it is only the central portion that is of any consequence in this case, we place them on a brass plate, 3 by 1, with the edges slightly turned up, and having a hole five-eighths of an inch in diameter in the centre. That part which lies over the hole is the only part which it is necessary to examine. Slides which contain air-bubbles, striæ or scratches, are at once laid aside to be used either for opaque objects or those of a very coarse kind. Those that are perfect are carefully stored away where they will not be subject to injury.

Covers.—After being properly arranged on the slide with a suitable preservative medium, the objects must be covered with a small piece of thin glass. Glass intended specially for this purpose is made in England, and imported either in sheets or cut into squares and circles of suitable sizes. Directions for cutting these covers would be out of place here. The beginner will always find it most economical to buy them ready cut. Of the two kinds—round and square—the former are, for all ordinary purposes, the most convenient, as covers of this shape are best suited to cells made with the turn-table, and they may also be finished more easily and neatly than the square ones.

Covers should be carefully assorted for thickness, since the thickness of the cover exerts a material influence on the performance of all lenses except those of the lowest power or quality. Where objectives which do not adjust for thickness of cover are employed, the microscopist should find out the exact thickness to which they have been corrected by the maker, and use glass of this thickness in covering all objects that are to be examined by means of these lenses.

The inexperienced student will be apt to find some difficulty in cleaning these covers. They are so fragile that it is difficult to rub them, so as to remove dirt, without breaking them. The best method is to soak them in a weak solution of potash, rinse them off carefully several times with clean water, and after pouring the last water off, give them a final rinsing by taking them up in a pair of forceps and moving them about in a tumbler of clean water. They should then be laid (singly, of course) on a wiping block and wiped. Wiping blocks are made by covering a flat block of wood with chamois leather or linen, drawn tightly so as to present a flat but somewhat soft surface. These blocks are generally made round and with handles, but we prefer them oblong (4 by 1½ inches) and *without* handles. One of them is laid on the table face up; upon this face the thin glass is laid and wiped with the other block. In this way the thinnest glass can be cleaned without risk of fracture.

CELLS—TURN-TABLE.—All objects that are mounted dry or in fluid should be placed in cells, as unless this is done it is difficult to arrange the object properly or to secure the thin cover permanently. In the majority of cases these cells consist of little more than a ring of cement laid on the glass slide and allowed to harden, and their depth does not exceed the thickness of a sheet of paper. Such cells are in constant demand,

and are almost always made by the microscopist himself by means of a little instrument known as a *turn-table* or *whirling table*, of which there are several different forms in market. A cheap and efficient form is shown in Fig. 62. The table is supported by a spindle upon which it turns, motion being communicated by means of a milled ring. The slide is held in its place by two spring clips, and it is brought to the centre by means of a guide or bar, c, with a square projection. This is carefully arranged, so that a slide 3 by 1 shall be accurately centered. Hence it follows that the rings and cells on all the slides put up by the owner may be instantly and accurately

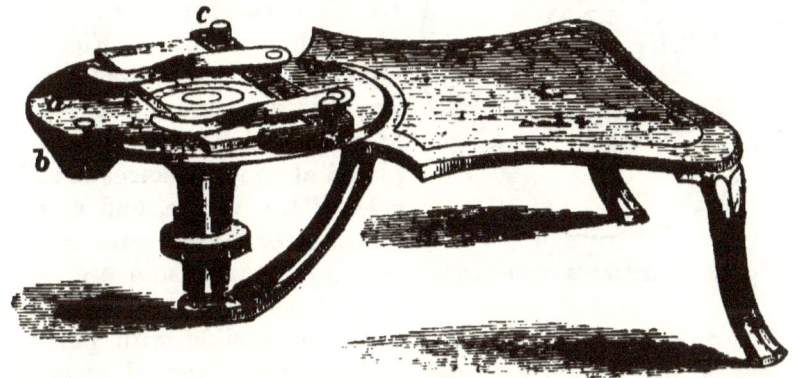

Fig. 62.—TURN-TABLE.

centered by simply placing them on the table and bringing them up to a firm bearing against the guide. This bar or guide may, however, be instantly removed when desired, and when this is done, *any* cell may be truly centered by the usual methods. This turn-table, therefore, enables us always to bring cells of our own make instantly to a perfectly accurate centre, while other cells can be centered at any time with very little trouble.

To most turn-tables there lies the objection that the devices for centering and holding the slide make one side heavier than the other, and consequently, as every mechanic knows, irregular and eccentric motion is the result. On many otherwise well-made instruments it is, from this cause, impossible to make a true cell, particularly if we attempt to work at a high speed.

In the turn-table just described, provision is made to obviate this difficulty. A heavy-headed screw, of the precise weight necessary, is screwed into the under surface of the table, and gives a perfect balance to the wheel. It then runs smoothly and truly.

Numerous attempts have been made to produce a self-centering table, *i. e.*, one in which the slides would be truly centered without requiring care and skill on the part of the operator. One of the earliest forms was that of Dr. Matthews, the centering part of which is shown in Fig. 63. Upon the surface of the table he arranges two triangular plates of brass, which rotate upon pins placed at equal distances on each side of the centre, and as the plates are of the same size, whenever their inner faces are parallel, these faces must be equidistant from the centre. Hence, when a slide with parallel sides is placed between them, and the plates turned so as to press upon the sides of the slide, the slide will be truly centered so far as its width is concerned. It is centered for length by a stationary pin, against which the end is always brought. Slides of irregular size are therefore centered only one way.

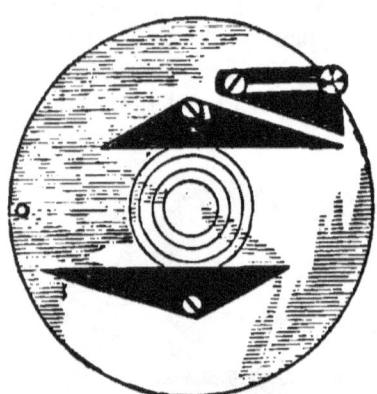

Fig. 63.—MATTHEW'S TURN-TABLE.

There are at present, however, before the public, two tables which centre slides accurately in both directions. One was invented by C. Mason Kinne, of San Francisco, who describes it as follows: "As will be seen from the engravings, Figs. 64 and 65, which are reduced one-half, the slide will be grasped automatically, upon removing the finger from the lever, the spiral spring causing the clutches to instantly clasp the slide, and retain it in a central position. One corner of either end of the slide projects sufficiently for the purpose of taking hold with one hand, while the other is pressing the lever, and can be fixed or removed without pushing along a circular disc to its edge. The slots are made to allow movement enough, so that the clutches can grasp any piece of glass from 1¼ to 3¼ inches in diagonal length, and the table is made of brass about a quarter of an inch thick, which gives weight sufficient to secure stability of movement. The whole rests on a small spindle 4 or 5 inches long, screwed into the centre of the brass stud, which is the fulcrum of the lever, and can be removed at pleasure to pack away. The pointed lower end of the spindle is stepped into a counter-sunk metal rest, and with a collar placed at a suitable distance above to allow of free movement of the hand, I find that a steady motion can be obtained with the thumb and finger, of any required velocity, and is under greater control than with any milled-head device."

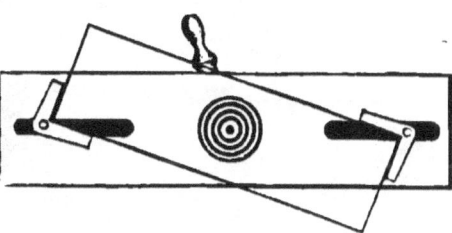

Fig. 64.—KINNE'S TURN-TABLE. (Upper side.)

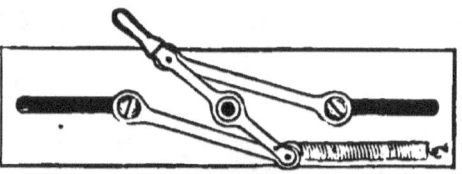

Fig. 65.—KINNE'S TURN-TABLE. (Under side.)

Mr. Kinne suggests a very simple method of constructing a home-made table on this plan: "The spindle can be fitted into any appliance, primitive or expensive, at the option of the worker, and I find that an old cigar box, with a portion of one end removed, is just as useful as anything else, though if made for sale, a cheap varnished box could be furnished, and in which the table and spindle could be packed when desired. If fitted up with the cast iron stand, the whole might present a neater appearance, but the additional expense would not add to its utility."

Slides which have been imperfectly centered on other tables, are recentered for varnishing by the use of two rectangular triangles and a little wedge. The inventor uses the corners of a broken slide and a piece of match.

The other self-centering turn-table was invented by Mr. C. F. Cox, of New York, and is shown in Fig. 66. The slide is

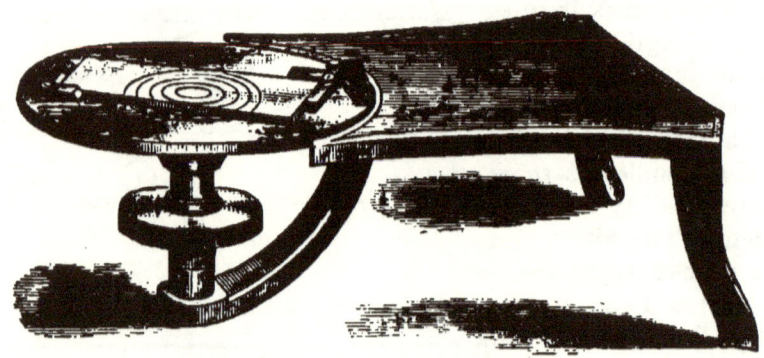

Fig. 66.—COX TURN-TABLE.

grasped by two angle-pieces, which are simultaneously moved to and from the centre by means of a right and left hand screw. When it is desired to re-varnish slides which have not been accurately centered in the first place, a pair of spring clips, attached to a stout bar, are fastened on. This can be effected in an instant. The arrangement is shown in Fig. 67.

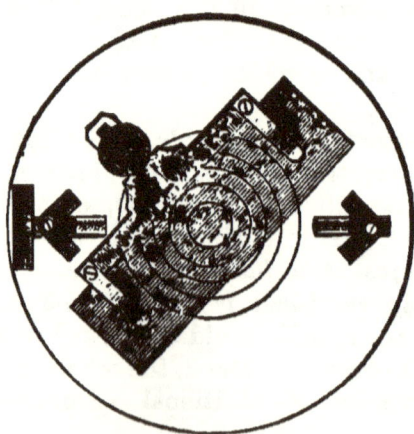

Fig. 67.—COX TURN-TABLE.

There is also a very ingenious device for placing a row of small cells along the middle of a slide. This consists of two equal right-angled triangles, the square corners of which fit into the clutches, thus allowing the long sides to lie parallel to each other, and at equal distances from the centre. A slide may thus be grasped between them, and pushed along longitudinally, as may be desired.

Those who once see a turn-table, will find no difficulty either in understanding the method of using it, or in putting this knowledge into practice. The slide, being held on the table either by springs or clutches, is made to revolve rapidly, and a brush, charged with cement or varnish, is held against its surface so as to leave a ring. There is a slight knack about making good cells, which it requires a little practice to acquire. The brush must be held in the direction of a tangent to the ring— that is, it must not point to the centre of the circle, but must lie so that the ring, as it revolves, will *draw* the cement away from the brush. Practice alone can give expertness in doing this, and we would advise the beginner to work steadily for a few hours at making cells on pieces of common window glass, strips of which can be had for nothing from any glazier. The chief points to be attended to are the position of the brush and the consistence of the cement. If the latter be too fluid, it spreads and does not form a well-defined circle. If too thick it does not leave the brush as freely as is necessary. The method of preparing the cement will be explained under the proper head.

Fig. 68.

Where a turn-table is not at hand, very good cells may be made as follows: On a card draw the outlines of a slide with a series of circles in the centre, as shown in Fig. 68; lay the slide on the card so that the centre of the circles will be at the centre of the slide, and then paint a circle of cement on the slide by hand, the rings beneath serving as a guide. Very good cells may be thus made, but the process is of course more tedious than that with the turn-table, and does not give as neat results.

A few precautions are necessary in order to insure the permanent adhesion of the cells to the glass. In addition to providing cement of good quality, we must see that the slide is dry and *recently heated*. It is difficult, with most cements, to use *hot* slides, as the cement is apt to flow; but the slide should have been recently heated, and after the cement has partially hardened, the cells should be baked by exposure to a temperature as high as they will stand. This is easily done by placing them on a board or plate, and leaving the latter for a short time in an oven.

Where cells of greater depth are required, rings of various materials are cemented to the slide. For objects mounted dry, rings of leather or cardboard answer well, provided they are carefully varnished so as to be impervious to air and moisture. For liquids, rings of glass, tin, ebonite, etc., are used. Rings of rubber and gutta-percha have been suggested, but they do not answer, as they soon become rotten. Full directions for making and using deep cells may be found in the works of Quekett, Carpenter, Beale, Frey, etc.

Hot-Plate.—This is simply a stout plate of brass or iron, which is supported over a lamp by suitable means. The common plan is to insert four stout wires to serve as legs, but a better mode is to support the plate on the ring of a retort stand, as its distance from the lamp can thus be readily adjusted and the temperature regulated. The hot-plate serves to distribute the heat, and thus to prevent the slides from becoming suddenly and unequally heated. Moreover, by means of it several slides can be heated at once, and thus much time may be saved. It should be tolerably heavy. The one we use is of cast iron, six inches long and three inches wide. The upper surface has been ground so as to be tolerably smooth, When a hot-plate is not at hand, a good substitute may be found in a smooth brick, or, better still, a plate of soapstone. These may be heated in the fire and will retain their heat for a long time.

LAMP.—Any lamp, or even candle, will answer, but we prefer a spirit lamp, the flame being free from smoke and easily managed. At night the kerosene lamp used for giving light will answer. Where gas is used, the Bunsen burner is a great convenience. Whatever lamp or burner be used, it should be surrounded with a chimney or shade, so as to prevent the flickering of the flame by currents of air. The best shade is a tin cylinder, with rows of holes at top and bottom for the admission and exit of air.

RETORT STAND.—A suitable retort stand is a very simple affair, and is best made at home. Ours consists of a board of hard wood, 5 inches by 4, into which is screwed a rod fourteen inches long, and a quarter of an inch in diameter. The rings have no screws, but are simply pieces of wire, one end of which is twisted round the rod, while the other is formed into a ring of the required size. Rings formed in this way are easily moved on the upright rod, but no weight placed on them in the usual manner can cause them to slip down.

CARDS FOR CENTERING THE OBJECTS.—Unless the objects are placed on the centres of the slides, the latter have a very awkward look. By drawing the outlines of a slide on a card, and marking out the centre, this difficulty is easily overcome. A card marked off in this way is shown in Fig. 69.

Fig. 69.

It is well to have two cards, one black with a white centre, and the other white with a black centre, as some objects, when immersed in the medium in which they are to be mounted, show best against a dark ground, while others are most easily seen against a light one. Those who use the self-centering turn-tables may readily centre their slides by painting on them a ring of some water-color, which is easily washed off. The ring is, of course, laid on the side opposite to that which receives the object.

MOUNTING NEEDLES.—These are similar to dissecting needles, but being used in balsam, varnish and similar substances, they cannot be used for dissection, and should be kept by themselves. They are most easily cleaned by being warmed over the lamp, and wiped with a piece of soft leather. When the balsam is burned on them, as recommended by some, it leaves a crust which is not easily removed.

COVER FORCEPS.—In placing the cover on the object, the ordinary forceps are very inconvenient. We have long used a pair of forceps bent as in Fig. 70, and with the points carefully adjusted. The mode of using the instrument will be obvious from the engraving. A very ingenious device intended to answer the same purpose has been invented by Dr. Fletcher. These forceps are self-closing, so that the thin glass cover is held without any effort. After the cover is in position on the slide, by pressing on the blades they open and allow it to slip out. If the cover should stick to the forceps in the slightest degree, it may be prevented from moving when the forceps are removed by inserting a common pin in the slit seen in Fig. 71. When using the forceps shown in Fig. 70, the same end may be attained by means of a wire fork (a hair-pin is as good as anything), which may be made to straddle the nose of the instrument.

Fig. 70.

Fig. 71.

SLIDE HOLDER.—The hot slides cannot be comfortably held in the fingers, and therefore a pair of wooden forceps become a necessity. Those usually sold are made by screwing together two thin slips of wood with a piece of brass or lead inserted between them at one end. To admit the slide, the slips are forced apart by pressing on pins arranged as in the stage forceps. When placed on a table the metal counter-balances the slide, and keeps it from touching the surface on which it is laid—a very important point. The English forceps, being all wood, frequently tip with a heavy slide.

A common spring clothes-pin is frequently used, but when we come to lay the slide down, the clothes-pin holds it in an awkward manner. The end of the hot slide is sure to lie on the table, and if fluid balsam or other medium should be present, the fact that the slide is not level produces bad results. By cutting off about half an inch from one of the limbs of the forceps part of the pin, however, this difficulty is avoided. The slide may then be grasped in such a way that when the clothes-pin is placed on the table, the glass will be held in a perfectly level position. A glance at Fig. 72 will show what we mean. A great advantage of this form of holder is that it costs but a trifle, so that the microscopist can supply himself with an abundance of them, and thus several slides may be cooling, while work on others is going on. When very heavy slides are used, it may become necessary to screw a plate of sheet lead to the under side of the clothes-pin, so as to prevent tipping

Fig. 72.—HOLDER FOR HOT SLIDES.

WATER BATH.—A water bath is indispensable in those cases where a certain very moderate degree of heat is not to be exceeded. Few persons fully appreciate the difficulty of regulating or even estimating the temperature of an object held over a naked flame, and mischief is often done before the operator is aware of it. A serviceable water bath is easily extemporized out of an old fruit can and a small beaker glass. This serves for exposing material and preparations to a temperature lower than that of boiling water. Where slides are to be so heated, the simplest contrivance is a flat tin box, with all the joints (cover and all, of course,) tightly soldered. A small tube, closed with a cork, serves to admit the water.

SPRING CLIPS.—One of the first of the needs which impress themselves upon the mind of the beginner, is the necessity for something to retain the thin cover in its place, until the cement, which is intended to hold it permanently, dries. An endless variety of spring clips have been invented for this purpose, but we have never seen anything that we liked better than the simple article shown in Fig. 73, and which we have used for

Fig. 73.

over fifteen years. It consists simply of a piece of brass wire bent as in the engraving. The slide being held in the left hand, the clip, held by the upper wire, is brought so that the projecting part of the ring is placed under the edge of the slide. The upper part is then lifted up so as to open the clip, which is then slid on to the slide until the vertical point is in the right position. When a broader surface than the point of the wire is needed, a piece of cork may be stuck on it, and if there should be need for greater pressure than that which the spring of the wire affords, this can be obtained by sliding a small brass ring on to the clip.

Various other forms of spring clip have been invented, but none that we consider more simple, or that we like better than the above, which has this great merit, that any one can make it for himself out of materials that may be obtained at any hardware store. It must be borne in mind, however, that all clips constructed upon this plan are apt to cause a slight displacement of the object, from the fact that the movement of the point is not quite perpendicular. With delicate objects this is a matter of importance. The only remedy is to use the end pressure of a rod moving in fixed guides.

CEMENTS AND VARNISHES.

A supply of carefully selected cements and varnishes is indispensable to the microscopist, and it is also well that he should understand the nature and properties of the materials used, otherwise he will be liable to make gross blunders. Thus, of the different articles in use, some are easily mixed with each other, while others separate as soon as left to themselves; some dry in one way and some in another. It would require a volume to detail the properties of the different substances which enter into the composition of the cements used by the microscopist. We have space for only the following hints, which, however, we hope will prove useful.

Cements become hard in three different ways—cooling, evaporation and oxidation. Shellac, sealing wax, electrical cement, etc., when melted by heat, furnish examples of the first process. Shellac and sealing-wax dissolved in alcohol, and asphalt and damar dissolved in turpentine, dry by the second process—the solvents evaporating and leaving behind the material which they had dissolved. Drying oil in all its forms, such as gold size, paint, etc., becomes hard by oxidation—not, as is generally supposed, by evaporation.

. In the case of varnishes which dry by the evaporation of some of their constituents, it is obvious that if a fresh layer

be laid over an old one, the old layer will be softened, and
if there should be any tendency to a vacuum in the cell,
the softened cement will be unable to resist the outside
pressure, and will creep in and spoil the object. So, too,
with varnishes or cements formed chiefly of drying oil or gold
size. If the different coats be laid on too thickly or too
rapidly, the part that is beneath cannot easily harden, but will
remain for a very long time in a semi-liquid condition. We
have just removed some brass rings from slides to which they
were attached four months ago by means of gold size, and
although the outer surface of the cement was hard and dry, the
interior was quite liquid, freely soiling the fingers.

GOLD SIZE.—The most extraordinary recipes have been given
for the preparation of this cement, which is in reality nothing
but good linseed oil rendered very drying by the usual
methods. Gilders frequently make it into a semi-paint by
adding coloring matter, thus forming a ground of a shade
similar to the gold they use, and this seems to have misled some
of our best writers. There is no ochre, litharge, or anything
of the kind present in good gold size. It does not pay to prepare gold size in small quantities, and it may be obtained from
any color dealer. The older it is the better, and it is well,
therefore, to lay in a good stock, which must be kept carefully
corked. The working supply should be kept in a small bottle.
This is the favorite cell making material employed by Dr. Carpenter, and it is certainly the most reliable cement we have.
It adheres firmly to glass, and if laid on in very thin successive
layers, tolerably deep and very durable cells may be built
up, but the process requires considerable time, otherwise the
under layers will remain soft. It has this great advantage over
asphalt, damar, and other cements composed of solid materials
dissolved in some menstruum, that fresh coats have but very
slight action on the old layers on which they may be laid. It
mixes with turpentine, and consequently with most materials
soluble in turpentine, but when once dry and hard, turpentine,
alcohol, ether, etc., have little or no action on it. It does not
mix with alcohol, and therefore cannot be mixed with the
solution of shellac in alcohol in any of its forms.

BLACK JAPAN.—When this can be procured of good quality, it makes a very excellent cell. It adheres very firmly to the glass provided the latter be exposed to a moderate heat after the cement has become dry. Black Japan dries up and thickens when kept, but may be thinned with turpentine.

BRUNSWICK BLACK.—This is simply a solution of asphaltum in turpentine. Occasionally it is rendered very black by the addition of a little lampblack. When good, it makes a very excellent cement. Its quality depends chiefly upon the character of the asphaltum that is used in its preparation. Now there are several varieties of asphaltum in market, the most common kind at the present day being that obtained from coal tar. This seems to be entirely unfit for the purpose. The proper kind is that which is found native in several parts of the world. The two kinds are easily distinguished by their odors.

SHELLAC.—This well known substance, when dissolved in alcohol, forms a varnish or cement of great value to the microscopist, and is the proper one to be used when glycerine is employed. Much of the shellac in market is artificially made from resin and wax, and makes a poor varnish. Real shellac must be employed if failure would be avoided.

BELL'S CEMENT.—Carpenter states that this cement is merely shellac dissolved in alcohol. With us it has presented no advantage over other cements.

SEALING WAX VARNISH.—This is prepared by dissolving the best sealing wax in alcohol. It unfortunately happens that all the fancy colored sealing wax in market is of inferior quality. Very excellent red wax may be obtained, but we have never been able to obtain good blue, black, green or other colored wax. We therefore make varnish of these colors by dissolving in alcohol the materials used for making the best red wax, substituting some other color, however, for the vermillion.

COLORED SHELLAC.—Bleached shellac, dissolved in alcohol, and colored with aniline blue, red, etc., makes a very fine transparent varnish.

DAMAR CEMENT.—This is a mixture of equal parts of damar varnish and gold size, mixed together. It should stand for some time before being used. It is said to be very excellent. It is very tough, and serves well as an outer coating over such brittle cements as shellac and sealing wax varnish.

MARINE GLUE.—This is undoubtedly the strongest cement in use for joining pieces of glass or glass and metal together. Skilful microscopists make great use of it; beginners do not find it so easy to manage as some others. In using it, the simplest method is to cut it in small pieces, lay it on one of the surfaces that are to be joined, melt it by heat, and apply the other surface, making sure of perfect contact by rubbing the two pieces upon each other, if they will allow of it. Marine glue may be obtained from most dealers in microscopes.

The cement known as *liquid glue*, is simply a solution of shellac in alcohol.

For attaching labels, paper covers, etc., to the slides, nothing is better than good dextrine. After having mixed the dextrine with water to the proper consistence, add six drops of glycerine to the fluid ounce of dextrine. This will prevent the labels or covers from cracking off.

Having provided himself with the necessary tools and materials, the next step is to learn how to use and apply them, and this will probably be most easily taught by describing a few characteristic examples. And first of all, selecting the most easily mounted of all objects, we commence with the scales on the butterfly's wings. Having prepared a cell of proper size, and allowed it to dry, the first step is to select a cover to suit it, and give a final cleaning to both slide and cover. When every particle of dust has been removed, breathe gently on the slide, and press the wing lightly against it, and within the cell. A large number of scales will at once adhere to the slide, and the next step is to attach the cover. Place the slide on the hotplate, (which must not be too hot, however,) and when it is thoroughly dry, and the cement somewhat soft, lay the cover on by means of the cover forceps. Press it into contact with the cement, and the operation is completed. It is not difficult to see when the cover and the cement are in perfect contact, and great care must be taken to close the cell all round in this way. It is true, this point is not of so much consequence with the particular object under consideration, but with some objects it would be quite important. The scales are now mounted dry, and may be kept for any length of time; no dust can soil them, and they are not liable to be injured by contact with other bodies. It only remains to label and "finish" the slide as hereafter directed.

Next to the above in simplicity is the mounting of such objects as the wings of insects in balsam. Suppose we wish to mount one of the smaller wings of a bee or wasp, so as to show the curious hooks with which it is armed: Place the warm slide on the centering card, drop a little balsam on the centre, and again warm the slide, so that any air that may be present may collect in fine bubbles which can be removed by means of a cold mounting needle. When the air-bubbles have been removed, seize the wing (previously well cleaned with a camel hair brush) with a pair of fine forceps, and lower the tip of it into the warm balsam. Then slowly lower the wing until it is entirely immersed. Drop, very little more balsam on it, warm the slide again (slightly this time), and remove air bubbles if there should be any. Then take a clean cover in the cover forceps, make it quite warm, and place it over the object by allowing it to first touch one edge of the balsam, and then to gradually fall down so as to exclude all air bubbles. In the case of the bee's wing it does not answer to apply much pressure as this would tend to distort the hooks. Press the cover into place as much as it will bear and no more, lay the slide in a warm place for some time until the balsam hardens, and then clean and finish the slide.

In mounting objects in balsam and fluids, the great difficulty to be encountered is the presence of air bubbles. Careful and judicious management, however, readily enables us to avoid them. In the first place see that they are entirely removed from the balsam on the slide. This is much more easily done before immersing the object in the balsam then afterwards. Next see that the air is expelled from the object. In the case of the wing, this is effected by *slowly* immersing the object in the balsam. Lastly see that no air enters with the cover. To do this see that the cover is hot, and that it is lowered on the balsam slowly, and from one side. If in any case there should be a vacant space under the cover as at *a* Fig. 74, and it should be desired to fill it, do not apply the fresh balsam directly at *a*. To do so would certainly be to inclose a large air bubble. Drop the balsam at *b*, warm the slide, and the balsam will creep in by capillary attraction, and expel the air.

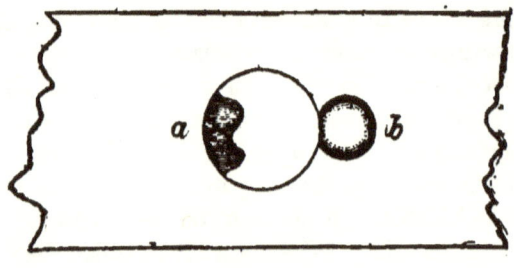

Fig. 74.

Let us now suppose that we have some small insect which we have prepared by soaking in potash, and which we desire to mount in balsam. Such a preparation if immersed directly in balsam, would be spoilt, since the balsam and watery solution would not mix. Therefore, proceed as follows: Wash the insect in pure water, and drain off the water; wash with strong alcohol, drain off the alcohol, and soak for twenty-four hours in the strongest alcohol you can get. Pour off the alcohol and soak for twenty-four hours in turpentine. The object may now be immersed in balsam without difficulty.

Air pumps and similar contrivances are generally recommended as the best means for removing air bubbles, but we never use them. If the object be dry, we soak it in alcohol until all the air has been expelled, then transfer to turpentine, and finally to balsam. This requires time, it is true but it does not occupy the time of the microscopist. The soaking process goes on without any attention from him, and while it involves far less labor, with us it has always given far better results, though we have used very fine air pumps, and followed the best published directions. Take the case of a dry shaving of wood, many of which are well worth mounting. It would be very laborious to get the air out of this by means of the air pump, while by soaking successively in water, alcohol, and turpentine, it can be mounted with great ease without a bubble.

Let us now take the case of an object mounted in fluid in a cell. Suppose it is the so-called tongue of a fly, which of course has been soaked for some time in the liquid in which it is to be finally mounted, viz., dilute glycerine. We make a cell of suitable thickness, which in this case may be made with shellac dissolved in alcohol. Several coats will be required, and as shellac alone does not adhere well to glass, we prefer to lay on first a coat of gold size or Japan, and when this is thoroughly dry, to lay the shellac on it. No difficulty will be found in making a cell of sufficient depth. The cell is now to be filled with the liquid, the object placed in it, and the whole carefully examined for air bubbles, which must be removed if they exist. The cover is now applied, all superfluous fluid removed by means of a camel hair pencil, which has been moistened and then squeezed dry, and finally the edge of the cover is to be coated with a thin layer of cement. After a day or so another layer of cement should be laid on, and this process repeated until at least three layers have been applied.

We give no directions for the construction and use of very deep cells as this is work that will hardly be attempted by beginners.

When opaque objects are to be mounted either in balsam, or in fluid, the process required is the same as that employed for transparent objects. Very many opaque objects are, however, mounted dry, and in this case all that is needed is to attach them to a slide, and see that they are properly protected. When thin they may be readily mounted in cement cells, and this is altogether the neatest and most secure plan where it can be used. Thicker objects require deeper cells, which may be made of card, ebonite or electrical cement. (3 parts resin, and 1 of wax, colored with ochre or any similar matter). Cells of card are made by first punching out a disc like a gun wad, and then punching a hole in this so as to leave a ring. The ring is to be cemented to the glass slide and carefully varnished.

Wooden slides with a cell bored in the centre, are recommended very highly, and seem to answer a very good purpose. The cells are not bored quite through the wooden slip, and as they are blackened on the inside, any small object that may be cemented to the bottom of them shows very well. For seeds, small shells, and similar objects, they answer admirably. In most cases it will be found unnecessary to cover the cells with thin glass. Several slides may be packed together face to face, and if held in firm contact by means of a rubber ring, dust will be entirely excluded. Or they may be arranged in the drawers of an ordinary cabinet, face down, the labels being placed on the backs. This will effectually exclude the dust.

Some years ago we mounted a large number of specimens of minerals on leather discs, which were cemented to glass slides. These leather discs were three-quarters of an inch in diameter, and we had a lot of pill-box covers which exactly fitted them. These covers, when slipped on to the discs, protected the objects perfectly, and the whole formed a very cheap, convenient and excellent mode of mounting.

A very ingenious cell for opaque objects, the invention of Prof. Pierce, of Providence, R. I., is shown in Fig. 75. It consists of a metallic cell, having a broad flange like the rim of a hat, which is cemented to an ordinary glass slide, as shown in section in the lower figure. To this cell is fitted a metal cap, which covers and protects the object. The object may be placed directly on the glass, or raised by means of a disc of any required thickness, so as to be more easily illuminated. The slide, with cell uncovered and containing an object, is shown in the upper figure. Uncovered objects may in this way be very perfectly protected from dust and mechanical violence.

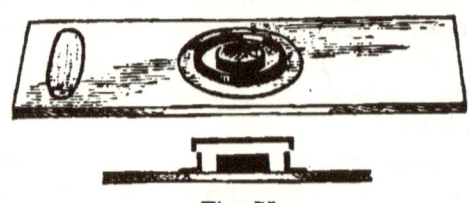

Fig. 75.

Some persons object to any slide that is mounted without a glass cover. It must be acknowledged, however, that while glass covers add to the appearance of the object and serve to protect it, they interfere somewhat with its examination, as it cannot be so brilliantly illuminated, and the rays in their passage to the objective are interfered with to a considerable extent. The objections to mounting opaque objects in cells with movable covers are that even during the short period in which they are exposed for examination they are liable to be contaminated with dust, the cover is liable to be lost, and the object when exposed is liable to mechanical injury. Therefore, while a few brilliant and striking objects, such as minerals, seeds, etc., may well be mounted in open cells, all delicate and valuable objects should be permanently covered.

Of late years the most popular cell for opaque objects is undoubtedly that devised by Prof. Hamilton L. Smith, and known as the wax cell. Various methods of making it are in use, the following being that originally published by the inventor: Take a circular disc of thin sheet wax, which is easily cut with a common gun punch from the sheet wax ordinarily used for making flowers, and attach it by means of heat to the centre of a glass slide. A brass curtain ring, of which the interior is the same size as the disc, is then slightly warmed and laid on the wax, to which it, of course, adheres. The object is fixed to the wax by slightly moistening the surface of the latter by a minute drop of turpentine. When dry, a cover, which exactly fits into the bevel of the ring is attached thereto with a little cement, and the whole may then be finished off on the turn-table.

The appearance of objects mounted in this way is very elegant, and consequently it has become a general favorite. It has, however, recently been condemned in most unsparing terms by the inventor, who has found that the under surface of the cover becomes in time coated with a deposit which causes a glare that entirely prevents clear vision. As soon as this difficulty was announced, an animated correspondence took place in the scientific journals, and it was found that while some microscopists had experienced this difficulty, it had never occurred to others. The final conclusion seems to be that the difficulty arises from the kind of wax used, and the method of attaching the object to it. The wax should have been thoroughly melted at a temperature as high as it will bear, so as to drive off all volatile matter, and instead of using discs punched from sheets, the wax should be applied in a melted condition, by means of a brush, to the warm glass slide. The object should not be stuck on with turpentine or similar cement, but should be attached to the wax after a small spot on the latter has been softened by bringing near it a hot wire. Objects mounted in this way, in cells so prepared, seem to remain in good condition for years.

A very ingenious cell has been devised by Mr. D. B. Scott. This cell is punched out of thin sheet metal, as shown in plan and section in figures 76 and 77. The cell is formed by the

Fig. 76.

Fig. 77.

METAL SLIDE AND CELL FOR OPAQUE OBJECTS.

central depression, and there is a turned-down edge all round the slide which gives it strength, and causes it to lie steadily on any flat surface. The cell has a ledge, or rebate, as seen in figure 77, for the purpose of supporting the thin glass cover. When made of tin the whole slide is japanned; those made of brass are lacquered, and the interior of the cell is covered with black asphalt, or some similar dark varnish. The objects are attached to the surface of the varnish by means of gum water, to which a very little glycerine has been added, and the thin glass cover may be cemented down and varnished on the turntable in the usual manner.

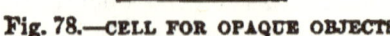

Fig. 78.—CELL FOR OPAQUE OBJECTS.

The alleged failure of the wax cell gave rise to a great many devices, one of which, proposed by Mr. Atwood, consists of a vulcanite or hard rubber cell, of which a sectional view is given in figure 78, the dotted lines showing the thin glass cover. The base is solid, thus giving a black back-ground of rubber; around the top is a ledge fitted to receive a one-half inch cover glass; this being secured by a trifle of shellac or any similar cement, completes the mounting. The cell may be attached to a glass slip by any cement, before or after preparation. For exchanges it offers superior advantages, inasmuch as the cell, with objects enclosed, may be sent through the mails independent of the glass slips, the recipient attaching them.

Cells similar in construction to the hard rubber cell may be moulded out of melted shellac by any one who is possessed of a proper die or mould. The die is easily turned out of a piece of brass, and with two or three moulds of different sizes, and a little shellac colored black, the microscopist may easily and cheaply provide himself with a supply of cells suitable for almost any object. The idea is due to Dr. Dayton, of Cleveland, and the details of the process may be found in the *American Journal of Microscopy* for June, 1881.

A cell which we have found very durable, easily and quickly made, and very neat, is constructed as follows: Having procured some good gold size and pure litharge, grind the latter to a very fine powder. Mix the litharge and gold size to the thickness of cream, and color either black or dark olive by adding lamp-black. With this cement it is easy to make as many cells as may be wanted, by laying on a ring with a brush while the glass slide revolves on the turn-table. As soon as the rings or cells are made, dust finely-powdered litharge over them until they are covered a sixteenth of an inch deep; allow them to stand a few minutes, and then shake off all the loose litharge by means of a few smart taps. The surface of the cell will now be quite rough. Allow it to stand a few hours, and then press it against a plate of glass. If this be done carefully, a smooth, level, solid ring will be left on the slide. If the edges should not be as smooth as they ought to be, it is easy to trim them off on the turn-table by means of a small chisel. Any turn-table with stout spring clips will hold a slide with sufficient firmness to allow of such soft material being turned quite true and smooth. Of course the tables which grasp the slides by the corner are best for this purpose. Such cells, after a few weeks, become very hard, and may be finished so as to be very neat. When covered with a few coats of shellac varnish or pure gold size, and completely dried, they hold liquids very well. They adhere so firmly to the slide that on several occasions when the slide has been broken by a fall, the cell has not parted from the glass. The only objection which we find to them is the length of time which it takes them to harden.

Tin foil, which may be had of various thicknesses from that of thin paper to a sixteenth of an inch, makes a capital material for cells. It is difficult to get the inner and outer circles which form the ring, concentric, except by the use of special tools. Prof. Chester avoids this difficulty by placing a large number of rings on a rod or mandril which just fits the opening, and after screwing the rings tightly endwise, he turns off the outside so as to leave it perfectly true and even. Mr. A. Y. Moore cements the sheet of tin foil to the slide by means of shellac, and cuts out the ring on the turn-table by means of a sharp knife or chisel.

Finishing the Slides.—The appearance of a collection of slides depends very much upon the style in which they are finished, and although in some instances it may be said that the finish does not affect the intrinsic value of the object, it is generally the case that a well-finished slide is more durable than one that has not been properly completed. The old system of covering the slides with paper is now entirely obsolete, and properly so. It was troublesome, unsightly, unless in professional hands, and not very durable. Fortunately slides with ground and polished edges are now so cheap that there is no occasion to resort to the paper cover. Objects mounted on these slides, whether in cells or otherwise, are in general covered with round covers, which are adjusted on the turn-table so as to be perfectly central. After the mount has been completed so far as fastening down the cover is concerned, the edge of the latter is finished with a neat coat of varnish. This varnish serves to do something more than merely ornament the slide; it secures the cover in its place, and prevents the drying up of the medium used for mounting. Even in the case of Canada balsam it is of use, for if gold size be used as the varnish, it prevents the evaporation of the turpentine, and the ultimate drying and cracking of the balsam. Where glycerine jelly, glycerine, or glycerine and gum are used, it becomes indispensable.

The process employed for finishing slides in this way is as follows: The objects having been mounted, the slides are laid away until the balsam, cement, etc., have been hardened, when all superfluous matters of this kind are easily removed with a small chisel made out of a brad-awl ground thin and sharp. A small chisel-pointed piece of hard wood, and a little water, will remove the last traces of balsam or varnish, and if necessary a final cleaning may be given with a rag moistened with alcohol. The slide is then placed on the turn-table, and a neat ring of varnish, either plain or colored, is run around the edge. The varnish used for this purpose should be selected according to the material in which the object is mounted. Thus, for objects in glycerine, glycerine jelly, or gum, the best coating is shellac varnish, which may be left quite transparent and colored with some of the aniline colors. Shellac also answers on Canada balsam, when the latter has become hard, but gold size is better, and the gold size may either be colored with the ordinary artists' colors, which are sold in tubes, and which give an opaque-colored ring, or transparent colors may be used.

Labeling the Slides.—The proper labeling of slides and material is a most important matter. All bottles should be labeled, not only on the bottles themselves, but on the corks or stoppers, and the slides should be kept labeled or numbered during every stage of their progress. Our system is as follows: Before the object is mounted the slide is labeled on the *under* side with a very thin gummed label. Numbering with the writing diamond is deferred until the mount is completed, because, if spoilt, the whole may be thrown into a jar to be soaked off, and this cannot be done with figures written or scratched in with a diamond. As soon as the slide is finished the regular label is attached, and the slide numbered with a writing diamond. Of this number a record is kept, so that even if the label should fall off or get soaked off, a new label may be provided;

and unfortunately it sometimes happens that labels drop off either from exposure to moisture or excessive dryness.

As regards designs, etc., for labels, the variety is endless. Each microscopist will probably select the one that accords most nearly with his own taste. The only suggestion that we would make is that severe simplicity be adopted as the rule. Complicated and fancy labels look well at first, but they soon pall, and we get tired of them. It is well to have a large blank label at one end, on which memoranda may be written, such as the power best adapted to show the object; whether it is best seen by reflected, transmitted, or polarized light; the location of interesting points as determined by the Maltwood Finder, etc., etc. An important point also is the direction in which the reading should run—whether across or lengthwise of the slide. There seems to be no rule on this point, and it would be well for our societies to discuss this subject, and establish a rule for the benefit of exchangers. Nothing is more aggravating than a lot of slides labeled in different ways. The direction will depend, of course, upon the kind of cabinet used. For cabinets with racks, either way will answer, though the lengthwise direction is somewhat the most convenient. For the old style English cabinet, in which the objects lie flat and endwise to the front of the drawers, the writing should run across the slide. For our American cabinets with drawers having spaces divided off for each slide, the writing should be lengthwise of the slide. In short, when the slide lies in its proper position in the drawer, the lines of writing should run parallel with the front edge of the drawer.

Cabinets.—The value, either for work or for exhibition, of a collection of microscopic objects, is greatly enhanced when they are properly arranged and easily accessible. Consequently every microscopist who possesses even a small number of slides, should provide some kind of a case or cabinet for keeping them.

The simplest form of case is one with racks, and these are made in a great variety of styles, forms, and sizes, from the simple mailing box, holding two or three slides, to large and expensive cabinets. The common box, with a hinged lid, and holding twenty-five objects, answers well for carrying a few objects to exhibitions and the like. The chief objections to this style of cabinet consist in the difficulty of lifting out any particular slide and of reading the names. The latter difficulty may be obviated by writing the names on the bottom of the box on a line with the slide; the first objection may be *mitigated* by placing the spaces in the rack as far apart as possible. These rack boxes make altogether the cheapest cases, and when placed in cabinets holding, say, a dozen boxes, or three hundred slides, they form a very economical and convenient arrangement. The cabinet, or outer case, should, of course, be so made that the boxes will stand on end, as in this way the slides lie flat—a most important point.

Cases or cabinets of shallow drawers in which the slides lie flat, with the labels fully exposed to view, are, however, altogether the best. They have been made of various forms. A cheap, simple case, holding about six dozen slides, may be had, in which the drawers do not slide in grooves, but lie one above the other. The only objection to this plan lies in the fact that all the drawers must be taken out if we wish to get at the lowest one; but where there are not more than a dozen drawers this is not a very serious difficulty, and the compactness, lightness and cheapness of the arrangement make it quite a favorite.

In the English cabinets the slides lie with their ends towards the front of the drawer, so that the motion of pulling the drawer out or pushing it in, does not cause the slides to slip over each other. This is a very excellent arrangement, and one which we like better than any other. In the American cabinets as hitherto made, the slides lie with the long edges towards the front of the drawers, and are prevented from slipping over each other by small partitions which divide the rows into spaces one inch each in width. This is, theoretically, the most perfect arrangement, but it requires a little more room than the other. The American cabinets have, however, one feature which is a most important one: The spaces in which the slides rest have a depression under the ends of the slides, and by pressing on the end, the slide is lifted so that it is very easily grasped. In the English cabinets this feature is wanting, and it is only with great trouble that a tightly-fitting slide can be taken from its place. Fortunately, any drawer which is deep enough, may have this device applied to it by simply gluing a thin strip of wood or pasteboard on the bottom of the drawer so as to raise up the part on which the slides rest, but leaving a space of about three-quarters of an inch under the end of the slide, into which the latter may be tipped.

The Maltwood Finder.—This is a most important accessory to every microscope, as it not only facilitates interchange of notes between microscopists living at a distance from each other, but it enables observers to make an accurate record of the position of any object, and thus make sure of its identity when under examination at different times.

Fig. 79.

It consists of a glass slip, a little wider than an ordinary slide, upon which is a photograph occupying a space 1 by 1 inch, as shown in figure 79. This space is divided into 2,500 squares (50 divisions on each side) and each of these small squares contains two numbers, one of which indicates its position from bottom to top, while the other marks its position from right to left. Thus the square which lies on the tenth line from the bottom, and the fifteenth from the right-hand side, would be $\tfrac{1}{1}\tfrac{0}{5}$.

The method of using the Finder is as follows: Placing on the stage an object mounted on an ordinary slide, with its lower edge against a ledge of some kind, and its left-hand edge against a stop (the stop and ledge both being movable as regards the stage), we bring some particular spot into view. Removing the slide, we now place the finder in its place, and read off the two numbers. It is now evident that if at any future time we should place the finder against the movable ledge and stop, and bring the same numbers into view, then on removing the finder and placing the slide on the stage and against the ledge and stop, which, of course, must occupy the same position that they did when the finder was in place, the precise spot originally under examination will be in view. We can therefore easily register the location of any object of interest, and so be certain of finding it at any future time.

The mechanical stage, or the ordinary movable glass stage, described at page 110, or that shown in Fig. 24 (page 111) affords special facilities for using the Maltwood Finder. But unless fitted with some special contrivance, microscopes which have only the ordinary clips, are unsuitable for this purpose. A movable ledge and stop, which may be used with the common spring clips, is, however, easily devised and made. We often use a simple wooden slide

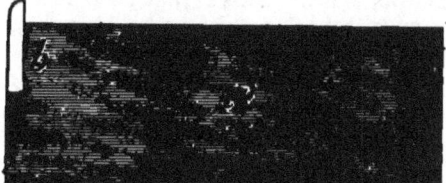

Fig. 80.—STOP FOR MALTWOOD FINDER.

with a little projection on the edge near one end. The wooden slide must be thicker than the glass slide which carries the object to be registered, as it is necessary that the springs should hold the wooden slide firmly in place, while the object-slide moves freely below the springs. A piece of vulcanite or hard rubber about the eighth of an inch thick and the size of the usual 3x1 glass slide answers admirably. It should have a stop fastened to one end, as shown in figure 80, where a is the hard rubber slide, and b is a small piece of brass, let into the end and screwed fast.

Microscopical Misinterpretations.—The observer who uses the compound microscope labors under certain disadvantages which do not affect those who examine large objects which can be handled, and thus subjected to the scrutiny of several senses. The fallacies to which the microscopist is liable in this way deserve special attention and special precautions. We have already (page 198) alluded to certain fallacies of another kind, which must be avoided by such careful and extensive study as will enable us to recognize foreign matter when we see it; the fallacies now under consideration can only be avoided by careful study of the laws of optics, and by introducing considerable variety of methods into our examinations. One of these sources of fallacy arises from the liability which most persons have to see objects *pseudoscopically*, as it is called —that is to say, hollows appear to be elevations, and elevations appear to be hollows. The extent to which this tendency exists is not generally recognized. Taking a gold coin, on which the letters, etc., were known to be raised, we placed it under the microscope, and submitted it to seven intelligent persons. Out of these, five declared that they saw the letters sunk into

238 SELECTION AND USE OF THE MICROSCOPE.

the metal; two said they were raised. In objects too small to be felt, and where sections cannot be made, the truth may be ascertained by watching the effect of raising or lowering the object glass in focussing.

Another fallacy of this kind has led to the belief that hairs and many similar bodies are hollow. Seen under the microscope, a hair looks just as if it were a tube—but then, so does a wire, which is known to be solid. The test in this case is to make a cross section of the object.

The true form of objects may frequently be determined by studying the effect of light and shade produced by sending the light across them in different directions. This is most readily effected by means of the revolving stage, which, for this purpose, should have very accurate rotation in the optic axis.

The most singular fallacies, however, are those arising from certain illusions of vision, which affect every one, and which in ordinary practice, are easily corrected. For a full account of these, the reader is referred to the works of Helmholtz; a brief account of the most common cases is given in the *Young Scientist* for 1881. The one which is of most interest to microscopists is the famous optical illusion of Nachet, of which a figure is given below. In the course of his examination of the markings on the

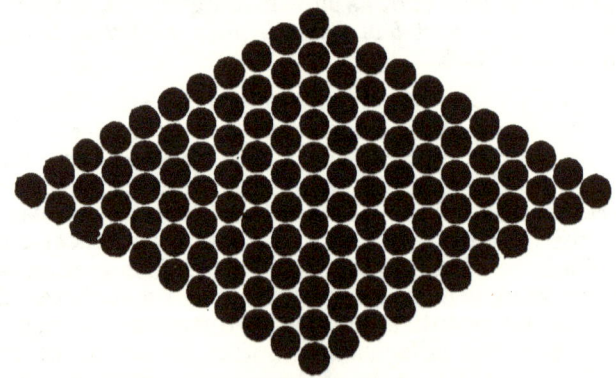

Fig. 81.—NATCHET'S OPTICAL ILLUSION.

P. Angulatum, M. Nachet found that if a series of round black dots be arranged on a white ground, as in Fig. 81, the dots, when viewed from a distance of twelve to twenty inches, will *appear* to be hexagonal, though we know that they are round.

FINIS.

Plate I.

ROSS MODEL.
As made by Ross & Co.

Plate II

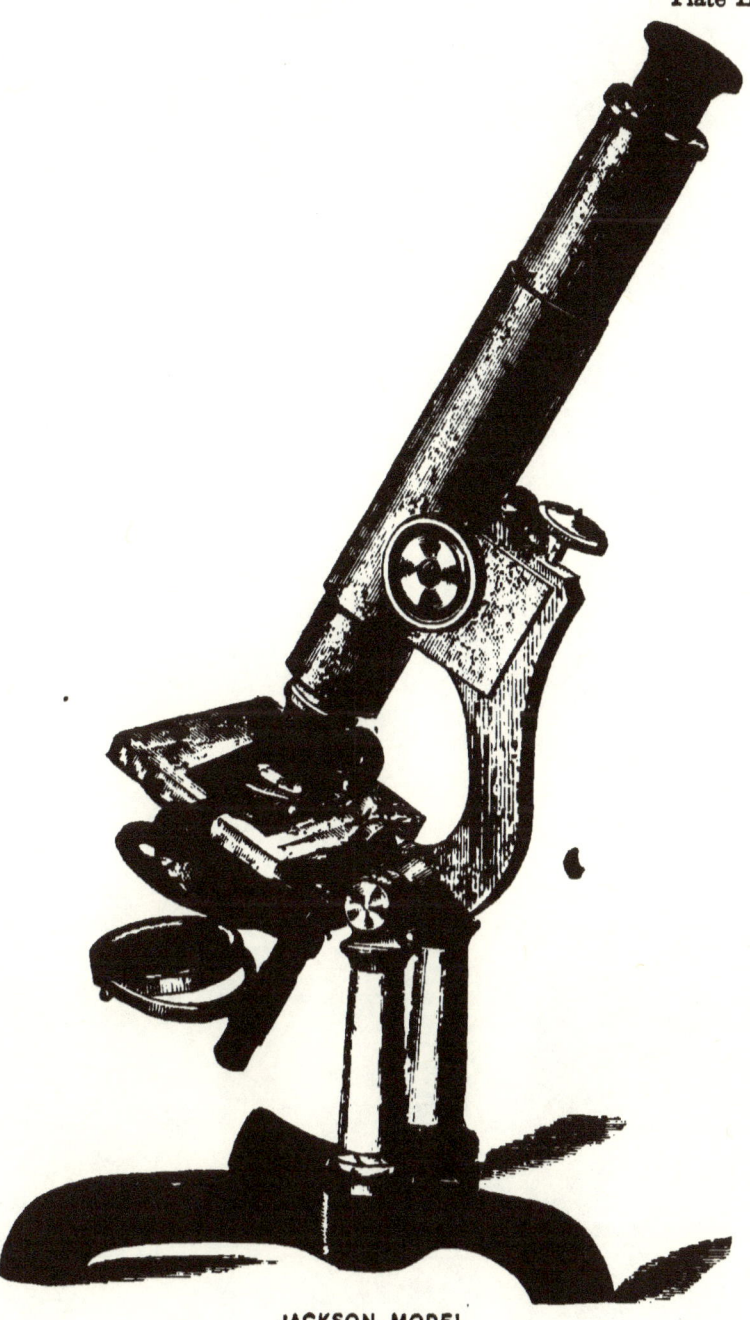

JACKSON MODEL.
As made by Bausch & Lomb Optical Company.

Plate III.

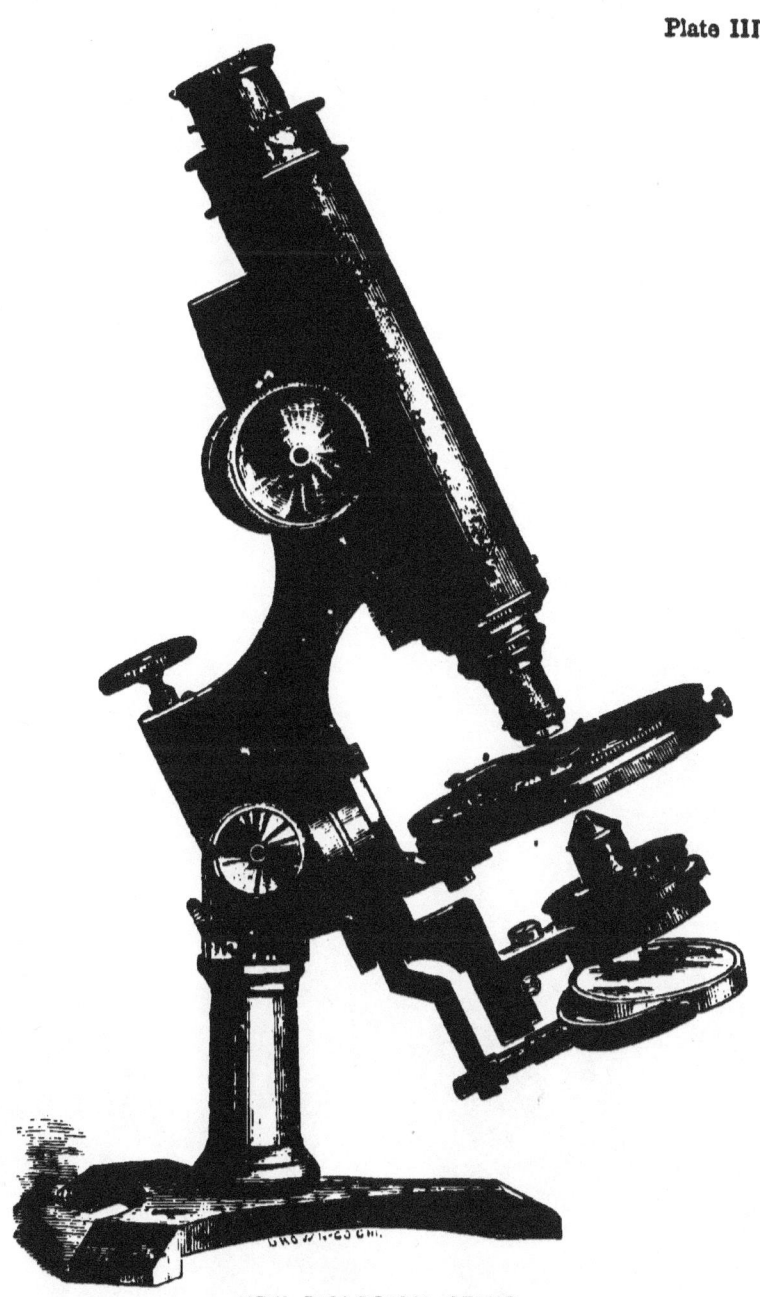

NEW BIOLOGICAL STAND.
As made by W. H. Bulloch.

Plate IV.

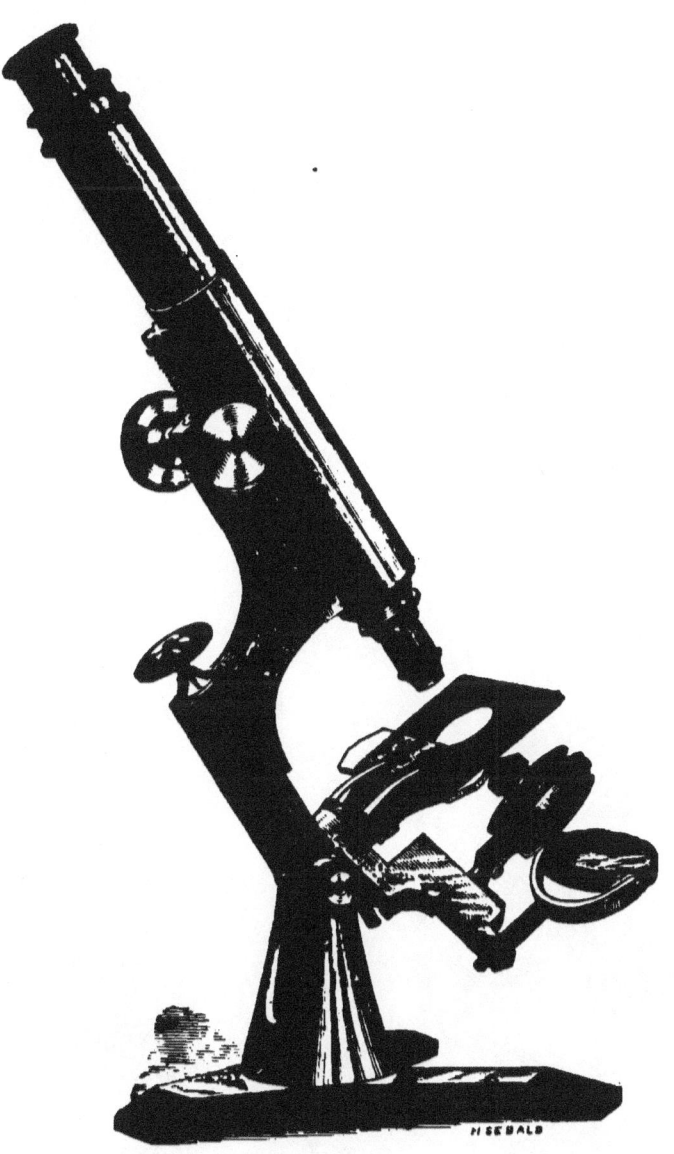

THE HISTOLOGICAL MICROSCOPE.
As made by Joseph Zentmayer.

Plate V.

THE INVESTIGATOR MICROSCOPE.
As made by Bausch & Lomb Optical Company.

Plate VI.

THE ACME BINOCULAR MICROSCOPE.
As made by J. W. Sidle & Co.

CATALOGUE

OF

Books and Periodicals

PUBLISHED AND FOR SALE BY

THE INDUSTRIAL PUBLICATION COMPANY,

14 Dey Street, New York.

☛ *Any of these Books may be obtained from any Bookseller or Newsdealer, or will be sent Free by mail to any part of the United States or Canada ON RECEIPT OF PRICE.*

The Amateur's Handbook of Practical Information,

For the Workshop and the Laboratory. Second Edition. Greatly Enlarged. Neatly Bound - - 15 cents.

This is a handy little book, containing just the information needed by Amateurs in the Workshop and Laboratory. Directions for making Alloys, Fusible Metals, Cements, Glues, etc.; and for Soldering, Brazing, Lacquering, Bronzing, Staining and Polishing Wood, Tempering Tools, Cutting and Working Glass, Varnishing, Silvering, Gilding, Preparing Skins, etc., etc.

The New Edition contains extended directions for preparing Polishing Powders, Freezing Mixtures, Colored Lights for tableaux, Solutions for rendering ladies' dresses incombustible, etc. There has also been added a very large number of new and valuable receipts.

Rhymes of Science: Wise and Otherwise.

By O. W. Holmes, Bret Hart, Ingoldsby, Prof. Forbes, Prof. J. W. McQ. Rankine, Hon. R. W. Raymond, and others.

With Illustrations. Cloth, Gilt Title. - 50 cents

Section Cutting.

A Practical Guide to the Preparation and Mounting of Sections for the Microscope; Special Prominence being given to the Subject of Animal Sections. By Sylvester Marsh. Reprinted from the London edition. With Illustrations. 12mo., Cloth, Gilt Title. · 75 cents.

This is undoubtedly the most thorough treatise extant upon section cutting in all its details. The American edition has been greatly enlarged by valuable explanatory notes, and also by extended directions, illustrated with engravings, for selecting and sharpening knives and razors.

A Book for Beginners with the Microscope.

Being an abridgment of "Practical Hints on the Selection and Use of the Microscope." By John Phin. Fully illustrated, and neatly and strongly bound in boards. 30 cts.

This book was prepared for the use of those who, having no knowledge of the use of the microscope, or, indeed, of any scientific apparatus, desire simple and practical instruction in the best methods of managing the instrument and preparing objects.

How to Use the Microscope.

"Practical Hints on the Selection and Use of the Microscrope." Intended for Beginners. By John Phin, Editor of the "American Journal of Microscopy." Fourth Edition. Greatly enlarged, with over 80 engravings in the text, and 6 full-page engravings, printed on heavy tint paper. 12mo., cloth, gilt title, - $1.00

The Microscope.

By Andrew Ross. Fully Illustrated. 12mo., Cloth, Gilt Title. - - - - - 75 cents.

This is the celebrated article contributed by Andrew Ross to the "Penny Cyclopædia," and quoted so frequently by writers on the Microscope. Carpenter and Hogg, in the last editions of their works on the Microscope, and Brooke, in his treatise on Natural Philosophy, all refer to this article as the best source for full and clear information in regard to the principles upon which the modern achromatic Microscope is constructed. It should be in the library of every person to whom the Microscope is more than a toy. It is written in simple language, free from abstruse technicalities.

The Microscopist's Annual for 1879.

Contains List of all the Microscopical Societies in the country, with names of officers, days of meeting, etc.; etc.; Alphabetical and Classified Lists of all the Manufacturers of Microscopes and Objectives, Dissecting Apparatus, Microscopic Objects, Materials for Microscopists, in Europe and America, etc., etc.; Postal Rates, Rules and Regulations, prepared expressly for microscopists; Weights and Measures, with tables and rules for the conversion of different measures into each other; Custom Duties and Regulations in regard to Instruments and Books; Value of the Moneys of all Countries in U. S. Dollars; Value of the Lines on Nobert's Test Plates; Table of Moller's Probe Platte, with the number of lines to inch on the several diatoms, etc., etc.; Focal Value of the Objectives of those makers who Number their Objectives (Hartnack, Nachet, etc.); Focal Value of the Eye-pieces of different makers; Magnifying Power of Eye-pieces and Objectives, etc., etc. The whole forming an indispensable companion for every working microscopist. Limp Cloth, Gilt - - - 25 cents.

☞ The "Annual" for 1880 is in a forward state of preparation, and will be uniform in size and price with that for 1879.

Microscope Objectives.

The Angular Aperture of Microscope Objectives. By Dr. George E. Blackham. 8vo., Cloth. Eighteen full page illustrations printed on extra fine paper. $1.25. Sold only by Subscription.

This is the elaborate paper on Angular Aperture, read by Dr. Blackham before the Microscopical Congress, held at Indianapolis.

Kutzing on Diatoms.—Nearly ready.

The Siliceous Shelled Bacillariæ or Diatomaceæ; the History of their Discovery and Classification; their Distribution, Collection, and Life-History. By Friedrich Traugott Kutzing. Translated from the German by Prof. Hamilton L. Smith, of Geneva, N. Y. 12mo., Cloth, Gilt, - - - - - - 50 cents.

Diatoms.
Practical Directions for Collecting, Preserving, Transporting, Preparing and Mounting Diatoms. By Prof. A. Mead Edwards, M. D., Prof. Christopher Johnston, M. D., Prof. Hamilton L. Smith, LL. D.

12mo., Cloth. - - - - 75 cents.

This volume undoubtedly contains the most complete series of directions for Collecting, Preparing and Mounting Diatoms ever published. The directions given are the latest and best.

Common Objects for the Microscope.
By Rev. J. G. Wood. Upwards of four hundred illustrations, including twelve colored plates by Tuffen West.

Illuminated Covers. - - - 50 cents.

This book contains a very complete description of the objects ordinarily met with, and as the plates are very good, and almost every object is figured, it is a most valuable assistant to the young microscopist.

Five Hundred and Seven Mechanical Movements.
Embracing all those which are Most Important in Dynamics, Hydraulics, Hydrostatics, Pneumatics, Steam Engines, Mill and Other Gearing, Presses, Horology and Miscellaneous Machinery; and including Many Movements never before published, and several of which have only recently come into use. By Henry T. Brown, editor of the "American Artisan." Eleventh Edition. $1.00.

This work is a perfect Cyclopædia of Mechanical Inventions, which are here reduced to first principles, and classified so as to be readily available. Every mechanic that hopes to be more workman, ought to have a copy.

The Six Days of Creation.
The Chemical History of the Six Days of Creation. By John Phin, C. E., editor of "The American Journal of Microscopy." 12mo., Cloth. - - 75 cents.

Stories About Horses.
Just the Book for Boys. With eight full-page engravings. In Boards, 15 cents. In Cloth - 50 cents.

Instruction in the Art of Wood Engraving.

A Manual of Instruction in the Art of Wood Engraving; with a Description of the Necessary Tools and Apparatus, and Concise Directions for their Use; Explanation of the Terms Used, and the Methods Employed for Producing the Various Classes of Wood Engravings. By S. E. Fuller.

Fully illustrated with Engravings by the author, separate sheets of engravings for transfer and practice being added.

New Edition, Neatly Bound.   -   -   30 cents.

What to Do in Case of Accident.

What to Do and How to Do It in Case of Accident. A Book for Everybody. 12mo., Cloth, Gilt Title. 50 cents.

This is one of the most useful books ever published. It tells exactly what to do in case of accidents, such as Severe Cuts, Sprains, Dislocations, Broken Bones, Burns with Fire, Scalds, Burns with Corrosive Chemicals, Sunstroke, Suffocation by Foul Air, Hanging, Drowning, Frost-Bite, Fainting, Stings, Bites, Starvation, Lightning, Poisons, Accidents from Machinery, and from the Falling of Scaffolding, Gunshot Wounds, etc., etc. It ought to be in every house, for young and old are liable to accident, and the directions given in this book might be the means of saving many a valuable life.

BOUND VOLUMES OF
The Technologist, or Industrial Monthly.

The eight volumes of THE TECHNOLOGIST, OR INDUSTRIAL MONTHLY, which have been issued, form a Mechanical and Architectural Encyclopædia of great value; and, when properly bound, they form a most important addition to any library. The splendid full-page engravings, printed on tinted paper, in the highest style of the art, are universally conceded to be the finest architectural and mechanical engravings ever published in this country. We have on hand a few complete sets, which we offer for $16.00, handsomely and uniformly bound in cloth.

We have also a few extra sets of Vols. III to VIII inclusive. These six volumes we offer for $8.00 bound in cloth. As there are but a very few sets remaining, those who desire to secure them should order immediately.

NOTE.—The above prices do not include postage or express charges. The set weighs altogether too much to be sent by mail.

Shooting on the Wing.

Plain Directions for Acquiring the Art of Shooting on the Wing. With Useful Hints concerning all that relates to Guns and Shooting, and particularly in regard to the art of Loading so as to Kill. To which has been added several Valuable and hitherto Secret Recipes, of Great Practical Importance to the Sportsman. By an Old Gamekeeper.

12mo., Cloth, Gilt Title. - - - 75 cents.

The Pistol as a Weapon of Defence,

In the House and on the Road.

12mo., Cloth. - - - - - 50 cents.

This work aims to instruct the peaceable and law-abiding citizens in the best means of protecting themselves from the attacks of the brutal and the lawless, and is the only practical book published on this subject. Its contents are as follows: The Pistol as a Weapon of Defence.—The Carrying of Fire-Arms.—Different kinds of Pistols in Market; How to Choose a Pistol.—Ammunition, different kinds; Powder, Caps, Bullets, Copper Cartridges, etc.—Best form of Bullet.—How to Load.—Best Charge for Pistols.—How to regulate the Charge.—Care of the Pistol; how to Clean it.—How to Handle and Carry the Pistol.—How to Learn to Shoot.—Practical use of the Pistol; how to Protect yourself and how to Disable your antagonist.

Lightning Rods.

Plain Directions for the Construction and Erection of Lightning Rods. By John Phin, C. E., editor of "The Young Scientist," author of "Chemical History of the Six Days of the Creation," etc. Second Edition. Enlarged and Fully Illustrated.

12mo., Cloth, Gilt Title. - - - 50 cents.

This is a simple and practical little work, intended to convey just such information as will enable every property owner to decide whether or not his buildings are thoroughly protected. It is not written in the interest of any patent or particular article of manufacture, and by following its directions, any ordinarily skilful mechanic can put up a rod that will afford perfect protection, and that will not infringe any patent. Every owner of a house or barn ought to procure a copy.

The Steel Square and Its Uses.

The Carpenters' Steel Square and its Uses ; being a description of the Square, and its Uses in obtaining the Lengths and Bevels of all kinds of Rafters, Hips, Groins, Braces, Brackets, Purlins, Collar-Beams, and Jack-Rafters. Also, its application in obtaining the Bevels and Cuts for Hoppers, Spring Mouldings, Octagons, Stairs, Diminished Stiles, etc., etc., etc. Illustrated by Over Fifty Wood-cuts. By Fred. T. Hodgson, Editor of the " Builder and Woodworker."

  Cloth, Gilt, - - - - - 75 cents.

Mechanical Draughting.

The Students' Illustrated Guide to Practical Draughting. A Series of Practical Instructions for Machinists, Mechanics, Apprentices, and Students at Engineering Establishments and Technical Institutes. By T. P. Pemberton, Draughtsman and Mechanical Engineer. Illustrated with Numerous Engravings.

  Cloth, Gilt, - - - - - - $1.00

This is a simple but thorough book, by a draughtsman of twenty-five years' experience. It is intended for beginners and self-taught students, as well as for those who pursue the study under the direction of a teacher.

Map of the Moon.

This is a copy of Webb's reduction of Baer & Maedler's celebrated Map of the Moon. It is engraved in the very best style, every feature being remarkably clear and distinct. It is accompanied with a small book, which contains a description of the various topographical features shown in the map, and forms an indispensable addition to the library of every Amateur Astronomer. Price of Map and Descriptive Book, - - - 50 cents.

☞ As the map was prepared for the purpose of illustrating the monthly papers on "Astronomy for Amateurs," published in the YOUNG SCIENTIST, it was given as a premium to all subscribers to that journal. Those who received the map with the Journal, and desire to procure the book, can obtain the latter, post-paid, for 20 cents.

SCIENTIFIC LIBRARY
FOR YOUNG PEOPLE.

MANUALS OF ELEMENTARY SCIENCE.

Fcap. 8vo., 128 pp., with Illustrations, Limp Cloth, 40 cents each.

☞ SENT BY MAIL, POST FREE, ON RECEIPT OF PRICE.

MATTER AND MOTION.
By J. Clerk Maxwell, M.A., Trinity College, Cambridge.

This work is a simple and yet thorough and accurate introduction to the study of Physical Science in general, by one of the ablest scientists of Great Britain.

ASTRONOMY.
By W. H. Christie, M.A., Trinity College, Cambridge; the Royal Observatory, Greenwich.

The illustrations in this book will give the young student a very clear idea of the actual arrangement of the heavenly bodies and of their motions.

CHEMISTRY.
By Albert J. Bernays.

Describes a great many simple and interesting experiments, as well as discusses the general principles of the science.

BOTANY.
By Robert Bentley, Professor of Botany in Kings College, London.

This little book on Botany has been prepared with the intention of supplying young boys and girls with a simple introduction to the study of plants. It is written in as plain language as possible, and is very fully illustrated.

ZOOLOGY.
By Alfred Newton, M.A., F.R.S., Professor of Zoology and Comparative Anatomy in the University of Cambridge.

Full of interesting facts, stated in simple and forcible language.

PHYSIOLOGY.
By F. le Gros Clarke, F.R.S., St. Thomas's Hospital.

The object of this elementary treatise is to teach some of the simple truths of Human Physiology, such as may be intelligible without any extended knowledge of other branches of science. But it is hoped, by the avoidance of technical terms, when possible, and their definition when essential, and also by a familiar explanation of any natural law which may be referred to, that there will be no material difficulty in understanding the simple principles and details which will be taught in these pages.—*Author's Introduction.*

FOURTH EDITION. *Greatly Enlarged, with over 80 illustrations in the Text and 6 full page Engravings, printed on Heavy Tint Paper.* 1 Vol. 12mo., 240 pages. *Neatly Bound in Cloth, Gilt Title. Price* $1.00.

HOW TO USE THE MICROSCOPE.

A SIMPLE AND PRACTICAL BOOK, INTENDED FOR BEGINNERS.

By JOHN PHIN,

Editor of "The American Journal of Microscopy."

CONDENSED TABLE OF CONTENTS.

THE MICROSCOPE.—What it Is; What it Does; Different Kinds of Microscopes; Principles of its Construction; Names of the Different Parts.

SIMPLE MICROSCOPES.—Hand Magnifiers; Doublets; Power of Two or More Lenses When Used Together; Stanhope Lens; Coddington Lens; Achromatic Doublets and Triplets; Twenty-five Cent Microscopes—and How to Make Them; Penny Microscopes, to Show Eels in Paste and Vinegar.

DISSECTING MICROSCOPES.—Essentials of a Good Dissecting Microscope.

COMPOUND MICROSCOPES.—Cheap Foreign Stands; The Ross Model; The Jackson Model; The Continental Model; The New American Model; Cheap American Stands; The Binocular Microscope; The Binocular Eye-piece; The Inverted Microscope; Lithological Microscopes; The Aquarium Microscope; Microscopes for Special Purposes; "Class" Microscopes.

OBJECTIVES.—Defects of Common Lenses; Spherical Aberration; Chromatic do.; Corrected Objectives; Defining Power; Achromatism; Aberration of Form; Flatness of Field; Angular Aperture; Penetrating Power; Working Distance; Immersion and "Homogeneous" Lenses; Duplex Fronts; French Triplets, etc., etc.

TESTING OBJECTIVES.—General Rules; Accepted Standards—Diatoms, Ruled Lines, Artificial Star; Podura; Nobert's Lines; Möller's Probe Platte, etc., etc.

SELECTION OF A MICROSCOPE—Must be Adapted to Requirements and Skill of User; Microscopes for Botany; For Physicians; For Students.

ACCESSORY APPARATUS.—Stage Forceps; Forceps Carrier; Plain Slides; Concave Slides; Watch-Glass Holder; Animalcule Cage; Zoophyte Trough; The Weber Slide; The Cell-Trough; The Compressorium; Gravity Compressorium; Growing Slides; Frog Plate; Table; Double Nose-piece.

ILLUMINATION.—Sun-Light; Artificial Light—Candles, Gas, Lamps, etc., etc.

ILLUMINATION OF OPAQUE OBJECTS.—Bulls-Eye Condenser; Side Reflector; The Lieberkuhn; The Parabolic Reflector; Vertical Illuminators.

ILLUMINATION OF TRANSPARENT OBJECTS.—Direct and Reflected Light; Axial or Central Ligh; Oblique Light; The Achromatic Condenser; The Webster Condenser, and How to Use it; Wenham's Reflex Illuminator, and How to Use it; The Wenham Prism; The "Half-Button;" The Woodward Illuminator; Tolles' Illuminating Traverse Lens; The Spot Lens; The Parabolic Illuminator; Polarized Light.

HOW TO USE THE MICROSCOPE.—General Rules; Hints to Beginners.

HOW TO USE OBJECTIVES OF LARGE APERTURE.—Collar-Correction, etc.

CARE OF THE MICROSCOPE.—Should be Kept Covered; Care of Objectives; Precautions to be Used when Corrosive Vapors and Liquids are Employed; To Protect the Objectives from Vapors which Corrode Glass; Cleaning the Objectives; Cleaning th Brass Work.

COLLECTING OBJECTS.—Where to Find Objects; What to Look for; How to Capture Them.

THE PREPARATION AND EXAMINATION OF OBJECTS.—Cutting Thin Sections of Soft Substances; Valentine's Knife; Sections of Wood and Bone; Improved Section Cutter; Sections of Rock; Knives; Scissors; Needles; Dissecting Pans and Dishes; Dissecting Microscopes; Separation of Deposits from Liquids; Preparing Whole Insects; Feet, Eyes, Tongues, Wings, etc., of Insects; Use of Chemical Tests; Liquids for Moistening Objects; Refractive Powers of Different Liquids; Iod-Serum; Artificial Iod-Serum; Covers for Keeping Out Dust; Errors in Microscopic Observations.

PRESERVATIVE PROCESSES.—General Principles; Preservative Media.

APPARATUS FOR MOUNTING OBJECTS.—Slides; Covers; Cells; Turn-Tables, etc.

CEMENTS AND VARNISHES.—General Rules for Using.

MOUNTING OBJECTS.—Mounting Transparent Objects Dry; in Balsam; in Liquids; Whole Insects; How to Get Rid of Air-Bubbles; Mounting Opaque Objects.

FINISHING THE SLIDES.—Cabinets; Maltwood Finder; Microscopical Fallacies.

THE WORKSHOP COMPANION.

A Collection of Useful and Reliable Recipes,
Rules, Processes, Methods, Wrinkles,
and Practical Hints,

FOR THE HOUSEHOLD AND THE SHOP.

CONTENTS.

Abyssinian Gold;—Accidents, General Rules;—Alabaster, how to work, polish and clean;—Alcohol;—Alloys, rules for making, and 26 recipes;—Amber, how to work, polish and mend;—Annealing and Hardening glass, copper, steel, etc.;—Arsenical Soap;—Arsenical Powder;—Beeswax, how to bleach;—Blackboards, how to make;—Brass, how to work, polish, color, varnish, whiten, deposit by electricity, clean, etc., etc.;—Brazing and Soldering;—Bronzing brass, wood, leather, etc.;—Burns, how to cure;—Case-hardening;—Catgut, how prepared;—Cements, general rules for using, and 56 recipes for preparing;—Copper, working, welding, depositing;—Coral, artificial;—Cork, working;—Crayons for Blackboards;—Curling brass, iron, etc.;—Liquid Cuticle;—Etching copper, steel, glass;—Eye, accidents to;—Fires, to prevent;—Clothes on Fire;—Fireproof Dresses;—Fly Papers;—Freezing Mixtures, 6 recipes;—Fumigating Pastils;—Gilding metal, leather, wood, etc.;—Glass, cutting, drilling, turning in the lathe, fitting stoppers, removing tight stoppers, powdering, packing, imitating ground glass, washing glass vessels, etc.;—Grass, Dry, to stain;—Guns, to make shoot close, to keep from rusting, to brown the barrels of, etc., etc.;—Handles, to fasten;—Inks, rules for selecting and preserving, and 34 recipes for;—Ink Eraser;—Inlaying;—Iron, forging, welding, case-hardening, zincing, tinning, do. in the cold, brightening, etc., etc.;—Ivory, to work, polish, bleach, etc.;—Javelle Water;—Jewelry and Gilded Ware, care of, cleaning, coloring, etc.;—Lacquer, how to make and apply;—Laundry Gloss;—Skeleton Leaves;—Lights, signal and colored, also for tableaux, photography, etc., 25 recipes;—Lubricators, selection of, 4 recipes for;—Marble, working, polishing, cleaning;—Metals, polishing;—Mirrors, care of, to make, pure silver, etc., etc.;—Nickel, to plate with without a battery;—Noise, prevention of;—Painting Bright Metals;—Paper, adhesive, barometer, glass, tracing, transfer, waxed, etc.;—Paper, to clean, take creases out of, remove water stains, mount drawing paper, to prepare for varnishing, etc., etc.;—Patina;—Patterns, to trace;—Pencils, indelible;—Pencil Marks, to fix;—Pewter;—Pillows for Sick Room, cheap and good;—Plaster-of-Paris, how to work;—Poisons, antidotes for, 12 recipes;—Polishing Powders, preparation and use of (six pages);—Resins, their properties, etc.;—Saws, how to sharpen;—Sieves;—Shellac, properties and uses of;—Silver, properties of, oxidized, old, cleaning, to remove ink stains from, to dissolve from plated goods, etc., etc.;—Silvering metals, leather, iron, etc.;—Size, preparation of various kinds of;—Skins, tanning and curing, do with hair on;—Stains, to remove from all kinds of goods;—Steel, tempering and working (six pages);—Tin, properties, methods of working;—Varnish, 21 recipes for;—Varnishing, directions for;—Voltaic Batteries;—Watch, care of;—Waterproofing, 7 recipes for;—Whitewash;—Wood Floors, waxing, staining, and polishing;—Wood, polishing.—Wood, staining, 17 recipes;—Zinc, to pulverize, black varnish for.

164 closely-printed pages, neatly bound. Sent by mail for 36 cents (postage stamps received). Specimen pages free.

INDUSTRIAL PUBLICATION COMPANY,

14 Dey Street, New York.

SCIENTIFIC LIBRARY FOR YOUNG PEOPLE. (*Continued*).

GEOLOGY.

By the Rev. T. G. Bonney, M.A., F.G.S., Fellow and late Tutor of St. John's College, Cambridge.

In the following pages I have attempted to set down briefly the principal facts of Geology, and the conclusions which have been drawn from them; to indicate the nature of the earth's crust, the processes which have acted and are still acting upon it, and the probable history of that little portion of it on which we live. I was requested, before commencing my task, to avoid the use of long words and the discussion of doubtful points, and have done my best to attend to this request.—*Author's Preface*.

CRYSTALLOGRAPHY.

By Henry Palin Gurney, M.A., Clare College, Cambridge.

Crystallography has been hitherto strangely neglected in this country as a branch of education. Its great importance to the chemist, the physicist, and the geologist cannot be questioned, and it is full of interest for all. No study is better calculated to sharpen at once the observing and the reasoning faculties of youth. There is nothing repulsive in crystals. Their beauty is often more attractive, as it is more enduring, than that of the fairest flowers. Their symmetry illustrates the rhythm and the harmony that pervade the universe. They have already suggested the most important law of modern chemistry. They tell us more about the properties of atoms than any other form of substance.—*Author's Preface*.

SPECTROSCOPE, THE WORK OF THE.

By Richard A. Proctor, Esq.

I have endeavored to make this little treatise on the Spectroscopic Analysis clear and simple for beginners, but at the same time accurate, and as complete as possible within so limited a space. * * * I have endeavored to give a full account of all the principles on which the application of spectroscopy depends, and also of all the chief methods of observation and their results.—*Author's Preface*.

ELECTRICITY.

By Fleeming Jenkins, F.R.S., Professor of Engineering in the University of Edinburgh.

Gives the most recent views of scientific men, and an account of the latest discoveries and the principles upon which they are founded—such as the telephone, microphone, photophone, etc.

☞ These ten volumes form the most complete popular Scientific Library now accessible to the student. If the ten volumes are ordered at one time they will be sent free to any part of the country for $3.50.

INDUSTRIAL PUBLICATION COMPANY,
14 Dey Street, New York.

Hand-Book of Urinary Analysis.

CHEMICAL AND MICROSCOPICAL.
For the Use of Physicians, Medical Students, and Clinical Assistants.
By FRANK M. DEEMS, M. D.,
Laboratory Instructor in the Medical Department of the University of New York; Member of the N. Y. County Medical Society; Member of the New York Microscopical Society, etc.

Illustrated, Limp Cloth, Gilt, 25 cts.

This Manual presents a plan for the Systematic Examination of Liquid Urine, Urinary Deposits, and Calculi. It is compiled with the intention of supplying a concise guide, which, from its small compass and tabulated arrangement, renders it admirably adapted for use, both as a bed-side reference book and a work-table companion. The author is well known as one who has had for several years a very extended experience as a teacher of this important branch of physical diagnosis, and he has compiled a manual which will serve to lessen the difficulties in the way of the beginner, and save valuable time to the busy practitioner. *Free by Mail on receipt of price.*

JUST PUBLISHED.

HOW TO SEE WITH THE MICROSCOPE.

Being Useful Hints Connected with the Selection and Use of the Instrument; also Some Discussion of the Claims and Capacity of Modern High-Angled Objectives, as Compared with those of Medium Aperture. With Instructions as to the Selection and Use of American Object-Glasses of Wide Apertures.

By J. EDWARDS SMITH, M. D.
Professor of Histology and Microscopy; Corresponding Member San Francisco, Dunkirk, and other Microscopical Societies, etc., etc.

Handsomely Illustrated.

Prof. Smith is well known as the most expert manipulator in this country, as regards objectives of wide aperture, and in this volume he gives, in a clear and practical manner, all the directions necessary to attain the surprising results which he has achieved. No microscopist that uses anything better than French triplets can afford to be without it.

Price, $2.00. *Free by Mail on receipt of price.* Address

To be completed in Six Monthly Parts. Price $15.00, payable in advance.

PART I. IS NOW READY.

A Manual of the Infusoria,

Including a Description of all Known Flagellate, Ciliate, and Tentaculiferous Protozoa, British and Foreign, and an Account of the Organization and Affinities of the Sponges.

By W. SAVILLE KENT, F.L.S., F.Z.S., F.R.M.S.

This important work, the result of many years' careful labor and investigation on the part of the author, will, it is hoped, meet a want which has long existed among microscopists. It will consist of a volume of text extending to about 800 pages super royal 8vo., and an atlas of 48 plates, containing upwards of 2,000 figures.

Wishing to lend what little assistance we can to the publication of this valuable work, we have subscribed for a large number of copies, which we offer to the microscopists of the United States at the prices named above. As the book is large and very expensive, the publisher will issue very few copies beyond those for which subscriptions are received, and consequently the price will undoubtedly be advanced after the work has been completed.

INDUSTRIAL PUBLICATION CO., 14 Dey Street, New York,
AGENTS FOR THE UNITED STATES.

The Carpenter's Steel Square,

AND HOW TO USE IT.

OPINIONS OF THE PRESS.

"This little work consists of a republication of some papers contributed by its talented author some time ago to the *American Builder*, and which were received with so much favor by artisans, for whom they were written, as to induce their author to collect them into the present volume." * * * * * * * "The work is well illustrated by upwards of fifty cuts which have been well engraved, and can hardly fail to give any one an idea of the capabilities of the steel square, and what can be accomplished from it when in skilful hands."—*Journal of Franklin Institute, Phila.*

"A most valuable little treatise of 70 pages upon that commonplace subject, the 'steel square,' being a description of that useful tool, and its uses in obtaining the lengths and bevels of rafters, hips, groins, braces, brackets, purlins, collar beams and jack rafters, and its application in obtaining the bevels and cuts for hoppers, spring moldings, octagons, stairs, diminished stiles, etc., illustrated by over 50 wood cuts. Mr. Hodgson has succeeded admirably in demonstrating that the study of the value and use of the square is by no means the dry subject one would suppose, and that as a tool in the hands of an intelligent workman, its possibilities are far beyond the standard usually conceded to it. It is a valuable book for the use of the carpenter, and should be upon the office desk of every retailer of lumber, from the valuable hints it will give him as a guide to his negotiations with his customers in figuring out their wants. It is, in fact, well adapted to the wants of every man who has a shed or fence to erect upon his premises, or who wishes to keep a check upon his builder."—*Northwestern Lumberman, Chicago, Ill.*

"This is a little book that no carpenter, joiner, cabinetmaker, or amateur woodworker, can do without, if they wish to keep up with the times in their several branches of trade.

"We believe this is the first and only book that has been written on this subject alone, and we must say, that the duty of writing it fell into good hands, as the author has handled his subject in a masterly manner. One is struck with astonishment at the number of difficult and apparently intricate problems this simple instrument—the square—is made to solve, and in such a manner that any mechanic who can read the figures on the tool can work out the solutions. The lengths and bevels of rafters, hips, braces, trusses, purlins, collar beams, and jack rafters are obtained as if by magic, and without thought or calculation.

"The work is handsomely gotten up, printed on heavy white paper, substantially bound, and cleanly turned out. The some fifty odd wood cuts are almost equal to steel engravings, and the whole get-up is a credit to both author and publisher, and the low price at which it is sold, (75 cents), places it within reach of every wood-worker, no matter how poor he may be."—*Enterprise, Collingwood, Ont.*

"It is a timely book on the subject in hand, and we can safely recommend it as competent to fill a long felt vacancy in the mechanics' library. The work presents a valuable collection of rules and data connected with the framing square, to the solution of roofing problems, braces, hoppers, etc., etc."—*Orillia Packet, Ont.*

"Some fifty engravings aid in the description of the square and its uses in obtaining lengths and bevels of all kinds; also, its application in obtaining the bevels and cuts for all conceivable shapes used in the wood shops. Any wood-worker possessing this book will find its cost, seventy-five cents, is not to be compared with its real value and usefulness in the shop."—*The Carriage Monthly, Phila.*

"The work is a very valuable one, and should be in the hands of every carpenter."—*Messenger, Collingwood, Ont.*

"The work will be of very great service to carpenters and builders."—*Bulletin, Collingwood, Ont.*

A New and Live Book on the Gun.

Just Published. Price 75 cents, in cloth.

PLAIN DIRECTIONS

FOR ACQUIRING THE ART OF

SHOOTING ON THE WING.

With Useful Hints concerning all that relates to Guns and Shooting, and particularly in regard to the art of Loading so as to Kill. To which has been added several Valuable and hitherto Secret Recipes, of Great Practical Importance to the Sportsman.

By AN OLD GAMEKEEPER.

Sent free by mail on receipt of price.

Opinions of the Press.

The directions are so plain that they cannot well be mistaken, and they are expressed in the fewest possible words.—*Turf, Field and Farm.*

Facing the title-page is one of the handsomest, best-executed woodcuts, we have ever seen. It is entitled "The Wounded Snipe," and almost equals a steel engraving.—*Baptist Union.*

From its pages we should think even the most experienced sportsman might derive some new ideas, while the beginner will find it an invaluable assistant.—*Country Gentleman.*

For concise instructions as to how to shoot, to select, load, carry, and keep a gun in order, etc., it cannot be surpassed.—*Western Rural.*

A pleasantly written, and, it seems, to us, correct and practical treatise on the sportsman's art; a modest little book, but one from the reading of which a good deal of the right kind of knowledge is to be gained.—*Appleton's Journal.*

A practical and well-written handbook, especially adapted for the use of young sportsmen, as it gives sensible advice on the manipulation of firearms, and the rules and etiquette of the field.—*Scientific American.*

GENESIS AND GEOLOGY.

The only really scientific and logical system of harmony between Genesis and Geology is to be found in a little work, just published, and entitled

THE CHEMICAL HISTORY
OF
The Six Days of Creation.

BY JOHN PHIN, C. E.,
EDITOR OF "HANDICRAFT."

1 vol., 12mo., cloth. 75 cents.

In this work an attempt is made to show that the account given of the Creation, in the first chapter of Genesis, agrees *literally* with the record developed by the investigations of modern science.

May be ordered through any bookseller. Single copies sent by mail, on receipt of price,

---

The following are a few of the Opinions of the Press:

This is a small book, but full of matter. The author believes in the book of Genesis as the work of Moses, and believes in the entire correctness of the statements made by Moses in regard to the work of creation. He defends the accuracy of the first chapter of Genesis, and defends it from a scientific standpoint. We think this book is full of interest and value; and as the discussions concerning the harmony of science and faith are rife at the present day, we commend the reasonings of Mr. Phin to the great number of readers and students who are investigating these subjects.—*The Presbyterian* (Philadelphia).

The author gives a new solution of this difficult question, and certainly presents many very plausible arguments in support of his theory.—*Sunday-School Workman.*

A very candid and ingenious essay.—*Christian Union* (H. W. Beecher's paper).

It is a topic which needs a calm and well-directed intellect to approach, and Mr. Phin has surrounded its discussion with thoughts of the deepest interest to all minds seeking rest on this much perplexing question.—*Journal of the Telegraph.*

The reasons and conclusions are clear, distinct, and natural. The book will interest and instruct, and is intended to lead the reasoning mind to firmer faith in the light of revelation.—*New York Globe.*

No one can read this book without compensation, without becoming more thoughtful concerning the phenomena of creation; and he need lose none of his reverence for the supremacy of the Divine Law.—*Rural New-Yorker.*

We could say much in commendation of Prof. Phin's little book. An intelligent reader can hardly fail to be interested in it, and many might be benefited.—*Country Gentleman.*

The book can not fail to interest even those who do not fully accept the theory it advocates.—*Boston Journal of Chemistry.*

It is a new scientific view of the matter.—*Phrenological Journal.*

The book, although not large, will prove exceedingly interesting to all who have ever directed attention to this matter, and contains more solid and suggestive thought than many voluminous treatises on the subject.—*Insurance Monitor.*

The work is ingenious and original, and presents many striking suggestions.—*American Baptist.*

We believe Prof. Phin has started upon the correct basis, and his theory is mainly tenable. His views are presented in a manner which, though terse, is easily comprehended.—*Paterson Daily Guardian.*

The Carpenter's Steel Square

AND ITS USES.

Being a description of the Carpenter's Framing Square, giving simple and easy methods of obtaining the Lengths and Bevels of all kinds of Rafters, Hips, Groins, Braces, Brackets, Purlins, Collar-Beams, and Jack-Rafters. Also, its application in obtaining the bevels and cuts for Hoppers, Spring Mouldings, Octagons, Stairs, and Diminished Stiles.

Illustrated by over Fifty Large and Clear Woodcuts.

By FRED. T. HODGSON,

Editor of the Builder and Wood-Worker.

Cloth, Gilt, - - - - - - - 75 cents.

This is the only work of the kind ever published, and must prove of great service to every person who may have to use a Carpenter's Square. Joiners, Cabinet-makers, Bricklayers, Stone Cutters, Plasterers, Lumber Dealers, Amateurs, and all who build a fence, tinker a gate, or make a chicken-coop, will find something in this little book that will help and aid them to do their work better and more intelligently than they could without a knowledge of its contents.

Many difficult and troublesome mathematical problems can be solved by the use of this tool, and the methods of solving them are shown in the work. It describes how Painting, Plastering, and Brick Work can be measured, and how many mechanical difficulties can be overcome with great ease. It explains how Ellipses, Parabolas, Octagons, Circles, and many other figures may be described by the Steel Square.

This is the "book of the period" for all who work in wood, and its low price places it within the reach of every journeyman and apprentice in the land. The engravings are of a high order, and the whole is printed on heavy calendered paper.

INDUSTRIAL PUBLICATION COMPANY,
14 Dey Street, New York.

SENT BY MAIL TO ANY ADDRESS ON RECEIPT OF PRICE.

The Only Practical Book Published on this Subject.

THE PISTOL

AS A

WEAPON OF DEFENCE,

In the House and on the Road.

12mo. Cloth. 50 cents.

This work aims to instruct the peaceable and law-abiding citizens in the best means of protecting themselves from the attacks of the brutal and the lawless. Its contents are as follows: The Pistol as a Weapon of Defence—The Carrying of Fire-Arms—Different kinds of Pistols in Market; how to Choose a Pistol—Ammunition, different kinds; Powder, Caps, Bullets, Copper Cartridges, etc.—Best form of Bullet—How to Load—Best charge for Pistols—How to regulate the Charge—Care of the Pistol; how to clean it—How to handle and carry the Pistol—How to Learn to Shoot—Practical use of the Pistol; how to Protect yourself and how to Disable your antagonist.

"No man is fit to keep house who is not fit to defend it."—*Henry Ward Beecher.*

"So long as rogues cannot be prevented from carrying weapons, honest men do not consult their own safety and the public good by totally discarding them."—*Recorder Hackett.*

"Such I hold to be the genuine use of gunpowder; that it makes all men alike tall (or strong.)"—*Carlyle.*

For Sale by all Newsdealers, or Sent postpaid by Mail on receipt of price

A NEW SERIES OF PRACTICAL BOOKS.

WORK MANUALS.

The intention of the publishers is to give in this Series a number of small books which will give Thorough and Reliable Information in the plainest possible language, upon the

ARTS OF EVERYDAY LIFE.

Each volume will be by some one who is not only practically familiar with his subject, but who has the ability to make it clear to others. The volumes will each contain from 50 to 75 pages; will be neatly and clearly printed on good paper, and bound in tough and durable binding. The price will be *25 cents each.*

The following are the titles of the volumes, and the order in which they will be issued. No. I. is ready for delivery, No. II. is in press, and the others will follow at short intervals.

I. Cements and Glue.
A Practical Treatise on the Preparation and Use of All Kinds of Cements, Glue and Paste. By JOHN PHIN, Editor of the *Young Scientist* and the *American Journal of Microscopy.*

Every mechanic and householder will find this volume of almost everyday use. It contains nearly 200 recipes for the preparation of Cements for almost every conceivable purpose.

II. The Slide Rule, and How to Use It.
This is a compilation of Explanations, Rules and Instructions suitable for mechanics and others interested in the industrial arts. Rules are given for the measurement of all kinds of boards and planks, timber in the round or square, glaziers' work and painting, brickwork, paviors' work, tiling and slating, the measurement of vessels of various shapes, the wedge, inclined planes, wheels and axles, levers, the weighing and measurement of metals and all solid bodies, cylinders, cones, globes, octagon rules and formula, the measurement of circles, and a comparison of French and English measures, with much other information, useful to builders, carpenters, bricklayers, glaziers, paviors, slaters, machinists and other mechanics.

Possessed of this little Book and a good Slide Rule, mechanics might carry in their pockets some hundreds of times the power of calculation that they now have in their heads, and the use of the instrument is very easily acquired.

III. Construction, Use and Care of Drawing Instruments.
Being a Treatise on Draughting Instruments, with Rules for their Use and Care, Explanations of Scales, Sectors and Protractors. Together with Memoranda for Draughtsmen, Hints on Purchasing Paper, Ink, Instruments, Pencils, etc. Also a Price List of all materials required by Draughtsmen. Illustrated with twenty-four Explanatory Illustrations. By FRED. T. HODGSON.

IV. Plaster: How to Make and How to Use It.

V. Hints for Painters and Paperhangers.

VI. Rules, Tables, Data and Memoranda for Mechanics and Others. (Part I.)

VII. The Construction and Use of Saws.
With Directions for Filing, Setting, etc.

VIII. Rules, Tables, Data and Memoranda for Mechanics and Others. (Part II.)

INDUSTRIAL PUBLICATION CO.,
P. O. Box 2852.   14 Dey Street, New York.

Thirty-seventh Year of Republication!

THE
London Lancet for 1881.

A Monthly Journal of British and Foreign Medicine, Physiology, Surgery, Chemistry, Criticism, Literature and News.

EDITED BY

JAMES G. WAKLEY, M.D., M.R.C.S.

☞ **The American Edition, as published by the Industrial Publication Co., contains EVERYTHING relating to Medical Matters that appears in the original London edition.**

THE LANCET is the oldest and most Practical Medical Journal published in the English language, and is the national British organ of Science in its relations to the human frame.

THE LANCET is edited by a corps of the most distinguished physicians of the British Metropolis, and numbers among its contributors, the best medical and surgical talent of Europe.

THE LANCET for 1881, will contain over 1200 double-column pages of closely printed matter, exclusive of the advertising sheets. The type is clear, and printed on the very best calendered book paper. Our pages contain nearly twice as much reading matter as any other monthly medical journal published on this side of the Atlantic. Every effort will be made to continue this Work, as it ever has been, the Standard Journal of Medicine and Surgery.

Illustrated with engravings by the best artists.

Subscription $5.00 per year.   Single Numbers 50 cts. each.

Specimen Copies (our selection), 25 cents.

For Club Rates, Subscriptions, Advertisements, etc., address

THE INDUSTRIAL PUBLICATION COMPANY,

14 Dey Street, New York.

THE YOUNG SCIENTIST,

A Practical Journal for Amateurs.

ISSUED MONTHLY.   Price 50 Cents per year.

It is characteristic of young Americans that they want to be DOING something. They are not content with merely *knowing* how things are done, or even with *seeing* them done; they want to do them themselves. In other words, they want to experiment. Hence the wonderful demand that has sprung up for small tool chests, turning lathes, scroll saws, wood carving tools, telegraphs, model steam engines, microscopes and all kinds of apparatus. In nine cases out of ten, however, the young workman finds it difficult to learn how to use his tools or apparatus after he has got them. It is true that we have a large number of very excellent text-books, but these are not just the thing. What is wanted is a living teacher. Where a living teacher cannot be found, the next best thing is a live journal, and this we propose to furnish. And in attempting this it is not our intention to confine ourselves to mere practical directions. In these days of knowledge and scientific culture, the "Why" becomes as necessary as the "How." The object of the YOUNG SCIENTIST is to give clear and easily followed directions for performing chemical, mechanical and other operations, as well as simple and accurate explanations of the principles involved in the various mechanical and chemical processes which we shall undertake to describe.

The scope and character of the journal will be better understood from an inspection of a few numbers, or from the list of contents found on a subsequent page, than from any labored description. There are, however, three features to which we would call special attention:

CORRESPONDENCE.—In this department we intend to place our readers in communication with each other, and in this way we hope to secure for every one just such aid as may be required for any special work on hand.

EXCHANGES.—An exchange column, like that which has been such a marked success in the *Journal of Microscopy*, will be opened in the YOUNG SCIENTIST. Yearly subscribers who may wish to *exchange* tools, apparatus, books, or the products of their skill, can state what they have to offer and what they want, *without charge*. Buying and selling must, of course, be carried on in the advertising columns.

ILLUSTRATIONS.—The journal will make no claims to the character of a "picture book," but wherever engravings are needed to make the descriptions clear they will be furnished. Some of the engravings which have already appeared in our pages are as fine as anything to be found in the most expensive journals.

Special Notice.

As our journal is too small and too low-priced to claim the attention of news dealers, we are compelled to rely almost wholly upon subscriptions sent directly to this office. As many persons would no doubt like to examine a few numbers before becoming regular subscribers, we will send four current numbers as a trial trip for

FIFTEEN CENTS.

CLUBS.

Where three or more subscribe together for the journal, we offer the following liberal terms:

3 copies for	....	$1.25
5 " "	....	2.00
7 " "	....	2.75
10 " "	....	3.50

Advertisements, 30 cents per line.

As postal currency has nearly disappeared from circulation, we receive postage stamps of the lower denominations (ones, twos and threes) at their full value. Postal orders are, however, much safer and more convenient. To avoid delay and mistakes address all communications to "THE YOUNG SCIENTIST, Box 2852, New York," and make all checks and orders payable to John Phin.

WHAT PEOPLE SAY OF US.

In a letter to the Editor, Oliver Wendel Holmes, the genial "Autocrat of the Breakfast Table," says: "I am much pleased with the YOUNG SCIENTIST. It makes me want to be a boy again."

"It is a little publication, calculated to call out and educate all the latent ingenuity and thirst for knowledge which the youthful mind possesses, and we hope it will win its way into every household in the land."—[Scientific Press.

"We have never seen a periodical, designed for youth, which came nearer to our ideal of what such a journal should be."—[Canadian Pharmaceutical Journal.

"The YOUNG SCIENTIST is one of the choicest publications for juvenile minds in this country. Every page treats on subjects of importance to young and old, portrayed in a clearly comprehensive manner, which at once interests the young idea in its careful perusal."—[Lapeer Clarion.

"It seems to fill the bill."—[Newport Daily News.

"It is pleasing to note that its youthful subscribers will not be misled by clap-trap advertisements or advertisements of patent medicines, which will not be received at any price. The YOUNG SCIENTIST is doing good work in setting its face against this class of humbugs."—[Manufacturing and Trade Review.

"The work is a copiously illustrated monthly, and is full of practical hints that will instruct and amuse the young folks."—[Industrial School Advocate.

"A small but elegant and very instructive monthly."—[Pittsburg Chronicle.

"Contains the best possible reading for the young of both sexes."—[Ottawa Journal.

"We can safely recommend this magazine as one of the very best publications for the young folks."—[The Independent, Fenton, Mich.

"This journal occupies a new field, and is needed to put the minds of our youth on the right track to secure a correct understanding of the nature of things."—[Wayland Press.

"It is ably edited by John Phin, who will make a large place in the heart of the rising generation, if he persists in his venture. We hope his success in the field will be equal to the article furnished—first best."—[Sunset Chimes.

"The articles are written in a popular, readable style, and profusely illustrated."—Akron City Times.

"The YOUNG SCIENTIST is excellent in conception, and well designed to amuse and instruct young people."—[Chicago Evening Journal.

"The YOUNG SCIENTIST is a handsome monthly magazine, each number containing about 16 pages, handsomely illustrated. It will supply a place which has been heretofore unoccupied. The copy before us comes fully up to the promise of the prospectus."—[The Times, Iroquois, Mich.

"It is a journal which should be in the hands of both young and old, and is a great benefit to the young scientist as well as the advanced professor. It is a thousand times more valuable than the dime novel series, so much read by boys. Parents would do well to have it in their households."—[The Iron Home.

"This publication is a new launch, and it is very gratifying to witness the ableness which pervades its pages."—Al. Horst Free Press.

THE AMERICAN
Journal of Microscopy.

PROSPECTUS—SIXTH YEAR—1881

The object of the JOURNAL OF MICROSCOPY is to diffuse a knowledge of the best methods of using the Microscope; of all valuable improvements in the instrument and its accessories; of all new methods of microscopical investigation, and of the most recent results of microscopical research. The JOURNAL does not address itself to those who have long pursued certain special lines of research, and whose wants can be supplied only by elaborate papers, which, from their thoroughness, are entitled to be called monographs rather than mere articles. It is intended rather to meet the wants of those who use the microscope for purposes of general study, medical work, class instruction, and even amusement, and who desire, in addition to the information afforded by text-books, such a knowledge of what others are doing as can be derived only from a periodical. With this object in view, therefore, the publishers propose to make the JOURNAL so simple, practical and trustworthy, that it will prove to the advantage of every one who uses the microscope at all to take it.

ILLUSTRATIONS.—The JOURNAL will be freely illustrated by engravings representing either objects of natural history or apparatus connected with the microscope.

TRANSACTIONS OF SOCIETIES.—THE AMERICAN JOURNAL OF MICROSCOPY is not the organ of any Society, but it gives the proceedings of all Societies whose officers send us a report. As the JOURNAL is devoted *wholly* to Microscopy, and is in good form and size for binding, no better medium can be had for preserving the scientific records of any Society. Matters of mere business routine we are frequently obliged to omit for want of room.

EXCHANGES.—An important feature of the JOURNAL is the exchange column, by means of which workers in different parts of the country are enabled, without expense, except for postage, to exchange slides and materials with each other.

Published Monthly at $1.00 a year.
SPECIMENS FREE.

Four copies for three dollars. Those who wish to economize in the direction of periodicals, would do well to examine our clubbing list.

FOREIGN SUBSCRIBERS.—The JOURNAL will be sent, postage paid, to any country in the Postal Union for $1.24, or 5 shillings sterling per year. English postage stamps, American currency or American postage stamps taken in payment. In return for a postal order or draft for £1 5s., five copies of the JOURNAL will be furnished and mailed to different addresses. Make all drafts and postal orders payable to John Phin.

Back Volumes.

Vol. I is out of print. We are occasionally able to complete volumes which, when bound, we offer for $1.50. Of Vols. II, III and IV we have a few copies on hand. Price $1.50 each.

Advertisements.

The JOURNAL OF MICROSCOPY, from its very nature, is a visitor to the very best families, and its value as an advertising medium has therefore proved to be much above that of average periodicals. A few select advertisements will be inserted at the rate of 30 cents per line, nonpariel measure, of which twelve lines make an inch. Address

AMERICAN JOURNAL OF MICROSCOPY,
P. O. Box 2852, New York.

NEW DESIGNS

FOR

Fret or Scroll Sawyers.

MR. F. T. HODGSON, whose admirable series of articles on the USE OF THE SCROLL SAW are now in course of publication in the YOUNG SCIENTIST, has prepared for us a series of

SEVENTEEN DESIGNS,

of which the following is a list:

No. 1.—This shows one side, back, and bottom, of a pen rack. It may be made of ebony, walnut, or other dark wood.

No. 2.—Design for inlaying drawer fronts, table tops, box lids, and many other things. It is a sumach leaf pattern.

No. 3.—Design for a thermometer stand. It may be made of any hard wood or alabaster. The method of putting together is obvious.

No. 4.—This shows a design for a lamp screen. The open part may be covered with tinted silk, or other suitable material, with some appropriate device worked on with the needle, or, if preferred, ornaments may be painted on the silk, etc.

No. 5.—A case for containing visiting cards. Will look best made of white holly.

No. 6.—A placque stand, it may be made of any kind of dark or medium wood.

No. 7.—A design for ornaments suitable for a window cornice. It should be made of black walnut, and overlaid on some light colored hard wood.

No. 8—A design for a jewel casket. This will be very pretty made of white holly and lined with blue velvet. It also looks well made of ebony lined with crimson.

No. 9.—Frame. Will look well made of any dark wood.

No. 10.—Frame. Intended to be made in pairs. Looks well made of white holly, with leaves and flowers painted on wide stile.

No. 11.—Horseshoe. Can be made of any kind of wood and used for a pen rack. When decorated with gold and colors, looks very handsome.

No. 12.—Design for a hinge strap. If made of black walnut, and planted on a white or oaken door, will look well.

No. 13.—Design for a napkin ring. May be made of any kind of hard wood.

No. 14.—Hinge strap for doors with narrow stiles.

No. 15.—Centre ornament for panel.

No. 16.—Corner ornament for panel.

No. 17.—Key-hole escutcheon.

These designs we have had photo-lithographed and printed on good paper, so that the outlines are sharp, and the opposite sides of each design symmetrical. Common designs are printed from coarse wooden blocks, and are rough and unequal, so that it is often impossible to make good work from them.

The series embraces over forty different pieces, and designs of equal quality cannot be had for less than five, ten or fifteen cents each. We offer them for twenty-five cents for the set, which is an average price of only one cent and a half each.

Mailed to any address on receipt of price.

INDUSTRIAL PUBLICATION CO.,
14 Dey Street, New York.

SHEET NO. 1.

SHEET NO. 2.

REDUCED FIGURES OF
NEW DESIGNS FOR FRET OR SCROLL SAWYERS.
SIZE OF SHEETS 28 BY 22 INCHES.
(For description see preeeding page.)

www.ingramcontent.com/pod-product-compliance
Lightning Source LLC
Chambersburg PA
CBHW031940230426
43672CB00010B/1986